Christopher Moore was born in Wallington but did most of his 'growing up' in Tonbridge Kent with his mum, dad and 'little sister' Bev. His school days really were amongst the happiest of his life and, after obtaining his first degree at university, he embarked on a career as a teacher, taking up his first appointment in 1979 and remaining in the profession until retirement. Chris has two children, Sebastian and Katrina, and four grandchildren. He has many interests, including politics, music, poetry and working as a radio presenter.

I wish to dedicate this book to all of the very kind people who helped me during my hospitalisation, to my friends, and to the two most important ladies in the world: my sister and my mum, both of whom I love so much.

Christopher Moore

A STROKE OF LUCK

Or a Beginner's Guide to Being Hospitalised and What
You Can Reasonably Expect!

WWW.THRIFTYOWL.COM

AUSTIN MACAULEY PUBLISHERS™

LONDON · CAMBRIDGE · NEW YORK · SHARJAH

A CIP catalogue record for this title is available from the British Library.

ISBN 9781528908504 (Paperback)
ISBN 9781528958950 (ePub e-book)

www.austinmacauley.com

First Published (2019)
Austin Macauley Publishers Ltd
25 Canada Square
Canary Wharf
London
E14 5LQ

Table of Contents

OR A BEGINNER'S GUIDE TO BEING HOSPITALISED AS A
MORE 'MATURE' PERSON AND WHAT YOU CAN
REASONABLY EXPECT!

Introduction

My name is Chris. If I'm being told off for any misdemeanour, be it a large one or a small one, then my name becomes *'Christopher'*, with a very strong emphasis on the *'Chris'* syllable. Conversely, if I had done something very good indeed, like popping up the road to buy some milk and *'The Daily Mail'*, or mowing the lawn, or attempting to sort out the computer, then, as if by magic, my name transforms into *'Chrissie Sweetie'*, or, at a push, *'My Darling'*, complete with a couple of house-points to boot.

'And who, pray (could be 'prey' when I think about it) is responsible for changing your name, depending upon your actions?' I hear you asking (that, too, is a pretty stupid thing to say really because of course I *don't* hear you in any shape or form, but I *guess* I can hear you asking that question, along with 'Is it your missus?').

To the supplementary part of the question, I can respond with a categorical 'No'. Nisi's, Absolutes and solicitor's fees put an end to my status as a married man after twenty-three years served as part of a life sentence. No—the guilty party is none other than my mum. I too can play the name-change game. If I need to offer a slightly formal response to one of her many enquiries, the term *'Mother'* comes into play. On the other hand, if I am thanking her for a cup of tea served to me in bed at precisely 06:45 hours, it's appropriate to use the title *'Mum', 'Ma', 'Mom'* or *'Mummy'*. These are generic terms of endearment and can be interchanged as often as necessary to avoid repetition.

We all have or had a mum otherwise we would not be in any form of existence. We wouldn't even be an *'ex'*. We certainly would not have been a glint in our mother's eye (or eyes, if she is blessed with two). And don't we love them! Of course, we do! I love mine to bits. Of course, they have their little foibles. For example, my mum will quite often (in fact, let's ignore the word 'quite') start a conversation like this:

"Christopher, you really *must* lose some weight—you're fat!" (Note the usage of *'Christopher'* and the unambiguous nature of her observation.)

"I'm doing my best Mum, honest…"

"Well, it's not good enough Christopher…"

She then proceeds to serve me a portion of dinner, which is large enough to serve an army and the opposing army too! Then, at the end of said meal, she will invariably say:

"Come on Chris, just finish those potatoes and broccoli up; you know I don't like to throw food away."

"But, you said I need to…"

"That's it son, you eat up…"

So, I duly oblige, stuff my face and get fatter and fatter by the day. A couple of hours pass in a drowsy, half asleep, wind-laden state, which is then followed by the statement from Mum which I have been anticipating:

'Come on, Christopher, wake up. You know your trouble don't you Christopher? You eat too much and don't exercise enough; you'll get fat, you know…'

Oh well. Worse things happen at sea, as it is so profoundly mentioned. You might hit an iceberg I suppose. Nonetheless, I fail to see how a non-descript item of rabbit food could cause considerable damage, 'cos (see what I've done there, clever or what? OK…*'what'*) as an item, it is not particularly substantial.

Mothers seem to live in a time warp whereby their offspring remain at the age of seven (*Sev-errnn,* as good old Len is prone to saying), totally ignoring the fact that the ravages of time have taken their toll. I AM 60. There. Said it. Am I bovvered? A soon to be OAP! Will get a bus pass soon. Get 25% off at *'Specsavers'*. I qualify for free medication now, which is saving me an absolute fortune. Also, I can apply for a Senior Person's Railcard (why don't they call it an 'old-has-been' railcard—seems about right to me?

And there, in a very circuitous fashion, is the main emphasis of my story. I might be 60. But, I don't feel 60. I like being in the company of young people. I volunteer five days a week at my local community radio station, *'Endeavour 107FM'*, (also available on line if you google it!) I present *'The Drive Show'*, Monday to Thursday, 16:00 to 19:00, and *'The Sixties Celebration'* on Sunday mornings, 11:00 to 13:00; a show which, as it implies really, celebrates the music of the sixties! A relatively new venture for me, but also directly concerned with broadcasting, is co-presenting a series of shows on a 'pod-cast' station based in Norwich called

'Deep Red Radio'. These are not jobs. These are hobbies. I give at least fifteen hours per week of my own time for no remuneration whatsoever. In fact, I pay a subscription, which is fair enough because you generally must pay for entertainment anyway in one form or another. I also enjoy writing stories and poems. I am also 'recovering' from my professional career as a teacher, which I started 'practicing' in 1979 (why is it called that, and why are GP's surgeries called 'Practices'; it hardly installs confidence, does it?). I am now retired from 'the noble profession' but that is another story altogether.

So, why do I do these things rather than just sit down with a pipe and slippers? As the Meerkats say *'Simples!'* I neither smoke a pipe nor wear slippers; I do a pretty passable Sandie Shaw impression within the confines and privacy of my humble abode.

The truthful answer is equally as straightforward—I love them. I would miss these activities badly. They keep me young, in spirit if not in body. I feel fit (not as in the attractive or sexy sense of the word), invigorated and ready for the daily challenges.

But, and this is a big 'but' (not as in bottom size, to clarify any misinterpretation), that was until recently.

I heard some dreaded words—only a few, but of major significance to me.

'I'm sorry Mr Moore, but it's best we take you in…'

'In' is a pseudonym for 'Hospital', very much with a capital 'H'.

'Oh! I've never been—'

'Anything you want to take, sir?'

I feel like saying *The complete works of William Shakespeare*, my entire *Pink Floyd* CD collection and Chairman Mao's *Little Red Book*, but I resist that temptation and settle for my mobile, without the charger (rendering it useless), some odd bits of cash, and, after having frantically locked the doors, my house keys.

I am 60. I've never been into hospital (except for when my ex gave birth and with a broken arm and a kidney removal, but that doesn't really count) and, to be honest, I am 'bricking it', as they say in the vernacular (or is it the Vatican?). I am a virgin of the hospitalisation game. I am a scared bunny.

What lies ahead? My little story will inform you and, hopefully, put your mind at ease, for a while anyway.

There is the slightest concern in what passes as my brain though that expresses itself like this: what exactly is it that makes a six-foot-five, eighteen-stone chap who, let's face it, is more than probably able to 'look after himself', resemble a quivering wreck when it comes to enjoying a little stay in a hospital? Be real Christopher: meals on tap, bed made, service at the push of a button—why can't you treat it as a little 'getaway' for a few days? You pay a fortune for that privilege elsewhere.

Perhaps my age has a misprint in it. If you knock the zero off at the end, then perhaps we are beginning to approach the reality of the situation! Perhaps I am demonstrating the unique ability to act my shoe size rather than my chronological age, which would make me thirteen—back to the days of being an impossible to argue with, stroppy, spotty individual, who would gladly argue that black is white and that the whole of humanity has simply 'got it wrong'.

Then, I get all sort of metaphysical and spiritual in mindset; is this simply a case of 'pay-back time', for all those mischievous and slightly naughty things I have done in the past as a child and as a big brother? Let me put the record straight, or clarify it, at this juncture. At no point in my years growing up with my dear sis did I do, or attempt to do, anything which would harm her—well, not much anyway!

I suppose the tone was set when Mum brought Bev back from the hospital, way back in 1960, when on being introduced to my little sis, I was purported to have commented—"what is that?"—or words to that effect. Not very nice of me was it? Perhaps not, but I was only three at the time, and I had been used to the undivided attention of Mum up to this point in history, which clearly was not to be the case anymore! Unfortunate for Bev, but of great advantage to myself, however, was the dynamic at play dictated by the fact that I was 'big' brother and she was 'little' sister, with all the rights that such a position of authority I was naturally embellished with! Beverley 'knew her place'! It was a typical brother-sister relationship, with the odds stacked in my favour!

As brother and sister, in our earlier years, we invented all sorts of weird and wonderful games, which basically involved Beverley 'coming off worse' than I did, shall we say, for arguments sake!

One such pastime was a game called 'Squeaky Cushion'. The concept around this activity was excruciatingly easy and simple to follow. It would involve Bev sitting herself on the sofa (or settee, as it was labelled in the Moore household, complete with an elasticised cover in a putrid shade of yellow if my memory is right). Once she had made herself comfortable on said settee, I would give myself as long a run-up as possible, then propel myself with as much force as I could muster, so that I landed on top of her, at which point, it was my role to make her declare 'I'm a squeaky old cushion' as she writhed in pain and giggled nervously!

What a nice brother I was! To be fair, I did give her every chance for revenge. Another game I/we invented was called 'Biscuit Wars'. Again, this was a very simple idea to grasp. It would involve both of us 'arming' ourselves, or literally 'mouthing' ourselves with a dry biscuit or two (plain *Digestives* were ideal for this purpose or *Rich Tea*). However, it was important not to consume the biscuit, rather to chew it up into tiny pieces, keeping the crumbs as dry as possible. On the cue, which was given by me, the aim of the game was to project the contents of one's mouth directly into contact with the other's face. If you pre-empted the cue, you were disqualified, and your opponent had a free 'go', unless of course you were *me,* in which case you were exempted from the rule; so, at times, it could be reasonably suggested that perhaps I was a little too trigger happy in retrospect!

I never did get to see who cleaned up the subsequent mess. I was inevitably partaking in 'a runner' away from the scene of battle!

Another firm favourite was a game entitled 'Slipper Match'. This needed a fair amount of preparation. Essentially, items of furniture were assembled to create what would be loosely termed as a 'boxing ring' (usually square or rectangular, but you get the idea I'm sure!). Bev would go to the red corner, because she was a little girl, and I would go to the blue corner, because I was big brother boy! Then, we placed our slippers onto our hands! Are you there yet? I would ring the bell; "*RING!*" I would declare, and at this point we would knock seven bells out of each other, or I did her! I'd never heard of *'The Queensbury Rules'* so this bout was generally a free for all, done and dusted within about thirty seconds, resulting in Bev shedding a little tear and muttering 'it's not fair'. Of course, it wasn't Sis; well done on pointing out the blindingly obvious! It was fun though!

Then, there was the case of Bev's favourite doll, called *'Rosebud'*. I pushed its face in so many times that it became stuck in a not very pretty pout! She had another doll too, which will remain nameless, from which I 'acquired' an item of its clothing, artistically altered said garment, and made it into a very fetching leotard for my Teddy Bear, called *'Tar'*, so named because it reminded me to say 'thank you' when convention dictated it of me!

My finest achievement in this respect though would occur in the summer months—lolly times! This was at the time when, if you collected enough ice-lolly wrappers, you could snip out the vouchers and send off for a pack of foreign stamps. I always was a budding philatelist, especially if it involved discomfort for 'poor sis'! So, of an evening, we would go out for a bike ride, stopping at every litter bin I could find, and Bev was tasked with rummaging through the bins, complete with vast numbers of deranged wasps, in order to retrieve the wrappers for my advantage. It's alright, she didn't get stung much!

Oh dear, looking back, I acted like a complete 'so and so' (add your choice of expletive here). For your information, Bev survived her 'trial by ordeal' and has a lovely family of her own! Thank God!

The Prologue

Wasn't 'the prologue' the beginning of Frankie Howard's story-telling about the naughty goings on in *'Up Pompeii'*? The name Ludicrous Sextus comes to mind as well but, on reflection, it's bound to really! It was a very funny series with interesting stories with a comedic twist. And that, my friends, is a comparatively apt way to describe this little tale. It has elements of sadness, exasperation, humour and disgust within its pages but, and this is important, hopefully it will provide you, the reader, with a valuable insight as to what happens in a hospital environment, especially if you've never had the misfortune to have been admitted into such an establishment before.

Let's start at the beginning then (this seems a reasonable plan to my way of thinking). OK, so you are about to enter the care of the big 'H', or you are there already, totally bemused as to:

- Why are you there, and
- What the hell is going on

It must be said, these are both fair and reasonable concerns. To be honest, I doubt whether you neither expected nor hoped to be where you are or are about to be. Join the club! You are not alone! You may well have risen out of your pit this morning, thinking, as Larry Grayson used to observe so adeptly whilst leaning against an old chair: 'What a gay day!'

On the other hand, however, you might have arisen as usual, drawn back the curtains, and thought: *Mmmm...I'm feeling a little queer this morning.* If Mr Grayson is acknowledged as making the first comment, I attribute the latter to my dear old Nan, bless her. Perhaps there was something in the water, and that is something I will come back to later. If you *did* feel a 'little under the weather' (the only way you can be above it is in an aeroplane, so that *is* a daft thing to say), I would wager my pocket money on what the psychologists refer to as your 'defence mechanism' kicked in. This, in turn, would probably elicit one of the following reactions;

- 'Oh well', or
- 'Just one of those things', or
- 'Bugger it!'

Or, indeed, all three, but not necessarily in that order. Who said something very similar to that? I'll give you a clue: he said it to a Mr Preview, a well-renowned conductor but not of the bus or train variety. Write your answer here:

After that, it was probably a case of just getting on with your daily chores.

As for my daily chores of the money earning kind, they are no more. They are like a dead parrot. They are 'fin'. They are 'over and out' and thank God for that. I have already fleetingly mentioned that I was a teacher but, just for the sheer hell of it, I will briefly return to subject.

I was 22 when I stepped up to the chalk face for the first time. That was in September 1979; I remember it vividly. On my very first morning, I got mistaken as a pupil. There I was happily (probably *not* happily; more like 'bricking it) cycling through the school gates, feeling proud, enthusiastic, optimistic and ready to educate the World and his Auntie, when a booming voice resembling a fog horn bellowed across the yard.

"Get off that bike sonny and milk it…"

"But, er…"

"It's either walking it or DT for you tonight boy."

For the uninitiated, regarding all things punitive, that means 'detention'. Good for the street credibility but not if you are a teacher.

Anyway, as ordered, I duly obliged and dismounted my vehicular transportation of choice.

"Good morning, my name is Mr Moore, and I'm the new history teacher."

"Oh, ah, I didn't realise…sorry Mr Moore…easy mistake…park 'round the back…staff racks are there…you don't want to come back to a flat tyre, do you?"

Of course, I do, I thought with a fair degree of cynicism.

Now, this little episode was causing somewhat of a rumpus as a gathering throng of pupils gathered. Unlike Victoria, they *were* amused. They were *very* amused. How many of 'the enemy', as I was later informed that is how you should refer to the pupils, would I meet today in my perfectly prepared lessons on:

1. What is History? ('all about dead things' I can remember the science teacher saying)
2. Why did the First World War start?
3. The Battle of Hastings
4. The Industrial Revolution
5. The Great Fire of London (it wasn't great was it, given the damage it caused!)

Random, or what? Random, I'd say.

Anyway, as predicted, the 'little sods', as I was calling them already, had a field day at my expense. The sense I had of 'making a difference for the good', the day before, had evaporated—shot dead on the spot. My stress levels started to rise from that day, along with anxiety, nervousness and goodness knows what. The PE Teacher was right.

"Take my advice," he said, "Remember that it is the survival of the fittest, and you must be the fittest—that's why I teach PE." I agreed with him but reckoned his teaching speciality was dictated by the lack of marking countless essays.

Fast forward thirty years and I resigned and took my well-deserved pension. I'd had enough. My tour of duty and service to God and the Queen had expired. There were so many events, both good and bad, which occurred over the course of my 'illustrious' career. Who knows, if I have the balls to write them down, you just might get to learn the story of *'The Teacher's torment'*. That, though, is for another time. Suffice to say though that when I woke up on my first day of retirement, something had changed, but I couldn't quite put my finger on it. Then, in a moment of Zen like enlightenment, I knew. I had *not* got a knotted feeling in my stomach. I was *not* filled with trepidation or dread for the day ahead. I was *not* stressed. My thoughts went back to that PE teacher's remark about survival of the fittest. I had survived, but was I fit? I certainly wasn't *the* fittest, but how had a life sentence in teaching left me health-wise? That, I considered, was questionable.

Don't get me wrong. I am not knocking teaching as a profession. My niece Annie is in her second year and, at present, she loves it. The point I am trying to make is this: do not underestimate the effect that your working life may have had on you, without you being aware of it. From brain surgeon to refuse collection operative, stress is everywhere, and it is feasible that it has caught up with you now. Do not bury your head in the sand.

I admit that the foregoing account has been one massive digression. However, there is a rationale to it. Just to remind you: I am an old 'shock jock' now. My soothing voice and razor-sharp wit can be heard by my listener in town, via the airwaves of Community Radio. But, here's the rub. It was a normal afternoon. I'd started the show and was playing Annie Lennox's *'Heaven Must Be Missing an Angel'*. I've always had a 'catholic' taste in music and might find myself playing *'The Bolero'*, followed by *'Mr Blobby'* and Right Said Fred's *'I'm Too Sexy for My Shirt'*.

In this instance, it was Annie Lennox. I walked across to the kitchen area to get myself a mug of water. Nothing like *Radio Two* here; if you want water, you damn well get water. I got back to the microphone and took a sip of said water.

WOW!

My lips began to tingle, bit like pins and needles. My mouth felt extremely hot and cold simultaneously. *Blimey!* I thought (or words to that effect) *...somebody has washed this mug with bleach and I've swallowed some.* Anyway, I got up again to get a replacement drink when, suddenly, my right leg turned to jelly. I wobbled, like jellies do, lost my balance and fell. It's a horrible feeling when you fall, isn't it? You are totally out of control, and it bloody hurts!

At this point in proceedings, 'Macho Man' and the 'stiff upper lip' philosophy took control, the latter being particularly valid! I pulled myself up, dusted myself down and got back behind the microphone again.

'...and that was the delightful Annie Lennox, singing about an absentee angel...it's four twenty-two on 107, your time checks being sponsored by *'Your Care'*...playing next it's the Robster, yes, Robbie Williams, with *Rock DJ...'*

So, the show went on; it *must* do, mustn't it? It had just turned six-thirty as I recall; time for *'Chris's Classical Cut'*. Nothing like a bit of Mozart or Bach to build in a tea break into the schedule! (Us DJ's must protect our vocal chords, darlings!) As before, I left the microphone and went to make a brew. Much to my chagrin, my right leg went weak again, my lips tingled, and I became acquainted with the floor again.

Shit! I thought. *Bugger it! Twice? You idiot!*

Picked myself up again, forgot all about the tea, went back to the microphone, and said:

'A bit of Mozart for you there on your very own community radio station; up next, oh yes, it's a knight of the realm no less, Sir Elton John with *I'm Still Standing,* here on 107...' I followed that up with a song which featured words about being continuously pushed over but repeatedly gaining one's former status.

1. Nobody out there in Radio-land would understand what I was subconsciously referring to, and
2. I thought it was funny

In fact, it wasn't funny in the slightest. Also, it might have been handy if someone *was* aware of what could be going on; I thought it was just a dreadful day at the office. If anything, it was strangely forewarning.

After the show, I made my way home in my *Fiat Siecento.* It was, and still is, a lovely car; to many, it seemed to be a physical impossibility that a 6'5", 18-stone man could get in it, or more importantly, get out of it! I live about only a mile away from the studio, and often, no, sometimes, no, very occasionally, thought about walking in. I could hear my mum saying "Christopher, you must do more exercise". I never did though. I was aware that, at a pinch, I could pass as *Mr Blobby!* Blobby, Blobby, Blobby...!

I felt OK, still a bit dizzy, mouth tingling and leg shaky, and I felt one of my heads coming on but thought nothing of it. I sat down in my favourite armchair to digest the jolly 'goings on' in *'EastEnders'.* As soon as the 'boomp, boomp, boomps' started to denote the end of another murder or stolen bench, I realised, that because there are no advertisements on the Beeb, I had a few minutes to fix myself a coffee before *'Casualty'* came on (such is the irony of life). Bugger me; I fell again. Same way. To the right. Leg gone weak. Lips tingling. This time, I collapsed via a collision with my all-singing, all-dancing electric chair (of the massage variety, not the ultimate in penal retribution!). It could have been worse; for example, I might have collided with my brand new 48" *Smart* TV. Perish the thought. I did notice the dirt on the carpet though and made a mental note to myself that I really should move the furniture when I am using the vacuum cleaner, and not work around it.

For the first time, alarm bells began to ring. One fall in a day is just silly. Two falls in a day is just weird. Three falls in a day and there seems to be an unwanted ominous pattern emerging. Then, something else came to mind. A couple of weeks ago, I went to go out my front door because I could see my new neighbours were outside, and I just wanted to be polite and say hello. I fell *out* of my front door with not even a modicum of grace.

"Good morning," I said whilst sprawled on the tar-mac, "my name is Chris; I'm your next-door neighbour. Don't hesitate to knock if there's anything you want."

I suspect three requests went through their minds as they looked down on me with a wry smile:

1. A new neighbour please
2. A way out of their contract
3. The men in white coats

It also occurred to me that on my latest visit to Mum's about a month ago, I fell for no apparent reason going up her steps. I could see the look of terror and worry on her face.

"Don't move Chris," she whispered in a type of silent despair.

"I'm fine, Mum," I replied, "...I just slipped, that's all."

To this day, I don't know if she took on board my excuse. But the fact was I hadn't slipped at all. I had gone base over apex, and I didn't know why. I felt that I had to be a bit economical with the truth, shall we say, because even though I am in my sixties, I still appear to be 'her little boy', and she worries about me. Bless her cotton socks.

So, back to the alarm bells, which were clanging away like 'Big Ben' now. I pondered and finally arrived at the conclusion that I *think, perhaps,* something could be wrong here. It was not an emergency; I thought and considered that the 999 providers would be none too pleased with me if I called to report a fall in the evening. They'd probably think: ...*another one who's had one over the eight...* and cut me off in my prime. Nasty!

Thus, I went for the 111, non-emergency, just advice, service. The adverts do say 'if in doubt, call 111', and I was in doubt, so I called 111. The operator posed a few questions which I answered honestly (no point doing otherwise) and then I was asked if I lived alone.

"I get 25% off my community charge, so, yes, I do," I quipped.

"Well, based on your responses Mr Moore, I think it would be wise to get the paramedics to you..."

"Really?" I said, with the image of Sergeant Wilson's astute comment to Captain Mainwaring in *'Dad's Army'* of 'Do you think that's *wise,* sir?' circulating in my brain.

They arrived in ten minutes and conducted a few tests.

Then I heard those dreaded words:

"We've got to take you in, mate." The phrase was repeated: "Sorry, mate, but you've got to go in, mate."

As we all know, 'in' equates to 'hospital' which in turn equates to something being wrong.

"Oh!" I said, followed by, "you stupid boy…"

At this point, here is a word to the wise for you. When the ambulance turns up, it will probably have its blue light flashing. This is guaranteed to get all the neighbours twitching behind their curtains. My tip to you is this: draw all *your* curtains. And when you get wheeled out to the vehicle, as you will be, even if you're suffering from a broken finger nail, place a sweater or pillow case over your head so that you are not recognised, just like criminals do when they are being escorted away from court! I would also suggest the following:

1.   Don't worry
2.   Don't be scared
3.   Don't fret
4.   Don't have negative thoughts
5.   You are not alone
6.   You are not the first and certainly not the last to have this little journey
7.   *'Always look on the bright side of life…'*

Seven points that are easy to make in retrospect but just how practical are they to take on board in the cold light of day? Let's try to elaborate on them.

How many times has someone said to you, during everyday conversation, "I shouldn't worry if I were you?" Sound advice—yes. Offered with every good intention—probably yes again! But the fact remains that the person regaling you with their words of wisdom is most definitely *not* you. It's a figure of speech, isn't it? It's an expression of empathy often routinely made without much forethought, along the lines of 'nice day, isn't it?' Nice? Nice? What does nice mean? Nice for whom? He who made the observation or the intended recipient? It would really take the dispenser of advice out of their comfort zone if their astuteness was commented on in the form of a verbal response! But we don't, do we? We grin and bear it and smile accordingly—the 'proper' thing to do.

Similarly, how can you *not* be scared given the immediacy of your predicament? If I was asked to 'wing walk' on a plane, I would be justifiably scared! The same applies if I had to perform a skydive, a tight wire rope walk, a climb to the summit of Mount Everest, or, in my case, a swimming lesson. People scoff at me when I tell them I am afraid of water.

"Oh…our baby can swim, and she's only four months old!" they say, as if it is something I should be ashamed about.

"Good for your baby!" I feel like retorting, but again, convention suggests that it is best not to do. 'Your baby has not been told that he is 'a miserable specimen of humanity' by one's swimming 'teacher' (and I use that term loosely) who took great delight in seeing me struggling in the centre of the swimming pool at Junior school, hence losing face amongst my classroom patriots, which, at the tender age of ten, is not the best thing to experience. One person's experience of being scared is another person's source of ridicule and enjoyment.

I love the word 'fret'. I assume it is a verb—the state of fretting! I love lots of words, you know! I particularly like 'knickerbockers', 'anti-disestablishmentarianism', 'coagulation' 'palaeontology', 'procrastination' and conglomerations'. These are long words, but I also like short words as well like 'bottom', 'fluff', 'bob', and 'maybe'. Words, in the main, are fun. But, we don't always understand what they mean! So, to fret may mean something to one person and something totally different to another. Fret, to me, means a state of self-induced moderate panic. I suppose what I am trying to say is don't fret/panic/scream/shout abuse/shout generally/implode/explode/become a self-appointed harbinger of doom—quite frankly, what's the point after all?

Negativity, in all its forms and guises, can cause problems too. Why look on the bright side when you can wallow in the darkness? Why even consider that there is a very good chance that, given the right attention, you will in time make a complete recovery, when you can sink into the depths of despair of unhelpful thoughts like *Come on, Mr Moore, your time is up* or *Why didn't I sign up to that private health insurance scheme?* Too late, my friend, tough—take it on the chins, you did *not,* and that, as they say, is that! Positive thinking, whilst understandably being a trifle difficult to achieve at this juncture, is certainly something worth *trying* to achieve. It is a lot less painful than the alternative—believe me!

No doubt, you'll be thinking to yourself—*Why me?* This is an entirely appropriate question to ask of oneself. However, it is a flawed question; it is a rhetorical question, even though there are a lot of rhetorical questions out there which need answering (think about it!) the answer, I suppose, although bleak and forthright, is: 'Why *not* you?' You are not alone. You are not the only one who has been taken ill. I bet that if a survey could be magically conducted at exactly the time that you felt poorly, countless (well, not countless, because in this particular circumstance, they are being enumerated for this mythical survey, in which case, they *would* be counted, and therefore, by definition, would not be countless, if you get my drift!) people would have suffered a similar fate simultaneously (now there's another word I should have included as a 'like'!), rendering you 'not alone'. There's a consideration for you to ponder, and while you are at it, you can turn your attention to other meaningful and deeply philosophical matters such as the meaning of life, the futility of the human state, what lies beyond the Universe, if God is omnipotent and created 'everything', where was He when he created it? Then, of course, there's the issue of whether you have fed the cat today, or have you taken yesterday's washing out of the tumble dryer? There's so much to think about, and you are not alone in thinking. Most people do it, with varying degrees of success, almost every day! Hard to believe at times, I know; but that is the crux of the issue. Neither are you the first or the last (if you want to be posh about it: the alpha or omega) to be questioning things right now!

Try to make light of the situation you are in. Make up some jokes that will make you chortle. Here are a few that I have prepared earlier to get you in the correct frame of mind!

Joke One: Why did the beach blush? Because the sea weed!

Joke Two: What did the grape say when he was run over by a lorry? He didn't say anything but just let out a little whine!

Joke Three: What did the big chimney say to the little chimney? You're too young to smoke!

Joke Four: What did the big telephone say to the little telephone? You're too young to be engaged!

Joke Five: Why is it pointless taking a frog to a library? Because every book he is offered, he just repeats "read it, read it…!"

Joke Six: Why did the tomato blush? Because he saw the salad dressing!

Joke Seven? "No, no, please no more!"
"Please, have mercy on us Christopher: stop! STOP NOW!"
"OK then!"

Houston, We've Got a Problem

Just by considering the above 'concerns' and depending whether you are a glass half full or half empty person indeed, you *have* got something to, at least, occupy your mind. Let's not deny it or beat about the bush: you have got key issues to contend with, yes, potential problems, which at best could be a major inconvenience or in a worst-case scenario, could drastically affect the lifestyle you have become accustomed to. But there are a couple of key words here to bear in mind: 'potential' and 'half full or half empty'. Look at it this way—problems are for solving, generally, they are not insurmountable. As for 'half full, half empty', read optimistic or pessimistic, and opt for the former. Positivism is a great healer. It is healthy even if you are not. I would also add to that 'perspective'. *Whatever* it is that you are being admitted for, there are countless others in a far worse position than you. You will become aware of this when you enter the hallow grounds of the hospital. I am not dismissing how you are probably feeling right now—believe me, I know, as I will tell you later. But try to adopt a mindset that says: "Yes, I have a problem or two here, but they won't get the better of me."

Mind you, that calm and collected approach is difficult to accept when your house is occupied by two paramedics whose very words imply that it is imperative for you to leave your premises with immediate effect. Your brain cells will start working in overdrive—'brainstorming' it is called apparently. In my case, this was accentuated when one of the guys said:

"There's no hurry, Mr Moore," immediately followed up with "Ready mate, we'll take you as you are." As an ex-teacher, under normal circumstances, I would have pointed out to the gentleman that his statement was self-contradictory, but I wasn't inclined to do that.

No. At that precise moment, I was having to process enquiries of my own making at a pretty alarming rate. In no particular order of importance, the thought processes went a bit like this:

1. *Take me as I am? You are kidding, aren't you? Oh, you're not kidding.* In theory, this would have been acceptable to me, but there I was, resplendent in my ripped PJ top, my dirty jogging bottoms, and my thoroughly worn-out slippers which had seen better days (bit like me really, really sympathetic my slippers were).
2. *House keys? God, where are the house keys?*
3. *Bloody hell, it's a mess in here. Please God, don't let anyone else come in!* A statement which, on reflection, might be just slightly inappropriate because if burglars did break in perchance, they'd probably consider the place had been done over already and therefore do a runner pretty damn quick.
4. *Cash; I'll need some cash.* I placed a few bits of coinage into my pocket, only later to find that it had fallen out. Again, a bit like me, except that I fell *over,* not *out.* A case of over and out it appeared. Leg before wicket. Tits over arse! For some reason, at that point, I had a flashback to my days at *Selhurst Park,* the home of the magnificent Crystal Palace football club, where on many an occasion, if a player was tackled and lost balance, the crowd would chant the refrain *'she fell over, she fell over'.* She? Female? As Frank Spencer used to claim in *'Some Mothers do 'ave 'em',* his maleness was not an issue!
5. *Mobile phone, mobile phone...* I freely admit to 'Moby', as I call it, being the most immobile mobile in the West, South, North or East. I never take it anywhere nor know its number. It's just there. I'm on this scheme called '£1 weekly', this gives me about 70 texts, an hour's worth of calls, and a certain amount of 'data' (whatever that is). It does not take pictures. It does not make your evening meal. You don't have to say 'OK Google' to it. It makes calls and texts. It suits me fine. Every time I go into the phone shop to top it up, the conversation flows as follows:
    "A £10 top-up voucher please."
    "How long will £10 last you mate?" (I'm not his mate; he's a moody so and so.)
    "Ten weeks, mate."

"Really?" he asks as if I'm talking a foreign language.

"Yes mate; I'm on a £1 a week scheme."

"Oh yes…well, would you like a free phone?"

It is said, of course, that nothing in life is free. But, in this case, it genuinely *is*, I think.

"Cool, mate; cheers!"

Upon which, he hands me a box containing a brand-new phone. It's the same as mine. I'll add it to the other six at home!

Now, a big tip here. Another very big tip. When in possession of a mobile phone, an essential pre-requisite is an item called the charger. If you possibly can, I would advise you to take said item with you always, especially if being admitted to hospital. The 'problem' was, I didn't, and, therefore, I was left with Moby rendered absolutely useless on my bedside table. It looked so sad and pathetic, so I hid it in a drawer. Christopher, you are officially a dick!

6. *Oh my God, the washing up; I haven't done it!* On this one, do not be too perturbed. As a very amusing 'Get Well' card that I received said: "It will still be there when you are back." True, but in what state? Covered in mould or slime and stinking the place out? Never mind, there's nothing to be done right now, that is, unless, you have a wife and/or a dishwasher, which are essentially the same thing. I have neither. That's not exactly true: there is a dishwasher sitting in the corner of the kitchen, but it seems to make the plates dirtier than when they were put into the machine. Yes, you've just got to resign yourself to a putrid, vomit-inducing mess when you return something to look forward to and something to persuade yourself to invest in a pair of rubber gloves like you've always said you would. And, of course, if you're anything like me, you are used to this scenario anyway!

7. *Did I? Did I?* Attempt to dispel any OCD tendencies you may have meticulously cultivated over the years. It really is of no benefit to torture yourself mentally by trying to recall whether you locked the door, closed the windows, set the alarm, put the security lights on, put the rubbish out, put the cat out, fed the goldfish and the like. None of this will be done by your good self whilst you are strapped down on an ambulance bed with seat belts! The chances

are that you *have* carried out these tasks with supreme diligence as a matter of course.

8. As for number eight onward: give up! Your mind will relish the opportunity to taunt you with further problems—imaginary or otherwise. The way I deal with this conundrum is by recalling Bob Dylan's song— *'Rainy Day Women # 12 and 35'*. I often wonder whatever became of women one to eleven, and thirty-six onwards? And why were they women specifically designed for when precipitation was apparent during daylight hours? It's a mystery to me and trying to work out just what is going to crop up in your mind with all those hours of leisure ahead, it inevitably will be a mystery to you as well. I wouldn't give it the time of day.

"Time to go, Mr Moore." My stream of consciousness is interrupted. "Your transportation awaits."

You're wheeled into the back of a very sterile looking ambulance with a blue light flashing. You've locked the door, hopefully. There's no turning back now, well, not for a while anyway. Your status as a hospital virgin has been taken away from you.

You're on your way to being 'In', with a big 'I'.

However, the thing is—what can you do about it, with a big 'D'? You can feel sorry for yourself; you can ask of yourself, "What on earth have I done to deserve this?" You can go down the 'blame route'; you can try to recall signs or indicators of the troubles which lay ahead but you decided to ignore them! Why didn't I cut down on those; why did I drink too much of that? With every possible respect, this line of enquiry is fruitless, futile and time-consuming. Why not use this enforced 'slow down' in your lifestyle to your advantage? Here's an idea—you are to set foot inside an Ambulance; it might as well be a fantasy land as far as you are concerned. Take a moment to familiarise yourself with your new surroundings. If you think about it, you are now the lead part in your very own medical drama programme which will be aired on prime-time Saturday night TV! Your first task, therefore, is to give your programme a name: something catchy like *'Ambulance'* for example! It's got to be a one word title, and in some way relevant, but it is probably best to avoid calling it *'Shit'*, or *'Bugger'*, or *'Damn'*—astute though these words are, they would probably not contribute to your cause when asking for your brainchild to be made into a series suitable for family viewing!

And then, of course, you need a plot.

Here is a plot I dreamed up earlier. I decided against it in the end because it seemed just a little bit contrived, but I have no doubt that, with a few adjustments here and there, it could be a massive hit in TV-land! Treat it as a gift from me to you as a mark of gratitude for you purchasing this book, even if you have dug it out of the bargain basement bin in your local charity shop!

The story centres around the notion that a fictional 'you' finally 'flips' when, on dashing to pick up the telephone which rings just in the crucial moment of your favourite film or treasured documentary entitled '*The Difficult Love Life of a Hedgehog*', discovers that it is the thirteenth call today from a Japanese, Chinese or Scottish salesperson enquiring after the 'recent accident you have suffered'.

The conversation goes something like this:

"Hello Mr… *(a pregnant pause whilst the surname is checked on their records)…Moo-er…*"

"It's Mr Moore actually, as in 'more', rhymes with 'bore', or 'chore', which it is, listening to you…"

The sarcasm is wasted, but never mind.

"We are calling about the accident you had recently…"

You want to say that you have *not,* to the best of your knowledge, either been involved in, or suffered from, an accident, recent or ancient. But then, there is an overwhelming desire to 'play along' with this anonymous person's claim that you have had a misfortune by taking it to a level of absurdity which would inevitably result in the caller slamming the phone down on you, after the penny (or Yen?) had finally dropped. *That would* guarantee the end of these incessant calls, wouldn't it? So, you play the game, with a wry smile.

"Do you mean the one where I tripped over a leaf?"

"Yes, sir."

"Which resulted in me breaking my leg in three places?"

"Yes, sir."

"And the tree, from which it fell, denied all responsibility?"

"Yes, sir."

"Saying I wouldn't be able to prove in a court of law that the leaf actually belonged to the tree I held responsible?"

"Where did this accident happen, sir?"

"In the middle of a lake!"

"Which lake, sir? We need to know to process your claim, and was the tree there voluntarily or against its wishes?"

"I would say against its wishes…"

"Why do you say that, sir?"

"Because it had been chopped down and was, in effect, a log…"

"A log, sir? You said it was a tree."

At this point, you realise that the game is 'up'. The joke is very much on you! Out of sheer and utter exasperation, you slam the phone down in disgust, with such brutal force that the entire piece of equipment and surrounding ornaments fall to the floor, create an obstacle, over which you fall ungracefully, and somehow manage to break your leg. Normally, you wouldn't mind: being an actor by profession, darling, the utterance of the phrase 'break a leg' is something you hear most every day and is intended to wish *you,* the greatly admired and respected thespian, every possible good luck! It is not intended to be a literal requirement!

There you have it then: the acorn of an idea for a storyline from which a massive Oak of a television blockbuster, nay, 'Gem' will grow.

Have that one on me!

Lie Back and Think of England

Or, if you're Scottish, Scotland; or if you're Polish, Poland. I am not going to go through my entire repertoire of countries, but I am sure you get my drift, so to speak. And, let's be frank, or Keith, or Sarah, or Wayne and Waynetta (Harry Enfield's 'slobs' I believe), there's two things you definitely will be doing for the duration of your stay—lying in your bed for countless hours, which sounds alright to start with but I can assure you that the novelty quickly wears off and contemplating the meaning of life and why you haven't swapped power supplier.

Never mind all that. Let's address some basics. You are not going to hospital for a laugh. You are either in for treatment on an injury or illness, or with extreme bad luck—both. In my case, as I've mentioned, it was a stroke. A small one, but enough for the experts to arrange my mini-break here. I had always been of the attitude that things like strokes happen to other people—me? Not a chance! Not in a month of Sundays! But, as the old expression so astutely refers to: "Well, there you go!" I'd *heard* about strokes, yes; but *knew* about them, no. I couldn't decide if a stroke was something you did to please a cat or was a swinging motion with a tennis racquet!

If you fall (sorry about the over usage of this word but it is kind of relevant) into the 'injured' category, you have my sympathy too. You're probably in excruciating pain, physically re-structured into an unnatural, uncomfortable position, joined in union with some weird and wacky machinery and perhaps 'plastered' in the literal sense of the word, probably wishing you were plastered in the 'other' sense of the word to make the pain go away! Life's a bugger, isn't it? I've got a mug in my kitchen cupboard. It's one of those novelty joke mugs that stands slanted. On the side of it are printed the words: "It's hard to keep things in balance." It is a very droll comment indeed, but quite right. It sometimes takes words on a mug to place things in their proper perspective. Hang on to this thought though—you are *not* ill. You may well be a bloody mess, yes, but you are injured. You stand a fair to middling chance of being reconstructed like *The Five Million Dollar Man*. In effect, you are temporarily incapacitated. Hopefully, in time, you'll improve and get back to running the marathon again.

The same, of course, applies if you are in the 'ill' category but, if you are anything like me, a little niggling doubt will be biting away at you. You too need to accept that, given time, *you* stand a fair to middling chance of making a recovery as well. This will enable you to re-commence your favourite pastimes too, be they fishing, bungee jumping, tight-rope walking or tiddlywinks. My goal was to re-impose myself to my undeserving listener over the local airwaves. I'm cruel like that!

Be *real* to yourself. Acknowledge the inevitable and blindingly obvious. If you are injured, someone will see it and give you all the sympathy in the world.

"Ahh! how's your leg, duck?"

"Fine, thanks, just shattered a wee bit and about to be separated from my torso…"

"Lovely, that's nice to hear Ducks! Don't do anything I wouldn't do, will you?"

If you are ill though, it is sort of impossible for you to be patronised in this way (which is clearly beneficial), nobody can see any real outward signs of it. You may even develop feelings of being a fraud. But remember, the experts 'strongly advised' you to come to hospital. You are here for a genuine reason. I've already mentioned my reason for admittance. Other conditions may well include:

- Heart attack
- Pneumonia
- Confusion
- Anxiety
- Stress
- Depression
- Diabetes
- Hypertension
- Blood disorders
- A rare tropical disease unknown to mankind

To name but ten! Now, here's a fun exercise for you. In the spaces below, firstly write down just *why* you are where you are. Then, try to think of five other reasons why other people are where *they* are right now.

1. I'm here because ………………………………….

2. Others are here because…………………………

3. And……………………………………………..

4. And……………………………………………..

5. And……………………………………………..

6. And, finally……………………………………….

Well done! I'm no Doctor (actually, I might be of the 'philosophy' kind if things progress with my research) but I guess you could think of so many more.

Next thing to do is this! In the space below, write down your condition again, but this time in big, bold letters, underlined, (always a favourite with teachers, ex or otherwise) with <u>PRIDE</u>, and, even if you are of a religious inclination, end it off with an expletive of your choice! (I'm sure your God will turn a blind eye or a deaf ear to your choice of phraseology!

'HELLO, MY NAME IS……………………………………

I AM IN HOSPITAL BECAUSE……………………………

AND I DON'T GIVE A……………………………………

There's an advert on the TV that says "Better?" and the reply comes "Better!"

Be assured, you have taken your first steps towards recovery! You are 'accepting' your condition, and this is good! If you can, think back to when Neil Armstrong took those first few strides on the Moon saying, "…this is one small step for man, one giant leap for mankind…" I wonder if that was scripted. I wonder if the conspiracy theory about the moon landing being a total hoax for propaganda purposes had any truth behind it. Whether it did or did not happen, it is the *sentiment* that is so relevant. Your journey back has begun. And concerning the moon landing controversies, I blame those pesky Russians myself!

Having achieved this, your first goal (let's hope you're not a Palace fan because that probably would be your last goal!), don't feel in the slightest bit embarrassed or guilty about lying back in your allotted pit and RELAX! Think of pleasant things! You've been through a lot already, and there's so much more to come, you lucky people. Let me tell you why I think this is valuable advice.

But before that, it's useful to consider the trials and tribulations you've been through already. By now, you are most likely the talk of the neighbourhood; despite your efforts, your attempt to maintain secrecy and/or anonymity would have failed spectacularly. You've endured the journey in an ambulance to your 'local' hospital (a term which covers a multitude of sins) with a fair degree of success despite discovering just about every single pot-hole en-route. No doubt, you've been bombarded with seemingly endless questions from the paramedic who sits next to you, which you really are not in the mood to answer.

On arrival, you are 'checked in', waited and waited in A+E for someone to acknowledge your existence, and you would have scanned the damage in front of you—drunks, junkies, the homeless, the time-wasters and a few actual genuine cases. You will also have noticed the neon sign that spitefully declares: "Current waiting time is four hours." Take no notice of that. I will be much longer. And then, when you've just about given up the will to remain functioning, you will report to the formidable figure of the 'Triage Nurse'. This is a lady or gentleman who deems whether you are worthy of putting the NHS further into debt. If you pass or fail her examination (depending on how you see it at this stage), you'll either be told to 'go away' or be informed that you are being taken to a specific ward—in my case, the stroke unit. You will be wheeled to your new base, at which point, you will again utilise your skills of perusal and judgement and quickly arrive at your very own judgement. It will either be "OMG", or "…seems all right; I've got the window seat".

Now, of course, one of the prime purposes of going to bed is to sleep; the other, I suppose is procreation, but to the best of my memory, that is not necessarily true. Here's another tip: be prepared for periods of 'unrelaxation'. You *won't* be sleeping like a baby or a log, in the case of the latter, I wonder how that is accomplished anyway, given that it is an inanimate object. This reminds me of *'The Four Yorkshire Men'* sketch when, John Cleese, to 'out-do' his friends and their reminiscences about life, declares that he rises from his pit before he has even got into it! There are an infinite number of reasons why your relaxation might be a trifle limited during your stay, or 'confinement', as they used to say about ladies. Here are just eighteen of them:

1. Blood pressure monitoring
2. Temperature readings
3. A thing that goes on your finger or ear to check you are ticking
4. Nurses to get you out of bed
5. Nurses to get you into bed
6. Breakfast, dinner and tea Trolley
7. Drug Trolley
8. *Horlicks* Trolley
9. Trolley for the other Trolley
10. Registrars
11. Consultants
12. Students
13. Pharmacists
14. Physiotherapists
15. Psychologists
16. 'Well-being' people
17. Bed makers
18. Gentle-folk of the cloth

In the next seven spaces, add your own; that will get it to a nice round twenty-five.

19..

20..

21..

22..

23..

24..

25..

Isn't that just so satisfying! "God's in his heaven; all's right with the world," as Robert Browning would have it.

I shall now suggest a few cardinal rules, which will help you to preserve your sanity. Ignore them at your peril! You have been warned, Oh, yee of little faith...

- Don't let numbers one to twenty-five 'get to you'
- Do not 'ear-wig' other patients' conversations with their carers. Honestly, it will freak you out!
- Make friends with *all* the right people: primarily, the tea/coffee lady!
- Ascertain where the nearest loo is, whether it is bi-sexual (you know, for men and women), and whether you will need a 'Sara Steady' +1 or 2 to facilitate said visitation. This will be written on the board above your bed so that everyone can have a right old giggle!
- Do not upset anyone you deem to be vital to your recovery. For example, do not complain that: "...the food here is crap...", or "...you're bloody hurting me...!"
- If you are not due any visitors, invest in a cheap pair of ear plugs or cotton wool balls. This advice also applies if you have a few visitors around *your* bed. There is a substantial likelihood that you will become invisible to them, whilst they happily engage in deep and meaningful conversations about this year's visit to the Algarve, the price of double-glazing, and any local gossip, it is humanly possible to dredge up. The other tactic is to fake, or even achieve, sleep; or at least a state of Zen-like meditation. *Medication* can work well too: just ask for a dose of intravenous morphine, for example, that will do the trick nicely.
- Develop a gigantic desire and hunger for grapes!
- Make no attempt to either disguise your farts; neither try implying someone else is to blame by looking accusingly at the person comatose in the bed next door!
- Prepare yourself for a daily dose of constipation relief, and then be ready for the consequences!

Rules, of course, are there to be broken though. Perhaps they should be re-designated as 'advisories'. And, if you are by nature a compliant sort of person who generally does what he or she is told to do, then at least take a hefty pile of salt, let alone a little pinch when reacting to the rule in question.

I have quite a catholic understanding, and I use that word purposefully and with valid intention, when it comes to someone, or something, telling me what to do. In this instance, I am now referring to a 'something'—a big 'something' unquestionably—the might of the Roman Catholic Church no less. I was born and brought up as 'Church of England'—created, ironically enough by one of the 'Henry' monarchs (I've lost count as to whom I specifically recall) who'd basically 'had enough' of the rules being imposed on him from a faraway place called the Vatican, which happened to be the HQ of the aforementioned 'faith'. It was something to do with marriage, and the ending of the same; it appeared that Henry took exception of being told that the Catholic thinking on marriage was that it was for 'life' and for 'sickness and health', and that therefore he was effectively barred from getting a divorce. I can just imagine his line of thinking:

How very dare you question me: I am the King of England (or, as my old History teacher implored us, his eager to learn pupils, to pronounce it as: 'Engg-Land! Bless him). He was labelled 'The Senior Master' of a Secondary-Modern school designated for 11+ exam failures; the establishment type where the pupils were destined for the scrap-heap of society! I should know: I went there as a pupil in the first instance, and latterly, as a teacher. He would not have been out of place as 'The Senior Master' of Harrow or Eton, but hey! That's another story, which will feature in my next foray into the world of publishing, so you will not need a 'spoiler alert' this time. No—you'll be required to buy my next book, which will be available at all good bookshops, some OK ones, some downright rank and dodgy ones and some re-cycling centres!

I've digressed! Where am I? Henry and the rule that said he must remained married.

Sod it!, or words to that effect I am sure he mulled over in his mind, *I'll set up my own church; it will be called the Church of England, and I'll write the rules!*

And, thus, a massive chunk of social history came into existence.

Move on a few centuries, and there I was, a young, naïve, freshly-qualified teacher, whose sole aim in life was to right the world's wrongs via my impeccable and inspirational teaching. It must be said that class 8Z, during the last lesson of the day on a wet, dark November afternoon, did not quite share my enthusiasm for all things educational, shall we say, can't blame them actually; I'd rather be in my local anyway, which indeed was where I was heading at the tolling of the 'day's end' bell. It was like a *Grand Prix*: '…and they're approaching the school gate, just the rubbish bins to avoid, and in the lead, we have John from 10C (not 10CC; that's a different concept entirely), closely followed by Ruth from 9Y, but coming up on the inside is your odds-on favourite, Mr Moore, aka 'Sir', whose gaining on the leaders at break-neck speed…!

Oh, so naïve, in so many ways! Basically, I was a good 'Sir', as I was in life generally. I used to panic, for example, if I was cycling at night without lights on—shock, horror—what a rule to break! If there was a rule in existence which said "you are now required to take a long walk along a short pier", I would have done it! It *might* have occurred to me that if I did follow this rule to its logical conclusion, I would, in effect, have fallen into the sea, which would have been particularly galling because of my inability to swim, but I *would* have done it, nonetheless.

What's that you're saying?

"No, you bloody wouldn't, would you? You flaming idiot!"

And my response would be: "Let me think about that one, and I'll get back to you. My 'people' can talk to your 'people' if you like?"

But, you see, in many ways, I liken myself to Henry. I proposed to the lady I wanted to be my wife. She said "yes" then came the 'B' word—'BUT'.

"But what?"

"Well…?"

"Oh, it's a 'W' word now, is it?"

"But, well… We'll have to get permission from Father at my church…"

Yes—you've guessed it. My wife to be was Catholic.

So, I went to these meetings, where several 'rules' were introduced to me, including that marriage is forever, despite all the trials and tribulations that life can test you with, and that if we were bestowed with any children, the rule said that I had to agree to them being brought up as Catholics.

I agreed to these rules—'no skin off my nose' was my mindset. Fast forward twenty-three years, and my wife then petitioned *me* for divorce! Funny old game, isn't it…Life!!

Rules *are* there for breaking, or for squirming out of, if you possibly can!

Ask Maradona if he broke the 'handball' rule in the Argentina versus England football match!

Ask the English goalkeeper, Gordon Banks, if Maradona was *justified* in breaking that rule?

Why is it 'the rule' that in Britain, we all drive on the left side of the road, whereas just about everywhere else in the world drives on the left-hand side of the road? Ho-hum!

Food, Glorious Food...

"While we're in the mood, cold jelly and custard." As a child, I used to get even the simplest of lyrics mixed up a bit, and happily sang of 'ripe cherries and mustard', which admittedly would not have been to everyone's taste buds. The only reason I mention this is because as I rested resplendently in my bed, this song came to mind, along with the confused words and caused me an immediate dilemma. The cherries would be served with a liberal coating of *Coleman's*. Similarly, said cherries would have stones in them, raising an immediate question—how do you get the stones out whilst retaining some sort of decorum within the hospital setting?

Option 1: Pick the stones out with your fingers, but your digits would then be covered with mustard leaving you with the only choice of wiping them clean on your nice clean bed linen, resulting in the bed makers (nurses) being none too impressed with you.

Option 2: Get the nurse to do it. However, it is somewhat questionable if 'cherry stone removal' is in their job specification. If I was a nurse, and I was asked to perform this duty, I'd immediately get my Union Rep on the case and call for an all-out strike, brothers, sisters, comrades (delete as appropriate).

Option 3: Not entirely viable this one, and best to be avoided, but as *The Beach Boys* declared: "Wouldn't it be nice." Work the stone around in your mouth, pucker up, take aim and 'fire!'. Award yourself points as follows:

- For hitting a monitor: 10 points
- For a direct hit into somebody else's water jug: 20 points
- A cool 40 points for a direct hit into another patient's cup of tea
- And a maximum 50 points, the jackpot, for a direct contact with that lovely young nurse's posterior!

Come to think of it, there are so many references to food in songs and literature, isn't there? "If music be the food of love, play on," said Shakespeare in *Twelfth Night. Matthew 4:4* states that "Man doth not live by bread alone", whilst Marie Antoinette is reputed to have said "Let them eat cake". In the case of the latter, let's not go into conspiracy theory number two, which suggests she never made such an utterance at all, but in all honesty, who gives a flying fig (well, I might if I knew what one was). Forget all that nonsense; here's another challenge for you—try to list six songs, musicals or references with some connection to food.

1. ....

2. ....

3. ....

4. ....

5. ....

6. ....

Now, let's get back to the main emphasis of this chapter. Once admitted, the chances are you will be partaking in at least a couple of NHS meals. My guess is that you've heard horror stories on this very subject before. But my advice to you on this one is to remember exactly where you are—that is, right here, right now, you are in hospital. You are *not* in any of the following establishments:

- *McDonalds, KFC, Subway, Harvester, Beefeater* or any other such eating establishment, of which many others are available
- A *Michelin 3** Restaurant
- Your local Pub
- Your mother's abode for her beautiful Sunday roast
- The works canteen

Do not expect a cordon-bleu eating experience, because you won't get one. I'll tell you what you will get though—thoroughly good and tasty food with a good amount of choice. You will inevitably hear the moaning Minnies in nearby beds saying: "I can't eat this; it's disgusting", or "What on earth is this?", or "I didn't order this". I heard one patient say: "This tastes like shit!"

Really? I wonder if he'd ever partaken of a plate of poo! Perhaps dung beetles do, and I know that dogs have a fascinating tendency to roll in the stuff to apply some sort of delightful perfume, but humans eating it? I would seriously doubt it, which in turn leads to doubt the relevance and accuracy of the statement and, on the scale of wrongness, he is very wrong indeed. In fact, I'd go on to say that rather than tasting it, he is talking it!

My typical diet at home goes something like this. If I am up before 10:00, I'll have a slice of toast with marmite and a cup of tea. If I have risen later than that, I skip it! Lunch tends to be a fried-egg sandwich, or beans on toast, with coffee—something like that. And for dinner, it's something out of the freezer—pie, fish, meat, sausages, oven chips, and mixed vegetables perhaps, and I never have a sweet/pudding/afters (depending on how posh you are). I try to treat myself on a Sunday; so, it is *Aunt Bessy* to the rescue.

I am hardly chef of the year, but I am not bad. I have not poisoned anyone yet—to the very best of my knowledge.

But now, look at what happens in hospital. The day you are admitted, OK, your choice is going to be very limited because, like you, they did not know that you were becoming a guest today; it was a very last-minute booking shall we say. You could well end up being offered what the person, who had occupied the bed before you, had ordered, before he knew he had made good his exit. The NHS kitchen staff has an excellent scheme going here. Sometime in the afternoon or evening, you will be given a menu for the next day's meals. I invariably chose a cooked meal for lunch and another cooked meal for dinner. All right, if you're used to a 'full English' for breakfast, forget that; you will be going all continental! In addition to this, hot or cold drinks are served at regular intervals during the day.

Let me give you an idea of the choices that faced me on a Wednesday.

For the first course of Lunch, you could select from:

- Roast Lamb with mint sauce
- Chicken a la King
- Lentil crumble
- Gravy
- Creamed potatoes

- Roasted potatoes
- Cabbage
- Diced Suede
- Pilchards
- Salad bowl

For the second course, the following was available:

- Bread and Butter pudding
- Custard sauce
- Ground Rice Pudding
- Fresh Orange
- Fruit cocktail in natural sauce

Moving on to supper, for the first course comprised:

- Minestrone Soup
- Orange juice
- Plain Omelette
- Croquette potatoes
- Baked beans
- Eden Cheese
- Salad bowl
- Ham sandwich (wholemeal)
- Ham sandwich (white)
- Tuna mayonnaise (wholemeal)
- Tuna mayonnaise (white)

Followed by:

- Victoria Sponge (such a nice lady!)
- Fresh Yoghurt
- Ice cream
- Pears in natural sauce
- Cheese and biscuits

You can choose portion size, whatever bits you want (I suppose within reason!), and each element of the menu is described as 'a healthy option' 'high energy' 'soft diet' and 'vegetarian', or a combination of some or all of these. I, for one, was very impressed. The point here is—be realistic with your expectations.

To round off this discussion, here are another couple of useful tips.

1. If the staff serving up the meals offers to open the marmalade or margarine packs or fruit juice containers, let them do it! Basically, you need fingers like pincers to accomplish this task, and it can get messy!

2. There's always a space on the form that says: "If you wish to make a comment on any aspect of the catering department, please do so here." I'll tell you what! Make somebody's day! I'm not advocating telling porkies, but the occasional 'thank you', or 'the chicken Kiev was lovely', or 'I appreciate your cooking and the meal was really tasty', sentiments like that, go a long way. You never know, but it just might bring a smile to somebody's face that's got used to a diet (sorry about the pun) of 'I wouldn't give that to my cat'.

At this juncture, I am going to be as bold to make a 'prediction'. This is something I never do lightly or indeed with much success. When I was a wee young 'nipper', my dad, bless his heart, took on a part-time job to supplement the family income at the time when the Moore household needed it most—I had Gannet like tendencies when it came to food, and little Bev wasn't that too far behind in the food-eating stakes as well. (Please excuse the pun, but it is clever, is it not; I'm sure that the great literary giants of our time and before splattered a few puns across their manuscripts for the general enjoyment of the reading public—the customer! My mantra was if it wasn't breathing, mooing, or bleating, eat it! I never was very good at being Vegetarian. Even during my 'peace and love and goodwill to all mankind' phase, that never did stretch to animals of the eating type! In balance though, I did not pose any kind of threat to the family pets we had over the years. The first was *Georgy Porgy, Pretty Boy*—this was a budgerigar that had obviously made an attempt for freedom from his previous owner but had clearly decided that freedom wasn't all that it was cracked up to be, so basically flew himself, without deviation, repetition or hesitation, into a spare bird cage, that the neighbour at the bottom of the garden *happened* to possess, as you do. I was at a bit of a loss as to why Mum and Dad had chosen to call him *Georgy Porgy, Pretty Boy.*

"That's a silly name for a bird," I said.

"No, it isn't," Mum retorted in the way that only your mother can do. "It's his name!"

"Ah, but how do you *know* that's his name?" I replied triumphantly.

At which point, said bird opened his beak and declared "*Georgy Porgy, Pretty boy*".

I was upstaged by a bloody bird! *How* embarrassing! The story of my life, I suppose!

The next pet was a stray from London; we 'acquired' (cat-napped) it—sorry—her, on one of Bev and my regular summer holiday week at Nan and Auntie Amy's place in London.

"Can we take it—sorry—her home please, Mum and Dad? Please…!"

Mum and Dad agreed, I guess under duress. Mum drove the car home. Dad held on to the cat for sheer life and was scratched to smithereens as a result. Unlike the bird, the cat could not speak, but, after a few days of hiding behind the boiler, and generally 'relieving itself for all cats everywhere', we decided on a name—another silly one—*Cinders*. This, I was subsequently informed, was to be the shortened version of her name, which would appear as *Cinderella Cleopatra Annabella Moore* on her passport. Said feline also learnt to respond as *Tin-Tin; Tin-Sin, Puss-Puss* or any other suitable variation on a theme.

Cinders lived the life of Riley. She was treated to boiled rabbit, fish and cheese—three of her culinary favourites. Your average 'cat food from a tin' did not suffice, I am afraid. And over the years, *Cinders* went from being a scrawny old stray with no fur on her back legs, to a fat, obese, 'thing' with a huge undercarriage that wobbled when occasionally she saw fit to raise from her slumbers and take a step or two by way of exercise!

No diet for *Tin-Tin;* she dined on the top table only!

Again, where was I?

Oh yes!

I was talking about predictions, food and the associated need for Dad to take a part-time job.

The part-time job he took was being a 'football coupons collector'. This was back in the day when you had to actually 'predict' the results of forthcoming football games. You could either select three 'draws', five 'away' wins or nine 'home' victories. I considered that the latter was the best way to have effective predictions so, I would study form, list nine times that were in essence 'guaranteed' to win at home, and hence result in a nice pay-out for me—a boost to my pocket money, shall we say.

Every Saturday, at about four forty-five, I would position myself in front of the TV as the football results were read out.

"Yep, got that, and that, and that and…"

Horror of horrors, it was a draw.

Bugger!

I also predicted that Man would never walk on the moon, that the world would be engulfed in a Maoist/Trotskyite/Leninist/Stalinist international Government, and that TV's were unable of depicting the real world because the pictures were only in black and white, being a gross misrepresentation of reality as it affects the working classes.

I learnt early on in life, therefore, that I was not very good at predictions.

In an equivalent way, I soon became to realise that because of my unwieldy and unconditional love for all things edible, I and the notion of 'dieting' were never going to be the best of bed-fellows. This is as true today as it ever has been. Just recently, I purchased (and, co-incidentally was 'given' by a person who clearly had my interests at heart!) a 'portion-plate'. In theory, this is designed to make you cut back on the sheer amount of what you ingest by dividing the plate into 'segments' for your proteins, carbohydrates and the like. This is an example of a valid concept not *quite* thought through; there is nothing to say that you can't load the plate vertically! OK, it does defeat the object of the exercise admittedly, and it does require the assistance of a forklift truck to transport the plate to the table, but that is a small price to pay, surely? And why am I telling you, dear reader, all of this? Well, I suppose the point I am trying to make is enjoy the hospital food but with realistic expectations!

A Stroke of Luck or, Alternatively, What I *Meant* to Say Was This

Have you ever experienced a 'nasty turn'? You know when you want to traverse in roughly a forward direction but instead of which, in some peculiar state of unawareness, your mind, your body, or maybe some concoction of the two intertwined, suffer from an outbreak of 'computer says no!'. The point is very much against your expressed personal wishes and desires, you begin to do a passable impression of the 'Leaning Tower of Pisa' (refer to the section on 'food' for more detail relating to this!). But there is one major difference—he is firm, but fair, by the way! Instead of *leaning,* you tumble. And let's not beat about the bush (Shepherd's or otherwise), tumbling is putting it rather mildly. Common expressions to describe this state of non-control include going 'base over apex', 'arse overhead', 'bum over tits' and other such niceties. Indeed, if the word 'spectacular' was invented to describe a fall, it would take the meaning of the word to uncharted territories in spectacular land—spectacularville!

And of course, anything could have caused this predicament. You might have fallen over your cat, which seems to be getting a lot of mentions in this story. You might have tripped over a leaf. You possibly slipped on black ice. You may have been just a little bit tipsy. I must tell you this little aside. Do you remember those advertisements on the TV which say, "Where there's blame, there's a claim?" And those phone calls constantly reminding you of the 'accident' you had recently. Well, in the case of the latter, out of sheer devilment really and total exasperation at the number of these beastly calls I was receiving, I thought I'd play a little game. I claimed that I had incurred serious injuries by tripping over a leaf! They *believed* me!

"How big was the leaf, sir?"
"Was it on or off the tree?"
"What type of leaf was it, sir?"

I could not believe my ears! My prank was being taken with every respect! At this point in proceedings, I lost the will to play and put the phone down.

Anyway, back to the plot. Falling is an undignified act. One second up, next second down; one moment compos mentis, the next moment sprawling on the deck. You'll be wondering 'how?', 'why?', 'when?', 'why?' and 'why?', because you do tend to repeat yourself in these circumstances. For a split second, you will no doubt consider your very existence and check for spiders, cobwebs, dirt, blood, injuries (approaching vehicles if outside on an icy night!) and a whole myriad of things that you've never wondered about, witnessed or considered (either actively or inactively) before. The next thing you look out for our fellow human beings, who will identify themselves as one of two types:

1. The 'Good Samaritan', who will gaze down upon you and ask: "Are you all right?" In this case, resist the temptation to answer with sarcasm like "oh, yes, never been better…"
2. The unsympathetic type, who will gaze down on you and giggle at your indignity.

Even your mother, whilst obviously being concerned about her son's immediate welfare, might well be concerned as to whether your well-cultivated weight of eighteen stone had crushed her beloved Petunias!

In my case, my fall was not due to physical conditions, but a concern of the medical type. No one to blame and nothing to claim. I will admit straight away—I have had a stroke of luck, given the severity (or lack of it) as to what happened to me.

The next event that generally happens in any fall is the 'check the contents of the pockets' ritual. Firstly, money. Have you been cruelly denied of it in the fall? Has it gone to meet its maker, rolled down a drain or generally out of sight? No! What luck! My 54p (at the last count) was neatly embedded within the confines of my snot laden excuse of a handkerchief, which was not seen in the inside of my washing machine since the dawn of time! "Your money is present and correct sir; it has attached itself to your rag." Good luck indeed! It has gone nowhere!

And so, to the next pocket wherein potentially lives the phone— yes—dear old 'Moby'! Well, it's *called* a phone in the broadest sense of the word. It is at times like this that I ponder the very validity of the word 'phone'. Is it a verb? Is it a noun? Is it a pronoun? Is it an adjective? Is it Superman? Call me 'stupid'.

"OK, I will, hello STUPID!"

But I always worked on the assumption that a phone—no—let's stop being lazy and give it its complete name, a telephone, was connected to a wire that in turn connected it to the telephone exchange. Apparently, not:

"Just look at my phone!"

"My phone's bigger than yours!" (This never used to be a compliment; the first mobile phones were the size of a brick on steroids!)

"Mine's an *XRJA, V.7.*" (A made-up name, but I think I'll slap a copyright on it anyway!)

"My phone speaks to God and the afterlife!"

"Look at all my pixels!"

"RIGHT!"

"My telephone makes phone calls. At a pinch, it can send a text!" Anyway, it is there too and in one piece.

And so, to the back pocket wherein a source of considerable pain lies. Oh yes, it is the key fob, attached to which are my car and house keys by some extraordinary twist of fate. Damn it! The keys have torn through my jeans and drawn blood (well, scratched) from my leg, what some might describe as 'man-injury' or 'just a flesh wound'. I've now got ripped jeans which to some in the fashion world represent the height of fashion, but not me. Never mind, they are from the *'George'* range, coming in at an almighty five English pounds! Another stroke of luck! 'Levi's' they are not. If they were, I might transform into 'Levi Man' who's in the launderette. There, he slowly removes his jeans to put them in the tub, leaving him standing there in just his undies. And the ladies therein, of the young and not so young variety, stare at him across the top of their steamed-up glasses, purring and pouting, as he displays his Adonis like body for all to witness. Would you really do that in a public space? *Really?* I suspect not, for fear of arrest if nothing else.

Also, whats a Greek Urn?

"A lot!"

How do you make a venetian blind?

"Poke his eyes out!"

What a digression! Which makes me think—what *is* a digression? Something off the point. But what point? Nothing's pointed in my immediate vicinity as I become aware that I am no longer in an upright state. There is absolutely nothing around here pointed, unless you consider the rose bushes, and I don't think I fell into them anyway. Does that therefore imply that if there is no degree of pointiness, it must be blunt instead? If, instead of lingering on the ground right now, but instead was in my kitchen, there I *would* find something blunt. My kitchen knives are blunt; I don't slice meat, I rip it! I have an electric knife, but that's blunt too. I call it James. I never could work out the rationale behind a knife; it starts sharp but ends up blunt. Why bother in the first place?

There is a purpose to these ramblings. As you await your fate in hospital, inevitably, you will have a lot of time to do some thinking. Your mind will go on random meanderings: don't be bothered by this, it happens to everyone in your situation, resulting in other guests possibly saying the strangest or most insulting things you've ever heard, even at *your* expense. You might find that you become blunted in some way too; you might feel that any sharpness you had is drifting away. This too is common: don't worry, it will pass. You might question yourself with doubts like "Why on earth am I in here; they can't do anything about it?" The response to this is that they can, and they will, if you give them the chance. So, play nicely. Finally, I would say that if you are really feeling down, take 'time out' for a few minutes—stop, listen, and look. You will gradually become aware that what you are suffering fades away into insignificance when you consider the plight of others. You will realise that despite your initial trepidations, fears and anxieties, you have had your own stroke of luck.

It is probably fair to say though, and I *do* say so from with the benefit of hindsight, that these 'brushes with the fates', 'encounters with chance' (call them what you will), can either be of great personal benefit, which is a good thing, or they can turn round and bite you on the posterior, which is not quite so desirable.

Let's think about the original understanding for a moment. I'm sure you've experienced it in the past: perhaps you have been just a teeny-weeny bit 'naughty' or 'mischievous' in the past. No, I'm not casting any degree of doubt upon your personal integrity, but we are all human beings in one form or another, and I suspect that if you put your mind to it, you will be able to re-call an 'incident', shall we call it, from way back in the mists of time, where you've done something a trifle 'dubious', the outcome of which has resulted in you offering up a silent prayer out of sheer relief that you 'got away' with it! I call this a questionable, dubious, perhaps unworthy, stroke of luck! You know, like the time when you smiled ever so sweetly at the member of Her Majesty's constabulary who pulled you over because you were doing ninety in a thirty mile per hour limit, and out the milk of human kindness, he offered you a place on a speed awareness course rather than points on your licence! Phew! 'Result' with a massive 'R'!

To illustrate my point, and to show you, the reader, that I am not 'holier than thou', I return to a more innocent time in my life's journey so far. They do say, don't they, that "your school days are the happiest days of your life". Two things perplex me about this oft quoted statement:

- Who are 'they'*?*
- Why this statement is never placed into its proper context? I would agree with it, in the main, with some glaringly obvious exceptions which I won't go into right now, from a *pupils'* point of view, but not from that of a *teacher.* I should know—been there, done that, got the T-shirt from both roles!

Anyway, I will tell you a tale from my time as a pupil. After an initial time of feeling all gloom and doom because I was a failure in the 11+ (only just, as my Junior school headmaster told my parents, but a failure is a failure nonetheless, and, whilst I am on a particular hobby horse of mine, the devastating effect that labelling a child as a failure on, or near to, the onset of puberty, was never properly thought through, in my very humble opinion,) I settled down in the top class, so my self-esteem was raised again, and I made friends with *Peter,* (his real name: he won't mind!) This was a friendship that was going to endure for years, and a fine image of pupil-hood we portrayed, getting us referred to by the staff as 'the two city gents', or 'the clergy of the school', or 'ambassadors'. How we revelled in our glory, and how badly wrong the staff had got us! Because behind our masks, shall we say, we 'cunningly corrupt' city gents, 'de-frocked Vicars', ambassadors of 'passing the buck!' Yes: we had become very adept at arranging pranks, at the teachers' expense, to the 'nth degree', arranging for lesser mortals to play the required roles, then standing back and lighting the blue touch paper! Did Peter and I ever get caught? The answer to that is a 100% 'no!' Did any of our fellow pupils get caught in the act? Again, the answer is 100%, but this time in the affirmative. And how we revelled in their disgrace and their ultimate downfall which came in the form of going 'on report' (this is a technique employed by teachers requiring the offender to have his (or her, we weren't fussed about the gender of the incriminated!) card signed at the end of every lesson, commenting on behaviour, attention and so on.) This was a surmountable problem: Peter and I had been 'supplied' with copious amounts of carbon paper. If you placed a sheet of it between two pages of A4, when you wrote one page of lines like: 'I shall never be a childish person again' (which was silly really, because much of a school's population is made up of children!), you had two copies as a result. Do the math on multiple copies of carbon paper then, which Peter and I sold at extortionate rates on the black market, thus living up to our 'city gents' image!

Another 'talent' Peter and I had both acquired was the ability to produce very passable counterfeit signatures of the staff, so, at a mutually agreed rate; we would sign the report cards in lieu of the teacher. All that was required of the purchaser was to keep his or her mouth well and truly zipped when it came to acknowledging whether they were on report or not!

I could tell you the story of *John* on the school roof, cling film over the staff toilets, teachers' classroom furniture turned upside down, deliberately singing alternative lyrics to hymns in school assembly which Peter and I had composed together, to name but four, but I won't!

Why? I suppose that, in hindsight, I find these episodes funny, yes: but also embarrassing. When I became a teacher myself, I discovered that there was a thing called *Karma*: essentially, what goes around comes around (or reverse the order of that; it makes no difference either way.) *I* became the butt of the pranks, which by now had turned into something more sinister and un-fun like.

Incidentally, you may be interested to know that when we left school, Peter and I went our separate ways. I saw him by chance a few years after I had got married: the city gent image had left Peter now, with his long, dread-locked hair, beads, ear ring and long leather coat.

About forty years later, I met him again. His dread-locks had gone, replaced by a rapidly balding head; he wore a sweatshirt and a pair of scruffy joggers, which mirrored my sweatshirt and my marginally scruffier *Levi's* (or were they a particular supermarket's own brand jeans costing £6; I can't remember, or refuse to say!) We exchanged tales about what life had thrown at us: what was *very* apparent though was that the school had singularly failed in its role as a Career Guidance Agency, since neither of us, it soon transpired, had been anything like a city gent, a vicar or in an ambassadorial role.

Over a cup of tea, well, mug of tea, and a few packs of biscuits, we reminisced about old times, and cringed. We'd done things and said things that appalled us now, but still raised a titter. It was Peter who came up with the expression: "You know, Chris, what I meant to say was…"

So true, so very true.

And here's the moral: when the Doctor enquires of you:

"Good morning, and how are you today?"

Don't say what you think might buy you a free 'get out of jail card'. Don't also be tempted to say what you presume the Doctor *wants* you to say. Similarly, don't 'overdo' your predicament. I overheard a gentleman really 'laying on' the agonies he was going through, again, for the benefit of the Doctor's ears, and amongst his list of complaints was a declaration that he couldn't 'pass anything': a claim which was blatantly untrue since to the best of my knowledge, he had visited the loo on at least three separate occasions with considerable success, I would suggest, looking at the smile on his face and the comment he made along the lines of 'that's a weight of my mind'!

But, you see, his come uppance was nigh, because the Doctor took sympathy on his patient and prescribed him an immediate dose of very strong laxatives which would 'do the job in no time'.

I can further tell you, that from this patient's experience, it is advisable not to request a certain type of medication if you really don't need it! Because of his consumption of said medication, it was not a case of how many times he visited the loo: rather, how *quickly* he visited the loo, and how long he stayed in there for!

I suppose that what *he* meant to say was:

_____

Or,

_____

I don't know. Correction: I do have a modicum of an idea!

The next exercise is to fill in the above spaces with possible alternatives of he genuinely wished to impart to all and sundry.

It's my professional training coming through! Once a teacher always a teacher! There is another saying to: "Those who can, do; those who can't, teach; those who can't teach, teach teachers!" Bah Humbug I say to that!

The Un-Magic Roundabout

Every child I can think of loves it when the fun fair comes to town. Oh, what fun can be had in The Ghost House, The Roller Coaster, The Dodgems, the slot machines and the Carousel. The countless days of waiting are now behind; pocket money has been saved; you're fit to go. You might even find an adult or two on the rides, justified by 'just to keep an eye on the kids'! As if! It is a case of adults regressing to their childhood, and, assuming it's been a happy one, there is nothing wrong with that. As well as the fair, I can remember that another big event was the annual arrival of the circus; the all-singing, all-dancing circus—guaranteed fun for all.

In either case, it was a magical experience.

Have you considered the alternative scenario though, where things aren't quite as you had happily anticipated? For the sake of argument, let's call it 'the un-magic roundabout'—not a nice thought indeed. Indeed, it could be a sham. One of my favourite circus acts was the one featuring a scantily clad lady adorned with a glittery and somewhat distractingly low-cut dress, who was attached to a rotating wheel. It didn't end there though: oh no! Whilst the wheel spun the pretty young lady at a fearsome pace, some guy also attired in a spangled outfit but altogether less easy on the eye, would be blindfolded and then he would proceed to propel knives at the target (I suppose), so that the objects landed equa-distance from each other around the lady but within a couple of millimetres of her torso. She was a human pig-roast; it *had* to be a fix. Didn't it? Just supposing it had gone wrong, with blood-curdling screams and blood everywhere. How would the audience react then? Scream? Run? Laugh, under the assumption that it was fake blood, when in fact, it wasn't? It was terrifyingly real blood. To consider the alternative scenario, of course, as a young male teenager with the associated raging hormones and acne, I used to conjure up in my warped mind an altogether 'alternative' scenario whereby one of the knives conveniently snapped one of the lady's straps, rendering her embarrassed, proud or boastful! "Look at me," she might have declared, "Aren't I beautiful?" Personally, I would have been inclined to consider the situation for some while, studying every detail, before proclaiming 'YES'. Wouldn't it have been funny if someone replied 'NO' though!

A case can be made for *everything* going around, either literally or in an unspecified way. Here's another brain teaser for you! See if you can list ten songs which feature the concept of 'going around' within them. If you're not too hot on songs but fancy another category, just substitute your preferred specialism for the undesired subject. Remember: 'what goes around comes around' or words to that effect, or the other way around! I never did know!

1...

....

2...

....

3...

....

4...

....

5...

....

6...

....

7...

....

8...

....

9..

....

10...

....

So, for the sake of argument, let's just take it for granted most things go around. It's the nature of that 'going around' which potentially can be problematic though.

On *'the magic roundabout'*, nobody falls off. On *'the un-magic roundabout'*, you are more likely than not to be jettisoned into the realms of outer space.

On the former, Dougal barks. Florence emphasises. Zebedee says, 'time for bed'. Dylan's got it right too. He sits. He sits and thinks and procrastinates and utters 'cool man' and 'far out'. Nobody even 'has a dump' in this marvellous place, apparently, there is no need.

But in the latter, Dougal may well bark to his heart's content, but no one will answer. Florence hasn't got enough time. Dylan is stressed out. No time for sitting and/or thinking either. And, as for the proverbial 'devil's dumplings', there is a constant need, but who will take you, bring you back or tell you where it is? Nothing worse than needing someone else's permission or help to get to the bog! These are thoughts that are playing with you, and they enjoy doing it so don't let them!

Something else that often bothered me about the *Magic Roundabout* was the very 'un-magic' nature of its setting—so unreal and quite surreal. There might be a few imitation flowers in the garden along with an artificial tree. Everything was not real. There didn't seem to have been a lot of imagination put into the design of the setting. But, says he, in a moment of understanding; perhaps that was the whole idea—the entire justification. Dougal and Florence weren't real either: I had forgotten that. Their 'realness' had been dreamt up and internalised by me; I imagined one thing to be true, when in fact it was the other. I had expectations, sometimes fulfilled and sometimes not. I can recall a comparable situation as well, this time, the characters are real enough; they are tramps. They too are bound by an existence with one false tree; at one point, this tree has a solitary leaf on it, and as time progresses, the leaf is no more. Their entire reason for existence is to 'wait'. In this case, for a person who never makes an appearance. Isn't that just the way of things: put it into terms of buses when you spend a subordinate amount of time waiting for one, then two turn up together! How frustrating! How annoying! But, there is absolutely nothing you can do about it! Ring any bells? Well, there is: accept that within your current situation, things are not going to be how you might have expected them to be. This could potentially put you in a very sour mood indeed: but why waste valuable time and energy which could be directed on speeding up your recovery on, let's face it, a futile pursuit? You might consider yourself right now to be in a 'magic' environment: however, the converse might be true whereby everything is distinctly 'un-magic'. Whichever way you look at it though, there is one common factor: you are going around and round on a roundabout of emotions at this time. Make it a happy ride, and not one, that when you get off, or even before, you 'throw-up'!

Adopt Dylan's perspective, that's my advice! No need take on his hippy tendencies by saying 'far out man' and 'cool' each time you are offered a hot drink, because that would be plain silly, and a hot drink by definition is not cool, which has the effect of making it appear as though you are away with the fairies (which, of course, you may be, in which case, I'd keep quiet and enjoy the trip!). But why was Dylan like this, even in the face of adversity? Personally, I blame the *Benylin*—the 'wabbit' drank it for fun, I'm sure! This is not as ludicrous as it might seem. When I was at University *all* those years ago, I had a mate and honestly, he was called Dylan too. Too wasn't his surname, but to ensure anonymity, you can assume that it was if you want. He was not a rabbit admittedly, but, and this is a big 'but' so let's make it a big BUT, he was the proud possessor of many rabbit like qualities and characteristics. Before your mind races well ahead of you here, this did not include the obvious one of procreation: he was far too 'laid back' for that. However, he did have big ears; he was partial to a raw carrot or two, and nothing ever seemed to faze him. He was the perfect embodiment of an archetypal Dylan character. Incidentally, he often seemed to have a bad cough which he self-medicated with *Benylin*as well. That was according to the best dinner lady in the world at Uni, who went by the name of Madge, or Auntie Madge, so, in that infamous phrase 'you could say that but I couldn't possibly comment'. I could, and I will: Madge was 100% correct! I wonder what happened to Madge and Dylan; I should imagine that the latter is a chief Guru in world peace and meditation now: bit like the 'Yogic flyers'.

Dear old Madge. I can recall her vividly. Once a week, me and my best buddy at the time, a chap called Mike, were required, as part of our course, to be bussed out to another university campus about one hour's drive away to partake of the wisdom of a world-renowned expert who was on a visiting professorship at another establishment. I didn't major or minor in maths; in fact, I barely passed '0' level at school (The place was so un-confident of my mathematical abilities that they 'double-entered' me for a CSE as well, and I ended up with a Grade Two in that!). However, this little ride out entailed a one-hour journey out, an hour's lecture and another hour's return voyage—a total of three hours minimum. The net result was horror of horrors; we would be late for our dinner at the canteen!

However, Auntie was aware of this. As if by clockwork, every week, she would remember that Mike and I would be delayed for our meal (Mike did a good line in 'home-brew' in his room, so that invariably but secretly, added to our lateness.). Anyway, when we finally rolled up (appeared after our intense travails and studies), Madge had already laid a table for us, complete with napkins and a vase of flowers, and she would treat us like royalty!

"Sit down, lads, take the weight, (she never completed the sentence), I'll bring your meal over. I'll wager you're both starving..." (We were drunk probably—a tad peckish, likely.)

"Thanks Auntie," we would say in union, with a degree of cuteness in our smiles that out-cutified the most cutest thing in the universe!

"You're good lads," she always said that.

"We know!" we always replied with that as well.

People are essentially 'good'. Certainly, this applies to the NHS, and ancillary, staff working in the hospital. There is a chance that you might catch them on a difficult day; unless you are a psychic, the chances are that you will be unaware of what is happening in *their* personal lives. They are required to put their emotions in check whilst they deal with the patients in the ward, including you.

My point here is that no one benefits from conflict. Ban the 'un-magic' logic from your mindset. Be an advocate for 'magic', good things will happen. I promise, even though you might be doubting it right now. I'm not suggesting that you jump with joy. If you take this course of action, you would resemble that North Korean newscaster lady on the TV who appears to be suffering from a bad case of over-excitement! Just be a 'Dylan' for a while!

In fact, I think that I've just had an idea: a very good idea indeed. Did you know that every day in our calendar is a national 'something' day? We have Pancake Day, Valentine's Day (which I abhor in abundance: it's a tax on men with a guilty conscience!) Christmas day, New Year's Day, Mother's Day, Father's Day and Easter Day—you know, the good old traditional ones, but to them you can add the likes of Pizza Day, National Fish and Chip Day, and probably any other specific 'day' you could possibly think of! So, here's my plan—let's institute a 'National Dylan Day': a day for celebrating all things 'Dylan', whereby the virtues of being 'cool and chilled' are to be aimed at, and the act of being so 'laid back' that you are horizontal is deemed as being next to Godliness!

I have a mate at *Endeavour* whose name is Dylan. He *is* a chum, but he's also the Managing Director of the operation, so it would be wise of me to exercise discretion at this point!

The thing is Dylan is as Dylan does; he is so un-phased on the scale that measures being un-phased, that nothing appears to bother him! He is immune from the stresses of 'Radio-land', whether it is a case of the transmitter going down, an impending flood, a presenter's revolt (because all radio presenters are revolting') or a mountain of OFCOM paper work which needs completing in twenty-four hours. It does not upset his equilibrium. I have often thought how nice and peaceful it must be to live in a 'Dylanesque' state—an existence whereby one can peacefully and leisurely peruse the situation one finds oneself in, and can reflect, consider, postulate, procrastinate and finally, at one's convenience, react!

I also had a mate at University called Dylan, strangely enough. He also seemed unaware of complications in his life—an assignment due in tomorrow? No worries to this Dylan. He would write it at four in the morning when most normal people, even undergraduates, were asleep, either because of consuming too much cheap beer at the Student Union bar, or as a natural result of putting in at least one hour of study that day!

This Dylan's natural habitat usually involved sitting in a field with his legs crossed, drinking '*Benylin*' from the bottle, playing unintelligible '*Captain Beefheart*' tracks on his battery operated C90 Cassette machine, communing with nature whilst stinking out the local environment with the incessant putrid and sickly fragrance of slowly burning *Josticks,* infiltrating the lungs of anything living around him, whilst reciting, perfectly verbatim, lines of poetry from the likes of Yeats, Wordsworth, Coleridge and Eliot. I mean—have *you* ever read T.S. Eliot's 'The Wasteland'? If so, have you ever been able to make sense of it, sober, stoned or otherwise? Dylan could—amazingly so; he was full of insights which I, or most of his fellow students-in-arms, could never have imagined or dreamt up.

Dylan was, how does one put it, 'far out, man!'. So is the Dylan at the radio station. So too have been other Dylans I have had the pleasure of meeting over the years. This has led me to the inevitable conclusion that the personal noun 'Dylan' is, in fact, derived from the verb—to 'Dylan', which simply means to exist on a slow heart rate and to let the world pass you by, with the option of jumping on board if you can be bothered to make anything resembling an effort—not too much effort mind; you wouldn't want to over-exert yourself!

Don't for one moment think that I am knocking this *Zen* like existence—too many of us get tied up in knots with comparatively insignificant things, which are taken out of all proportion.

Let me put this in perspective for you. Teaching was my career of choice; I went into it as a very naïve twenty-two-year-old and there I remained, in what is labelled as 'the noble profession' for my entire working life. Oh yes—I had been subjected to the claims made by non-teachers that I ought to get a full-time job, and didn't I get bored with the short working day and the long holidays. This I took in my stride and accepted it as harmless banter.

Fast forward many years—too many to recount or re-call. On the night after I had retired, I did not set the alarm. When I woke up, I *knew* there was something different; something felt strange. It took me a few minutes to work it out, but then I did; I realised that I did *not* have a knotting sensation in my stomach. It then became apparent to me that on every school day, over countless years of teaching, I took it as granted that I was going to wake up with this uneasy, unnerving feeling in the pit of my tummy. For once, I was not stressed the moment I woke up from my slumbers, whereas before, the gut feeling of trepidation and anxiety I had assumed was normal. God knows the toll that this was potentially having on my health.

I wish I could have been a 'Dylanesque' teacher!

There are other, more day-to-day and mundane situations, where the art of being 'laid back' is beneficial. Consider, for example, the following scenario. It is three o'clock in the afternoon on a Sunday. Your favourite Supermarket is compelled by law to close at four, and thus takes the opportunity to get rid of its perishable stock at rock bottom prices. Out comes the employee with what I call the 'price reduction gun'. You always know when someone is out with this labelling machine which drastically reduces the prices of anything that would not survive overnight, because a huge crowd gathers around the said, probably petrified employee, fearing that a case of major civil unrest is imminent!

Then, the fun begins, let the battle commence. A cake is reduced from two pounds to twenty pence. There is a scrum and lots of shuffling and cursing to secure it before anyone else can, and successfully place it in *your* trolley! This sport/ritual/torture/pastime continues whilst all the items are reduced to mere pence. Quite frequently, you get pushed to the back of the scrum, because you are deemed by others who are partaking in this melee that you have secured enough bargains.

Now, if one adopted the Dylan approach to bargain shopping etiquette, you would soon arrive at the conclusion that seeking the bargains is a futile and worthless pursuit, in the great scheme of things. This would result in you gracefully withdrawing from the occasion without any feelings of bitterness or angst aimed at the other participants, and you would be at peace with yourself.

Wouldn't you?

"No, the hell, I wouldn't!"

"Oh, yee of little faith; chillax!" (As the kids say, apparently!)

Thus, being a Dylan is a good thing to be.

Here's to the Royal approval of a 'National Dylan Day'—the sooner the better, I reckon!

Living 'with' the Ceiling

I seem to be quoting an awful lot of song titles or lyrics in this story, don't I? And guess what—here's another one! Do you remember a ditty called *Living on the Ceiling?* It was recorded by a band called *Blancmange* as far as I recall—not the foodstuff (which co-incidentally, I never saw listed on the hospital menu once, which was just as well, because I hate the stuff!). But given my dislike of the sweetly soft desert, I wouldn't have ordered it anyway, which makes my last comment irrelevant. Never mind!

And, of course, living *on* the ceiling is a physical impossibility except for two random suggestions. Firstly, if you are referring to a ceiling 'down under'; a place where every child knows, everything is upside down, and it seems right. That is a logical assumption for any child to make, with the possible omission of baby Einstein, who would had brought relativity into his deliberations. Secondly, referring to my University days, there is the well-respected prank of moving the entire contents of a fellow student's bedroom onto the hall of residence roof. If you are reading this, Lorraine, sorry! The other variation of this particular 'wheeze' is to turn everything in the room upside down, which is a pretty silly thing to do since it induces a considerable amount of anger aimed in your direction from the recipient of the jolly jape!

No—an altogether more constructive, viable and acceptable option is not to live *on* the ceiling, but *with* the ceiling. You are about to embark on a deep and meaningful relationship with the ceiling in your hospital, which might result in a proposal of marriage! You never know your luck. Let's just assume you happen to be confined to bed. This may be for all the morning, all the afternoon, or all day. Excluding the time you are asleep (this being a topic for discussion I will return to later), for much of the time, by definition, you will be gazing longingly straight upon this marvellous construction immediately above you. In the main, it will be white. In my case, it was divided into what appeared to be tiles—intersperse with light fittings and rails. Despite its plainness, and dullness, and lack of conversation, at first, I stared at it with contempt, thinking terrible thoughts like—*Come on, do something to shock me.* But as the hours turned into days, and the days into weeks, I began to like this feature that so dominated my viewing pleasure. Then, before I knew it, I had 'fallen' (the word used in a different sense this time) hook, line and sinker in love with it! To be honest, I didn't quite get around to the marriage proposal, but the yearning was there I can assure you.

The first sign that the ceiling and myself were in this state of bliss was when one morning, after having partaken of my medication, I began to 'draft' the kernel of a game I could play with the use of the ceiling. This is very *Alice in Wonderland* but bear with me on this one—it's worth it, I promise! I began to imagine the ceiling as a chess board, but without the alternate black squares. I began to think of characters to play on the board akin to chess, but hospital-based. So, the pawns would be the family visitors to the ward because they were numerous and often got lost. The Queen would be the matron. The King would be the Consultant. Other roles were up for debate, but you get the idea, I am sure. Having established the players, a set of rules was needed—particularly important as there were no black squares to move to. I had to work a scheme that would allow the characters to move, and this was a tricky one. In fact, I never did resolve it. I knew the purpose of the game though—you had achieved 'all clear' when the King was able to authorise your discharge. The strategy of the game was to convince the Queen that this was appropriate and desirable. It would be possible, of course, to be placed into a position of *'Really?'*. This was the equivalent to *'check'*, when you were forced into making a defensive move. For example, this predicament would occur if one of the Knights, in the role of Registrar, might say to you: "Why is it that you even vaguely consider you are remotely well enough to be discharged yet?" This, inevitably, would be a blow! But, it was not insurmountable. All that you needed to do was to bring some persuasive thinking into play. And, of course, you would need the inclination to embark on this whole game invention plan anyway.

So, I re-iterate. I found that a good survival technique was to live with the ceiling. If I hadn't have taken this course of action, I do believe that my mind would have been engulfed by the sheer 'whiteness' of it. This would have been not a good type of blank canvas to work with!

Going back to the *'Alice'* analogy, she twisted and turned and continued falling into a whole new world far beyond her imagination. Her tumble appeared to be never ending, but it was finite, and ended with a graceful Alice-type 'thump' onto the ground. She could take things to make her bigger. She could take things to make her smaller. She had tea-parties with a mad hatter and a rabbit that was always late. Time meant nothing in this place. Some people acted in very peculiar ways indeed. She had weird and wonderful adventures. But for Alice, ultimately, her adventure was a dream (wasn't it?). So, 'here's the rub' as they say (which begs two questions: who are 'they' and what on earth is the rub? Please put answers on a postcard.). Your situation is *not* a dream. You might close your eyes and pray to God that it *is*, but the answer will come in an emphatic negative—NON!

Potentially, you have found yourself in a place not of your choosing. As you lay inert on your bed, you may be thinking that you have landed in a very strange environment. There will be hissings and bleeps (no 'booster' though for all you *Blue Peter* fans of the sixties and the seventies—down, Shep!). They'll be bashing and crashing, wailing and moaning, monitors that flat-line by mistake, windows that don't open beyond a couple of centimetres, desks and files and notes, and, curiously enough, suspended TVs hung high from the ceiling which need a mortgage to operate (apart from two hours in the morning, which is free, and very good of the commercial suppliers who have nothing to do with the NHS.). In my ward, there were two wall clocks—each telling a slightly different time. This, I believe, was a deliberate ploy with one of two purposes, one of which is unlikely. Firstly, it was all down to a *Doctor Who's* time-shift portal for his 'Tardis'. Incidentally, did you know that the word 'Tardis' is an acronym. Each letter represents a word. So, here is your next task—what does the acronym represent? If you can be bothered, enter the appropriate words in the spaces below!

T..

A..

R..

D..

I..

S..

Here's a little clue for you all—it was suggested that Mr McCartney was a walrus!' One for *The Beatles'* fans there! No— here is the clue: 'A' stands for 'And'.

Back to the clocks being out of synchronisation. Secondly, they provide a false sense of optimism, or pessimism, depending on which way you are travelling of the time it takes to get from point 'a' to point 'b', especially if you employ the use of a Zimmer, a walking stick or a *Steady Sara.* On my first outing with the former, I had an intriguing conversation with my 'plus-one', which went something like this:

"Goodness, you're tall!"

"Yes—I'm six feet five and was born on the planet of Zog!"

"Really? Cute! My boyfriend's tall…"

"Oh, how tall?"

"Not as tall as you. You're tall, aren't you? How tall are you?"

"I'm six feet five and was born on Zog!"

"That's nice love; don't fall, will you?"

"Why not; it'd be a laugh!"

"Don't get out of bed now, will you?"

"I am!"

It's rather nice having two clocks telling contrasting times. You can choose what time you *want* it to be, and this can be taken to illogical extremities. It is well within the realms of fantasy to make evening into morning, Monday into Tuesday, one Millennium to the next Millennium. Say you forgot something in the evening—well, you could go back and get it in the morning. The possibilities are endless and great fun to consider. This can only be described as a philosophical enquiry of some importance. This, coincidentally and conveniently enough, reminds me of a conversation I heard, well, 'ear-wigged' (being a skill you should avoid refining at all costs in order to preserve your sanity, but strangely enough, you just *have* to tune in, for the entertainment value alone). It happened at a patient's bedside during visiting hours, a concept which seems to be 24/7 in my opinion! Anyway, it went like this:

"He's qualified in philosophy."

"Phil who?"

"No, he's passed his exam in philosophy."

"What is it?"

"I can't think."

Now, I wonder if Plato had this dilemma. Or Plato, or Aristotle, or Descartes or Kant?

I wonder who thought: "I tell you what: let's have positive realism and existentialism!"

"What's that?"

"The way out."

"Out of what?"

"From the way in!"

"But the way out is the way in!"

"Not if the way out goes the other way to the way out in which case it's not in, not out, not in and out, you see?"

This is an apt and valid exchange of thought processes; it is open to critical analysis and interpretation. Either that, or with every due respect, it is a load of old 'do-dah!'. It cannot be denied, however, that within the great scheme of things, of miracles that have and ever will be, such discussions are wondrous to behold, depending on two important criteria:

- What constitutes 'great' and 'greatness'
- I know that seven are known to exist, but in terms of 'wonders', is there room for number eight?

What does the preceding chapter amount to? "Not a lot!" as Paul Daniels said. The delightful Debbie had a million reasons to marry him apparently. You will, inevitably, at times, get bored and frustrated. You are not at home, but, right now, you are being cared for.

So, let's quickly consider the notions of 'being bored', 'being frustrated' and 'being cared for'—*not* from the usual perspective of your home but this time from 'another place' within which you do *not* feel 'at home', otherwise known as 'Hospital'. I have come to realise that the meanings of these everyday expressions change ever so slightly to correspond with the setting one finds oneself in, and I believe it is useful to bear this understanding in mind. Let's look at the one by one, then.

- How many times have you heard the gut-wrenching cry of 'I'm bored' coming from the nine-year-old occupant of the back seat in the car when you are just about ten minutes into a four-hour journey heading towards your summer holidays? Horrible, isn't it? A sort of whine from the wilderness! And of course, there is the ultimate horror of the alternative plea which goes along the lines of: "Are we nearly there yet?" which can be coupled with the former enquiry thus: "I'm bored, are we nearly there yet?" This declaration of boredom is enough to test the patient of a Saint but, let's be real here, you're no Saint, far from it, particularly when you struggle with the dilemma of deciding what you *want* to reply with and what you should. The antidote to being bored is to do something. In a nine-year olds case, they have multifarious methods of alleviating inertia—Playstations, iPods and mobile phones to name but three. And what about introducing the offending child to the joys of 'I Spy' and, best of all in my experience, a fascinating little pastime whilst in the back of a car heading to a holiday destination, is a game called Pub Cricket.

Admittedly, this game needs two participants in the back of the car who constantly claim boredom. But, here are the very simple rules. Whichever side of the car that the child occupies denotes the window they look out from. On passing a Pub or restaurant, anything with a name attached to it, the lucky person can claim the number of runs denoted by it. For example, a pub called 'The Cat and Mouse' would score eight runs: four for the cat and four for the mouse. You've really hit the jackpot of course if you encounter a pub called 'The Eleven Centipedes', but this is most unlikely! Where the number of legs is not expressed, for example, 'The Cats and Dogs', only the singular can be claimed—in other words, eight 'runs' again. The game is ended after an agreed time limit or a target number of runs have been achieved. Hours and hours of fun are guaranteed for all! Boredom is condemned to non-existence—at least for a few minutes anyway.

The trouble is though that at this present time, you are not in a car with complaining rear passengers. How I bet at this stage, you wish you were, all things being considered. I am afraid to say that at some point during your hospitalisation, you may well be bored—in fact, I would probably say that it is inevitable. So, how do you deal with periods of prolonged inactivity with getting bored and all het-up? Mindset and 'mindfulness' is the key in this respect—remain aware that your boredom is nobody's fault; everybody is doing their best for you, but delays, like access to the scanner and blood result tests, will and do happen in a hospital environment. "Fore-armed is forewarned" they say—again, I am still in the dark as to who 'they' are!

- Boredom and Frustration, of course, go hand in hand. They are best buddies. They are allies. They feed off each other. They revel in the angst they cause. They celebrate the generation of negative thoughts. 'Our work is done' is without any element of doubt, their mantra.

  We all get frustrated from time to time. Teenagers appear to have collared the market in it, but this is a gross misrepresentation of what being a teenager is all about. Take a few minutes to think about it, then jot down six times you have been frustrated. For example, you get frustrated when the toilet is blocked—you get desperate too, but that's another matter. You get frustrated when you turn the key in the car, but nothing happens; you might even be tempted to beat said car across the bonnet with a tree branch and threaten it with dire consequences, but again, that is another story as well! What about when you make meticulous preparations to meet someone, but they are a 'no show'. You've got it—frust-rate-ing! So, come on, provide six first-hand experiences of the art (or is it a science?) of being frustrated!

Satisfying, I think you will agree, now that you've got those off your chest! Now, take a breath, and relax. Were they *worth* getting all steamed up about, given what you know *now*? I would suspect not. And therein 'lies the rub' my friends; do not allow frustration to get the better of you; rise above it. It is an understandable human condition and one that everyone can relate to, regardless of sex, race, religion or the success of one's cocktail parties! Nonetheless, it is an emotion which can be transferred from a negative to a positive. This awareness is one of the keys of survival in hospital. Put yourself in the shoes of the myriad of people who are working for the benefit of *you,* and you will see things in a different light. You might even smile. Everyone likes a smile!

- This brings me to my ultimate point. Alright—I know that you are not in hospital out of choice; there are so many places you would rather be right now, with so many people, and probably having a whale of a time over a few glasses of *Rouge* or *Blanc.* I will tell you one thing for certain right now—there is no *Vino*, or any other alcoholic beverage, in this establishment. Your search for a bar, I can assure you, will be in vain, so save your energy and don't bother!

But you will still have a reason to smile.

"Why?" I hear you ask.

Let me tell you why. It may not be at the top of your thinking right now, but, in this environment called a hospital, you are being cared for 'twenty-four seven'. It's not the care you get at home, with all your comforts surrounding you. No, but it's a 'comforting' care; your health is their number one priority.

An awareness and acceptance of that undeniable fact should bring a smile to the face of the most cynical of people!

The Bard and Other Teams

I bet that you would not have considered just how important a part the ceiling plays during a stay in hospital. It gives you something to think about, fires your imagination (not, of course, in the football managerial sense, whereby you are out of a job if you lose three matches in a row!) and inspires you to arrive at a greater and deeper level of understanding. I wonder if Bill, otherwise known as William Shakespeare, took guidance from a ceiling when he came up with his immortal phrase "to be, or not to be, that is the question". Did he have an answer in mind? Did a ceiling of the time have any impact when he wrote—"alack, poor Yorick, I knew him well"? What did Bill mean the term 'well'? Was he able to quantify the expression, after all, he was talking to a skull?

Funny joke time—why didn't the skeleton go to the concert? Because he had nobody to go with! As *Basil Brush* might have said: "Boom, boom, Mr Geoffrey," with or without the aid of a ceiling.

What else did Bill say? What other little gems did he utter? As Bill once said, "All the world's a stage, and all the people on it merely players." There's every likelihood that he didn't say it once, but on many an occasion. It would have been pathetic of him to have given birth to such an awe-inspiring and insightful remark, only for him to have said it just the once. So, let's assume, he said it more than once—let's go with four times, for the sake of argument.

I am not really of a literary bent, but I do like Bill's ideas about 'stages' and 'players'. This is not a further addition to *Cole's Notes,* (for those without knowledge of said publications: these are little 'guides' written, in this case, about every Shakespearean word ever written, concerning themes, characterisation, plot and the like, aimed specifically at the "I can't be bothered to read a word of this incomprehensible rubbish anyway, but I want the GCSE in English Literature" brigade.

No, but it is an interesting way to consider the plot and characterisation of your field of play. As in any game, you need two teams—the home and away teams. The 'away' team must travel to their opponents 'manor'. Even with a modicum of intellectual activity, it is not difficult to imagine yourself as one of the 'away' team, with your fellow wardmates being the other constituent members. As for the 'home team', they far outnumber your lot and play a very different system, and the individual members of their team come in many guises, as discussed earlier in this book. And here is another weird thing: in this game, there is a strange rule which dictates that the home team must help the away team to achieve their goal, or victory, to the best of their ability. And this they do, with flying colours. You might feel that they deserve a yellow or even a red card at times for inexcusable offences like not getting you a bottle in time or waking you up at 3 am in a case of mistaken identity!

Now, the first thing to do is to give your team a name. Try not to use the obvious, like 'Man United Against Everything in Here' or 'Charlton Athletic I'm Not Very'. Having done that, you need a club nickname, and then a club motto. In the space below, fill in your club name, nickname and motto—it will provide a fascinating insight into your state of mind at the time when you inevitably reread this epic piece!

Team name...

Team nickname..

Team motto...

Which means...

If you feel so inclined, you could go into team kit, manager and ground name, but these are supplementary nuggets of information only. As for the former of these, the team kit, I am pretty sure that you will be playing in charming light blue gear, complete with poppers. A very fetching look indeed, with the kit being just one size (a phenomenon inspired by the ex-Crystal Palace player Fitz Hall, known as 'One-size' by his team mates: think about it!).

Every team has got its star players—the likes of Gazza, Besty and Pele. I mention this because the team I played for during my stay in hospital had several interesting characters which added to our overall un-predictability.

Playing to the right of me, because he occupied the bed to my right, was a lovely chap called *Bert*. Speed was not his main asset, since he was basically comatose, disturbed and confused, who had a tendency of addressing me as *'Auntie Joan'*. I wouldn't have minded this—all players refer to their colleagues by a nickname, and his, for me, was 'Auntie Joan'. Also, Bert's wife, on one visit to a match, came across to me and whispered in my ear:

"Take no notice of Bert. He means no harm. Auntie Joan passed on eight years ago."

I offered my condolences and assured her that Bert's uttering did not bother me at all. However, it got me thinking: *Exactly what was it that Bert saw as he stared at me when awake and facing toward me?* The last time I had checked, I was 'all man'. Perhaps I was growing a pair of 'moobs'? Horror of horrors!

I appointed Bert as team captain. He was inspirational. Despite everything, he had a cheeky smile that broke out every now and again. Apparently, in his younger years, he had been a boxing champion, and when I looked at this chap, clearly a shadow of himself, his spirit of determination shone through. He was a fighter then and a fighter now. He, too, had experienced a stroke, but not a minor one as was my case. At night, I shed a tear or two for him. I didn't want to during the day time because he was of the generation of 'the stiff upper lip' and all that, and probably a keen advocate of the 'big boys don't cry' mantra. Nothing seemed to keep Bert down. If he could beat this thing, and he was, gradually, then 'sod it, so can I' crossed my mind.

The next character I would like to introduce to you was a fellow named *Frank*. In footballing terms, he was a speedy little winger— difficult to get to. Because of *his* stroke, Frank needed his velocity in order to get to 'the little boys' room' at very short notice. This was an excruciating process to witness, because it was 50/50 whether he would successfully accomplish his mission or not. It was on these occasions when his name became very apt indeed; he was prone to give his audience a very basic and 'fruity' description of what he had failed to do, and the reasons behind any such failure:

"I'd bloody rung the bell you know, but no one came!" (To be fair, this usually consisted of about ten seconds notice; I doubt whether *Usain Bolt* could have got there in time!)

"They make me sodding sit down when all I need to do is sit, not shit!" (This comment, oft repeated, had me crying again, but this time with laughter!)

"I can't aim Percy at the porcelain properly when it's dark!" (It's *never* actually 'dark' on the ward, by the way.)

'It was the best of times; it was the worst of times' for Frank. He was the comedian of the team—inadvertently, he had everyone in stitches! This was good for team morale. Come to think of it, that quote comes from Charlie-boy, doesn't it, and not Bill? Never mind—to use another football term, we'll let that one 'pass'.

This leads me on nicely to our next star player who answered to the name of *Ken.* Now, Ken was our rock-solid defender and blocker. A self-confessed bed-blocker who, despite his various complaints, of which there were many, seemed to be enjoying his stay. He would not shift. He was a defender without equal; nothing would get past him. His mindset went along the lines of 'let others work it out'. He, too, was prone to blame others for the late delivery of the 'ball' (bowl, cardboard receptacle) for his usage thereof. I found myself admiring his tenacity and forethought though, perfectly exemplified by his re-cycling of his water jug into something else, which was sheer genius, if not disgusting. If anyone on our team deserved a red card, it would have been Ken (or at least just a warning in the form of a yellow card and a fresh water jug, which in the case of the latter, of course he got. Not that he drank water. I think he had an alternative source of liquid refreshment amongst his personal belongings!

Which leaves 'yours truly'. I must declare, from the outset, that my role in the team itself was minimal. I didn't play an active role: if anything, I was one of two things:

1. The manager. The *Arsene Wenger* type figure. Not very animated, constantly scribbling down notes on a constant supply of A4, and guilty of 'not seeing it'. I *did* see it, and hear it, and think about it.

2. The team's *sweeper.* This was a very acceptable role for me to play because in this surreal, clinical environment, I became a grateful recipient of little snippets of conversations which occurred between *Frank* et al at feeding (visiting) time. How my mind went into a blissful state of overdrive as I attempted to internalise and make sense of the dialogues happening all around me.

"Gonna find out why he's not a Sarah steady!"

"What a palaver; I want it very firmly in!"

"Over-growing, hanging baskets everywhere."

"I was looking at it; it needs doing now!"

"Nurse, nurse, too late, bugger, I've shat myself!"

"Stick your bottom right out; there...that wasn't painful, was it?"

"They're putting the bog in first!"

Words expressed by members of a team. Words expressed by the average person. Words which reflect our uniqueness, our quirks and personality traits. An acceptance of the human state in all its glory is an essential contributor to a happy and beneficial stay in hospital.

Pulse!

During my time presenting on a radio station (by the way, John Peel I am not!), I have often been asked to name my favourite all-time album ever. This has always provided me with a great challenge and a huge amount of thought. I am a lover of music full-stop (or, period, as our pals from across the pond say.). I get great enjoyment from all genres: classical, Punk, Rock, Reggae, and drum 'n' bass, to name but a few. However, there is one album for me that stand apart from other 'greats' such as *Pet Sounds* and *Sergeant Pepper's*. From the moment I first heard it, right up to the present day, I am captivated by the sheer uniqueness of Pink Floyd's *The Dark Side of the Moon.* If you perchance have never heard this musical masterpiece, I urge you to do so at some point: preferably in a darkened room, with a fragranced jostick smouldering peacefully in the background, at about two in the morning, complete with your favourite tipple. The production values are out of this world. If you close your eyes, the music transports you into an altogether different place, and for me, it is a different place every time.

Apart from the music, there are deep and meaningful lyrics, which are open to interpretation in a whole variety of ways. And there are mysteries surrounding the entire concept of it as well. In other words, what is it about? Theories abound on this topic: critics sometimes quote a spoken 'aside' which appears on the album, claiming that the whole of the moon is dark, not just one part of it. Intriguing and bewildering. Make of it as you will. It is like the conspiracy theory 'doing the rounds' during the 1960s (before the moon landing conspiracies came into the public consciousness) that Paul McCartney, yes, he of 'The Beatles' had, in fact, died. He was no more. He was an ex-Beatle, and that the person who replaced him was a Paul McCartney 'lookalike' rumoured to go by the name of Billy Shears. Furthermore, the remaining band members teased their audience with little clues on the album sleeves and via their lyrics. Visually, there were clues too on the sleeves of albums such as *Sergeant Pepper's* and the zebra crossing artwork on *Abbey Road.*

What a load of.................. (you insert your choice of vocabulary here), I hear you cry. "Go back to your radio station or start a whole new career as a music journalist!" Total and utter............... (again, insert your word).

But, wait—hold your horses! There is method in my madness and my umpteenth digression! Just bear with me for a minute. Allow me to return to my opening gambit, which was... oh, I've forgotten. Only kidding! Of course, I haven't forgotten! I may have had a stroke, but I haven't lost my marbles! No, I was talking about my favourite album, and therefore my favourite band. It was *The Dark side of the Moon* by Pink Floyd (or, for any fellow avid Pink Floyd fans out there, *The* Pink Floyd as they were originally known, but they dropped the '*the*' for musical reasons!). Amongst my CD and vinyl collection back at 'Moore Towers', I have most of the band's albums, amongst them being: *Animals, A Momentary Lapse of Reason* and *Welcome to the Machine.* I could set you another task here to name three other albums by the band, but that would be cruel because not all the world and its mother are fans of said band. So, I will:

1 ....

2..

3..

Done it? No? I will let you off! I am gregarious by nature, you see!

And finally, before I embark upon the main premise of this section, if you are stuck for a number three on the above list, I'll give you an answer: *Pulse.* Yes, that's the name of another Pink Floyd album and very good it is too. Also, it doubles up as the title for my forthcoming discussion, for a variety of reasons that should become abundantly clear, with 'should' being the operative word really. Time will tell.

So, where to begin?

We've talked about you, as a member of the 'away' team. It is only fair that we highlight some of the star players of the 'home' team (usually referred to as 'the opposition' but not in the game you are playing right now—probably best to describe them as 'the facilitators' of your recovery.

Now, this lot are swift: very fast indeed. It is hard to keep up with them. It can be a bit confusing as well, because they don't all wear the same kit. But each has a well-defined role to carry out. They sort of employ a 'roll-on, roll-off' tactic, and they are prepared to play the game at any time of the day or night; under floodlights or not. As a rule of thumb (another expression which means absolutely nothing, unless a thumb *did* rule at some point in history somewhere), this team kicks off at about six in the morning, perhaps when your senses are not at their most alert, shall we say. You know that the match has started because the pitch is invaded by the whiff of cheap perfume or inexpensive aftershave utilised by the 'water change' lad or lass. Theirs is a vital role—to exchange your water from the night before with a brand new one with as much noise as is humanly possible—not *humanely*: humanly. They also are vital in preparing you for the arrival of their next 'ace' on the team—it's the prodders and the pokers!

"Morning Christopher," a cheery voice declares

Avoid the temptation to retort by saying: "Well, it's hardly afternoon, is it?" That would be just too sarcastic, wouldn't it? (Wouldn't it?)

And bear in mind that this player probably meant to pre-fix the word 'morning' with 'good', but, as you arouse yourself into some kind of life-like state, that might be debatable as well.

Besides which, it's not so much the 'Morning Christopher' that perturbs me. It is the fact that written above my bed on the whiteboard behind me (which contains vital information like 'nil-by-mouth', which means that feeding time at the zoo, is accomplished via a drip in your case, or 'D.N.R', which means what it means), there is an instruction to address me as 'Chris'. This is written boldly, underlined, and in capitals, like this:

'ADDRESS AS CHRIS'

So, I fail to see why, at five past six in the morning, when I am not really at my best, I am greeted, ever so cheerily of course, with a "Morning Christopher".

I deem this to be a yellow card offence at least. It is designed to catch me 'off guard'. But, being the decent chap I am, I consider it wise not to kick up a fuss. Why? Well, for two main reasons:

- It's too bloody early, and
- Worse things happen at sea.

This, of course, gets me thinking. What things happening at sea could possibly be worse than being referred to as Christopher when I specifically requested that I be called Chris? Enduring a Force ten storm I suppose, or being be-calmed: '*Water, water everywhere, but not a drop to drink!*' The lack of wind must be a terrible thing. A predicament not necessarily the case in *my* ward during *my* stay. Warning: for those of a squeamish nature, or those who are offended by reference to all things pertaining to bottoms, I would skip the next paragraph!

Oh, to have been be-calmed on the Stroke Ward! No wind would have been a blessing. But, there was loads of it. It was one mother of a windy stay (with apologies to my mother and all mothers everywhere; we owe our very existence to you, along with our wind!)

Yes, a lack of wind would have been beneficial to all. You would be amazed at the variety of textures, aromas and velocity of said outbreaks of the phenomena. And why is it called 'wind'. I never have been able to get to the bottom of this one! And how is it that something which comes forth from the human posterior can register so highly on *The Richter Scale?* Why is it the cause of so much mirth, humour, embarrassment or disgust? Why do we, as English-folk, try to pass the blame of such an occurrence onto someone else by looking very disapprovingly in their general direction when, let's face it (full on, if we have to, complete with nose and the associated ability to smell), an entirely natural act has taken place? Why is it that the most awkward place for ones of these happenings to take place is within the confines of a lift? The Europeans don't seem bothered by it. They do it all the time without a blink of concern. I had a Professor once, who appeared to take immense pleasure in 'letting one out' in public and during lectures. It was most disconcerting.

And, I would be intrigued to know, who created the terminology around these events? Below is a list of words or phrases to describe 'wind', as I understand it to be (or not to be, that is the question again), either picked up during my stay or previously known:

- Farts
- Bottom-burps
- Guffs
- Blows
- Omissions

Can you name another three? If so, fill in the bullet points below:

- Descriptor one..
- Descriptor two..
- Descriptor three...

Also, why are people compelled to say, after passing wind, "Oooh, more tea vicar?" What is the association between tea, vicars and farts?

What I am saying is—be prepared for windy conditions. And, if you feel compelled to pass wind, do so, with pride, safe in the knowledge that at least you can create one!

So, where was I?

"In the loony bin!"

No, that is an incorrect observation. I was making astute and witty observations about the main players on the home team.

Another player appears.

"Can I take your temperature please, Christopher?"

"Take it where? For a walk? And call me Chris, I prefer that!"

"Sorry, Christopher. Put this under your tongue please!"

The implement for recording your temperature, known as a thermometer, (from the Latin 'thermos' meaning heat, as in thermos flask!) can be placed in one of three places. If you have been a good boy or girl, it can be placed into your mouth. Alternatively, if you have not got a mouth, it can be inserted in your armpit, which can be embarrassing if you have neglected to clean said area for a couple of days. Similarly, if this key player is having a bad match, or considers you to have a mouth, but a far too vocal and well-exercised one, the implement can be situated up your bottom, which may bring about a bad case of farting, as discussed earlier. My tip to you is—play fair and insist for the mouth option whenever possible!

Funny, isn't it! Funny how things work out! There you were one day, just going about your daily chores when 'BANG!'—for whatever reason, you have found yourself where you are right now—in hospital. "You have to laugh though, don't you?" That's what my Nan used to tell me. That, indeed, is what they said—make the best of it, which is good advice indeed. But, deep in the recesses of what passes as my mind, I ask: "Who are 'they'?" For the poetry lovers amongst you, this can be put another way:

"Who, or where, or why, or what, is the akond of Swot?"

'They' have got a lot to answer for. 'They' can say anything they want: any place, anytime, anywhere. Like the *'Black Magic'* man. Do you remember him? You know, the idiot from the advertisement for a certain brand of chocolates. What possesses him to dive from a mountain top into a raging sea beneath him clutching a box of chocolates for his lady friend confounds me. Surely, there are safer alternatives? And, how is it that the chocolates do not get the slightest bit wet, or even a tad salty? It's not as if he's dived into a freshwater lake, which would be particularly silly, given that he might hit his head on the bottom (of the lake!). Why does the box not disintegrate?

Diving anywhere in order to deliver a box of chocolates to his lovely lady, on the scale of irrationality, is pretty significant on the irrational front. Plain daft, if you ask me! But *Black Magic* man annoys me, you know. Everything in his world is perfect with a capital 'P'. Is his hair wet? Nah! Is it out of place? Not a chance! Does he appear dishevelled? Maisnon, monsieur! Does he maintain his rugged good looks? Oh Yes? Does he ooze sexuality? Definitely! Is he suave and sophisticated? He struts around like a peacock carrying a box of chocolates!

He proceeds to calmly and quietly enter the lady's boudoir—not a drop of water to be seen.

He then calmly pulls out (wait for it; this is not *Lady Chatterley's Lover*) his immaculate calling card from his pocket; this too defying any sort of reasoned logic in terms of stiffness, and places it serenely and carefully next to his intended recipient who, of course, remains asleep and blissfully unaware during the entirety of his manoeuvres. Mission accomplished, he makes good his escape by jumping into the sea again to retrace his steps, which presumably includes scaling the mountain he dived into the sea from. You never get to see that bit though. Shame, that part would be fun, but the advert is too short—it merely concludes by saying that the reason he does this is because the lady of his dreams is a little bit partial to a particular brand of confectionary!

I can't understand why he doesn't wake the lady up before going. After all, he has gone to an awful lot of trouble to deliver the edible goodies. You think he might have expected a peck on the cheek (facial or otherwise) as a reward for his endeavours. Or even a snog, *with* tongues! Nothing like a game of good old 'tonsil-tennis' to spread the germs! It might not have been unreasonable for him to expect a 'leg over' at a pinch! But no—like a ship in the night (I emphasise the usage of the word 'ship' and not its possible misprint, although that might be more accurate), he is gone. He has disappeared into the world of 'advert land'.

And as for the lady, well, she is mysteriously aroused from her peaceful slumbers. Complete with satin negligee, she surveys the scene with those marvellously intoxicating 'come to bed' eyes (too late, he's gone, my love!), spies the chocolates and whispers in her sultry tone:

"Shit! Not again! If I've told him once, I've told the twerp a thousand times, I'm Type 2!"

And with that, they are propelled with gusto into the nearest bin!

But now—back to reality.

"Christopher, pulse!"

"No, Christopher Moore!"

"Can I take you pulse please Christopher?"

"Where to? Is it going with my temperature?" (a funny joke, I thought!)

"No, your pulse, Christopher, not your temperature; you've had your temperature read already!"

Read? I thought it had been taken, perhaps as a hostage. I am getting confused.

"Will you give me a finger Christopher?"

"Sure: which one do you want? Which one are you missing?" (another mildly amusing comment)

"Doesn't matter Christopher; any one will do!"

"Call me Chris!"

"OK, Chris."

Eureka! I've cracked it. I have found a way of getting someone, anyone, to call me Chris.

Anyway, this character places what can only be described as a vice-like gripping device onto one of my digits.

"Oooh that is good, Christopher."

Perhaps I haven't cracked it after all.

"What's good?" I enquire

"Your pulse is good, Christopher."

"Good," I think to myself, trying to work out a definition of 'goodness'.

"Pressure!"

"Pressure?"

"I need to take your blood pressure, Christopher."

I fight the urge to come up with any witty comment now, and I have given up on the possibility of being called Chris.

"Can I have an arm please, Chris?"

Again, I want to say, nay, I feel compelled to say, something highly amusing, but I arrive at the conclusion that discretion has a greater purpose in the overall scheme of things here. I proffer my right arm. That makes sense really given that her monitor on wheels is on my right-hand side. It would be a bit of a stretch to offer my left arm, not to mention, clumsy, painful and irrational.

"Have my right arm."

Upon which, a rubber cuff is wrapped round and secured with Velcro—that sticky, rough feeling material which is used to keep one part of an item securely attached to the other. The machine is switched on. Your arm becomes increasingly strangulated and the Velcro is being tested to its limits. The machine, having taken your arm to the point of no return, then takes pity, and gradually deflates itself—a bit like *Autopilot* in Airplane. Then, a series of numbers proudly display themselves on the screen:

"Oooh; these are good too Christopher."

"In what sense of the word good?"

"Your blood pressure, it is good Christopher."

Good, I think again. One of my main strengths is the deepness and originality of thought I possess.

"You can have your arm back now, Christopher."

"Why, isn't it good enough for you?" (I can't resist this quip.)

"Your pulse and your pressure, they are both good."

"Good."

And with that, I got my arm back. In theory, I hadn't really given it, as such, to anyone. Arguably, I had 'loaned' it. To have given it would have been a permanent thing, which led me on the trail of thinking—if I *was* able to 'give' my arm, just how could I give it? Presumably, it would need severing from my body, a la *Texas Chainsaw Massacre.* Either that, or through the purchase of a good hack-saw from *'B+Q'* (other DIY stores are available.). I bought a good one recently; a very reasonable £6.99, to do battle with the 'Butterfly bush' which has grown to dominate my back garden. I didn't even plant it. Me and gardening do not compute. I hate gardening with a vengeance. The whole idea of me actually 'planting' anything is alien to me. However, the damn thing flowers every year, and the butterflies gather every year. I have nothing against butterflies (why aren't they called 'flutter-byes', by the way, because that describes exactly what they do?), but I see it as my mission to rid myself of this undesired plant. So, every year, I have attempted to 'prune it' or 'cut it back'—basically, nice ways of saying 'get rid of' the Triffid. But, despite my valiant efforts, every year it makes a return appearance saying, "Hello Mate" or, if it's feeling particularly theatrical, proclaiming "here's Johnny"!

Somebody offered me some invaluable advice in my attempts to rid myself of this black spot.

"Cut it open and pour paraffin into it!" I was told.

"You don't want to do that; it kills cats!" someone else informed me.

Kills cats! We have hundreds of them in the neighbourhood. Fat ones, thin ones, noisy ones, lazy ones—creatures that make you stop *your* car as it sits in the road and thinks, until it is of a mind to wend his weary way home. I have no desire to be known as 'The cat and bush killer' of old Boston town. Imagine the gossip! My immediate neighbour loves cats; I like cats, but my brother-in-law would have them all lined up and shot at dawn! I suppose that I am ambivalent towards them; I'd probably veer towards taking them rather than leaving them. As a child, we had a pet cat. She was called *Cinders,* or *Sin,* or *Tin-Tin,* or *Tin,* or *Sin-Sin.* No wonder she suffered from a split personality disorder. She also had a show name: *Cinderella Cleopatra Annabella Moore.* The irony of this, though, was that she was never entered into a show.

"Why is that line flat nurse?" I asked mischievously.
"What line, Christopher, oh, that line?"
"Am I dead?"
"I don't think so Christopher."
"But can you be sure?"
"Sure of what Christopher?"
"Sure that I'm not dead."
"Sure I'm sure, Christopher."
"Sure?"
"It was flat with that guy too, I'm sure of that."
"Surely that means he is dead as well?"
"It's a malfunction on the machine, Christopher."
"Sure?"
"Sure."

Nice to be assured that it was a technical error and not a case of the both of us 'flat-lining' simultaneously. I gazed at both clocks in turn. Both concurred to within some degree of accuracy. It was either six thirty-five, or six forty, in the morning. It made no difference really. There's a long day ahead.

And that is the point here.

This game does not adhere to any time regulations. Also, there are no restrictions on the number of players on the pitch at any one time.

If you accept this premise, play fair, and only stop when you hear the final whistle, you will do just fine. Don't become aggravated by the complexity of the game; no-one understands the 'off-side' rule in any sport that I am aware of, and you do not want to be caught 'offside'. It is not worth getting the red card either, which results in an immediate 'sending off', despite any protestations.

No—*do unto others as you would have done to yourself.*

Maintaining Your Good Looks

Good old *Popeye*. He had rugged good looks, didn't he? Just check out those rippling muscles, that well-toned torso. I bet he had a great 'six-pack'. *Olive Oyl*, bless her heart, went weak at the knees at the mere thought of him. Single-handedly, Popeye performed wonders for the spinach industry (a vegetable sometimes to be found on the hospital menu and, as an elderly acquaintance of mine used to say: "It's delicious and nutritious!") He was a figure all males of the species aspired to be like in some shape or form; he was a role model of manliness and good looks. I don't know who the female equivalent would be: Carole Vorderman, Marilyn Monroe or Katie Price perhaps? Here's your next exercise, write down the name of six people, celebrities, cartoons (I always fancied Penelope Pitstop from *The Wacky races*, for the ladies, I suppose, it was Peter Perfect!) or real-life Mr or Mrs Joe Average who, in your opinion, have maintained their good looks, for whatever reason.

1. ....

2. ....

3. ....

4. ....

5. ....

6. ....

Do *you* appear on the list? No! Well, you should. Because of your stay in hospital, you will see yourself in a whole new light when it comes to 'keeping up appearances', and, in my case, that was no bad thing. Let me explain.

In 'hospital-land', everything is squeaky clean. And I mean 'everything'. Cleanliness is most clearly next to Godliness here, and that, my friends, includes YOU! The days of 'oh, I won't worry about shaving today' or 'I'll leave my hair until tomorrow' now become mere figments of your imagination. You can't have 'bath night' on Wednesdays and Sundays now!

It is an enforced exercise, dome at a time before breakfast is served, but after you've had your first cup of tea or stiff gin! There appears to be two purposes to this exercise, which is conducted with military precision, obviously, to get you clean and comfortable after what passes as a night's sleep, and secondly, to ensure you look your best for when the whirlwind, better known as the consultant and his entourage, sweep through the ward with alarming and frightening speed.

Working on your experience, 'washing', as we shall call it, at home, is done in a leisurely and carefree way. You perhaps yawn your way through the motions and rituals of whatever a wash means to you. But, in hospital, be prepared for the rigidity, the tight scheduling and the vast array of wash 'types' that are made available to you.

When I was a child, a treat for my sister and I was to stay a week at our Nan's house—a little terraced house in South London. This was an annual occurrence in the summer—considered a treat for Sis and me, and no doubt, thought of as a holiday for my mum and dad, who would gleefully deposit us at Nan's place, and then make good their escape with a great big grin on their faces as we waved them off into the distance. We smiled too. Nan did at first, along with *her* sister and therefore, our Auntie, with whom she lived. That would be on a Saturday. By the Wednesday, the smile would have transfigured into a marked frown. Funnily enough though, by the time 'pick-up' time arrived on the following Saturday, both she and Auntie were overwhelmed with unbridled and child-like joy, whereas my parents' countenances were decidedly enigmatic!

This was a week when Sis and I 'got down in the dirt'! We developed some marvellous wheezes over the years. One such event will involve the both of us wandering up and down the local streets, picking up any discarded cigarette butts we could find on the pavement. These were then returned with us to Nan's, after which we picked them apart, separated any remaining morsel of tobacco therein, combine the contents into a workable whole and acquired some *'Izal Medicated'* from my Nan's outside loo. For those of you unaware as to what *'Izal'* is—it was hard, scratchy, unsoftened, lacerating loo paper, the type not really fit for the job, since it was essentially tracing paper and did not possess any of the absorption qualities of today's three-ply super soft! Going to the loo outside was a hoot for Sis and me, but a way of life for Nan and Auntie.

Anyway, back to the baccy! We would then proceed to tear each sheet of *'Izal'* into strips, and then carefully placed the discarded tobacco remnants into these strips, rolled them up into a thin tube, and lo, we had created our very own 'roll-ups', a fine art we had witnessed our Uncle Albert, who was a driver on a big red London bus, accomplish with some ease. The last act in this task would require either of us getting access to a box of matches to ignite these creations. To the best of my recollection, Nan, who was probably suffering from a bad case of frayed nerves right now, and with a heightened sense of awareness, usually intercepted us. I never took up smoking. It seemed to me a filthy habit. Sis, meanwhile, has progressed onto a hundred plus per day complete with patches as well! (Only joking, Sis!)

The point of the foregoing aside though is this—we got dirty. Pretty damn filthy! And we loved it! Nan, however, would get her revenge (if you've ever seen *The Hell's Grannies* sketch on Monty Python, you'll know exactly what I mean!)

In my case, she would lure me into a sense of false security by offering me the usage of 'Mauve Soap! The very concept of a bar of soap being 'mauve' both intrigued and excited me (it *was* 'the swinging 60s though, in my defence!). I was then grabbed, very much against my will, and placed/situated on the kitchen sink, whereby I was presented with another proposition. This was not pleasant though! It entailed opting for one of four wash options. These, in order of kindness, are listed below:

1. A 'cat-lick'
2. A 'neck-wash'
3. Something bad
4. Something very bad indeed!

I think I found God during these dilemmas:

"Please God, I haven't been very naughty; it was mainly Sis, please let it be one or two. Oh! And yes, A-men!"

Invariably though, option three or four was the outcome. In fact, I would go as far to say that I had no choice in the matter at all! A 'cat-lick' was nothing really; options two to four increased in severity and were best avoided if possible. The trouble was that I never *did* avoid them; however, my sister sometimes did!

This childhood encounter with mauve soap did serve a useful purpose though: it taught me that there are degrees of washing, and that it is always 'nice' to look and smell like '*4, 7, 11*' or however mauve soap smelt. Never did I once contemplate that this experience would come back to haunt me over fifty years later—not on a sink top, but in a hospital!

Now, for Bert, the ex-boxer, I had learnt, this was a surreal start to yet another day. Two lovely nurses, with the patience of a saint, would gently whisper into his shell-like:

"Morning Bert, would you like a wash? We've come to wash you."

Trouble is Bert was hard of hearing. He never reacted, so the act was done to him without his knowledge, but with such love and care, it almost brought another tear to my eye (just the one eye in this case). In his state of confusion, Bert had taken to calling any female nurse as Paul—that was his favourite. A close second came Peter. It gradually dawned on me that perhaps he was working his way through the twelve disciples, and that during the afternoon, we might all be entertained by a man with a beard who could walk on water and turn water into wine during visiting hours! He would be a very popular visitor on the grounds of his 'water into wine' routine alone!

(Watch out Christopher, there's a huge bolt of lightning developing overhead with your name on it...)

CRASH!!!

"Missed me!"

Now, where was I? Oh yes! I was talking about these lovely nurses who performed washes on the gentleman on the ward, and they performed their duties with such care and diligence, that it was lovely to witness. A bowl of soapy warm water, just right, would be placed at his bed-side, and they would proceed to gently caress and clean his frail skin. Not that I witnessed it directly, you understand. A curtain was drawn around every patient whilst this act of love, compassion and caring, took place. Bert maintained his dignity, bless him. This would have been of prime importance to him, and, although he was unaware and confused, he deserved the very best of treatment, which he unfailingly received.

I referred to these nurses as 'the wash ladies', only privately and in my mind, but taking not to make the obvious mistake of calling them 'washer ladies', which, to me, had entirely different connotations. They're a different breed altogether. As a spotty youth and awkward teenager, I used to have a little part-time job in a local laundry. Well, to say that what I heard these ladies say about 'what they'd do with me, and with what' was an education in itself: an 'eye-opener'. Poor innocent me! It was 'effing this and effing that!'. I used to blush very easily apparently. I just have done again at the memory of it—woe, and thrice woe, I am damaged goods!

Then it would be my turn:

"Morning Chris, we've come to give you a nice wash."

"What's a nasty one?" I quipped.

No answer. My talent as a comic is clearly not appreciated.

"Do you want a bowl ducks?"

"No, I prefer to bat!"

This one raised a slight titter.

"You're on good form this morning, Christopher."

Damn it, the name's gone back to Christopher; have I done something wrong? I imagine my mum bedside, tutting at me and saying 'Chris-topher'!

"I don't need a bowl thanks; I wash myself."

"So, you don't want a bowl, lovely?"

"No, I wash myself in the wash room."

"That's nice ducky, and how will you get there?"

"Thought I would fly today!"

Another titter, a bit larger this time.

Basically, these ladies were implying whether I needed a Zimmer, whether I needed assistance getting there (because it did say 'mobilises himself + 1' on the board behind me.

"Don't you go falling again now, will you?"

"Yes, if I can possibly arrange it!"

No titter at all to that one.

And with that, the ladies depart to their next victim (client/patient). Bless them!

I then had time to ponder before my first outing of the day. I *had* said I would fly to the wash room on that occasion. Of course, I was just having a laugh, but three other alternatives did pop into my grey matter.

1. I could go via *'The Maid of the Mist'* on the Niagara Falls (get it?).
2. I could go via a trip (get it?) with Richard Branston to outer space, but that would land me in a bit of a pickle! (Ps. I know it's Branson, before you complain about an error to the publishers!)
3. I could use inter-planetary tele-porting like Dr Spock and Jim did in *Star Trek*, but, in retrospect, I would be uncomfortable with this mode of transportation when bearing in mind that my molecules might not re-construct themselves as 'Me!'. I might come back as John Major, for example. This would be understandable because he, like me, enjoys peas (and pees) and his favourite colour is grey too. However, it would afford me the opportunity to say 'Beam me up NHS'; I would like that (not a lot) but I would like it.

With my flights of fancy well and truly exorcised, I gathered my stick, staggered ten yards to the washroom, saying 'Morning' to every patient I passed en route (this being a statement of the blindingly obvious actually, so why I actually said it, I don't know), reached my intended destination, entered the room taking care not to lock it, sat on the chair by the sink lovingly placed there just for me and proceeded to wash with all the equipment they had provided. Finally, I sat on the toilet but to no avail—not even the thought of an enema proved decisive. 'Fear ye not' in this respect, there's only so much your tummy can take!

It was nice to have a peaceful sit (I said *sit!*) anyway. Here I could sit and think in peace, in splendid isolation and consider the meaning of life.

But only for a brief while.

There is a loud knock at the door, followed by an anonymous voice asking:

"Are you alright in there Christopher; you've been in there quite a while?"

"I'm just finishing off!"

"Let me know if you want anything dear."

"I'm just coming; give me a few seconds."

And with that, I prod the door open with my walking stick, very reminiscent of Noel Coward and make my grand re-entry onto the stroke ward. I feel like singing *'TRA-LA!'* but don't. I am too bloody tired.

I look at one of the two clocks—it's six forty! I look at the other—it's six forty-three!

I'll finish this section with a very useful tip for all the men folk reading this, (and, I suppose, for any unfortunate lady!): take this opportunity to exercise your lazy tendencies and grow a beard. In terms of time saved, it's worth its weight in gold, along with the added benefit of it stopping the 'would you like to shave this morning?' question, because, at six thirty in the morning, at a time not of my choosing, the answer would be an emphatic 'No'. Sorry—I mean "No thank you but thank you for asking so sweetly and with such concern for my wellbeing and appearance".

Good manners cost nothing you know, and they can potentially reap dividends.

Also, all the staff around you, in whatever capacity, have your interest at heart and deserve to be treated politely and with respect.

Have a lovely day!

The Trolley Without
the Fringe on Top

It's probably fair to say, that in the overall scheme of things, the grand design if you wish, the inspirational quality of the last chapter was perhaps a little dubious. So, to address the balance, I will introduce this section with some rip-roaring, slap your thighs, yee-haa! Up-beat words with the 'feel good factor'! There is a famous music-hall type of song which describes the movements of various farmyard birds when a loved-up couple enjoy an afternoon's excursion in what passes as a vehicle!

Do you remember the song? Do you remember where it came from? Yes, you've got it (and, if you haven't, I'll tell you), it's a song from the musical *Oklahoma,* where it is rather breezy apparently and the crops smell very nice! It reminds me of Boston actually—not Boston, Massachusetts but Boston, Lincolnshire on a wet Wednesday afternoon, particularly when the Brussel sprouts are being harvested!

This song is well and truly etched onto my brain, and it has been since the age of eleven, when I moved up to secondary school. The image contained within my thoughts is indelible, never to be removed, despite many efforts to wipe it out and replacing it with the lyrics from a *Slipknot* or *Napalm Death* track, for example.

"And how did you arrive at this predicament?" I hear you asking. Well I don't, but let's just imagine I do.

At the age of eleven, I was deemed a failure. I failed my 11+. For the uninitiated, this is a selection process whereby you are either deemed fit for a career in law or medicine or, God forbid, teaching, and you subsequently transferred to the local Grammar School. However, the other side of the coin was that you did not meet the necessary academic requirements and you were therefore consigned to the scrap-heap at the local Secondary-Modern, where boys learnt manly things like woodwork, metalwork and car maintenance. Or, in my brother-in-law's case, printing with moveable objects or words to that effect. The study of academia in all its forms was not necessary for the likes of me. Shame, really, because I considered myself to be something of a 'luvvy'—a thespian darling, a lover of the arts.

This yearning was partly catered for in the music lessons. Bear in mind that these were pre-National Curriculum days, and the specialist teachers could 'deliver' essentially anything they wanted to within the broadest of definitions of the subject. I had a smashing teacher who had a 'thing' for all things theatre. Hence, we were fed a diet of all the classic songs from *Oklahoma, The Sound of Music* and the Gilbert and Sullivan operettas like *The Mikado* and *The Pirates of Penzance.* This, for me, was wholesome fun. I even partook as a member of the chorus line in a couple of school productions of these shows—firstly, because, as I said, I saw myself as a Laurence Olivier in the making, and secondly, because I had a crush on the music teacher's daughter, so I was given the opportunity to couple up with her (in the biblical sense: purely platonic, despite my hormones advising me otherwise) on stage, without incurring the wrath of the music teacher, who regarded her daughter in highly angelic terms. She was a little tease: a right Minx!

Anyway!

I have digressed.

Again!

There is a method to my madness though.

You see, whilst in hospital, my mind drew a positive correlation between the song I used to sing all those years ago and the Drinks/Breakfast/Lunch/Dinner Trolley that was wheeled around the wards. Indeed, this mobile contraption would announce its arrival with a whole array of rattles and clangs and squeaks as it meandered its way around the various wards, or units, or even bays, as some people referred to them. The term 'bay' sent me into another stream of consciousness as well. The word 'bay' brought to mind images of *Montego, Hudson* and even *Herne.* Long, hot days spent soaking up the rays on a sun-kissed beach. That did not apply to *Hudson*, of course, or even *Herne,* but the mind was willing to suspend reality and 'go with the flow', so I let it! Outside of the increasingly steamed-up window, I could see it was pissing down and was blowing a howler!

So, here is a typical scenario. In this instance, the trolley is 'in role' of the breakfast deliverer, along with its driver—one of the ancillary staff who is desperately trying to maintain its general direction—a bit like those supermarket affairs, that have a mind of their own too!

The operator looks at each of the boards above the patients' beds, the ones containing vital information such as 'nil by mouth' and 'type 2 diabetic', that type of thing. She starts with Bert.

"What you having for brekky, Berty love?"

Now, Bert is asleep. He has a feeding tube stuck up his nose, and 'NBM' clearly written in bold letters on the board above him. This means he can't eat or drink anything—'nil by mouth'.

"Oh, yes, sorry Bert love, bet you can't wait to eat and drink again, can you duck?"

"Quack, Quack!" I can imagine Bert saying, if he was so inclined. But, as far as I could tell, he was asleep anyway and therefore, by definition, he would be disinclined.

Then, it's my turn.

"Morning Christopher, what do you want my dear?"

What do I want? Now, there's a thing. How about complete world domination for a starter?

Anyway, there is no chance to respond.

"Its tea, isn't it? White. Three sugars."

Again, no chance to answer.

"And it's cornflakes with milk and sugar?"

Wrong on all counts.

"No, it's coffee, black, with sweetener; *'Weetabix'*, no sugar, and a slice of toast, please. Oh, and instead of milk, can you pour Vodka on the *Weetabix* please?"

"Butter or margarine ducks, marmalade or jam? Do you want me to do it for you chuck?"

Do what, I wonder. Deconstruct the Eiffel Tower and reassemble it in my back garden? Arrange for a Ferrari to be made available to me at no personal cost? Bring Mozart back to life so that he could finish his unfinished symphony? (If he has an unfinished one needing finishing; I know that quite a few of these composer chappies did tend to leave things undone.) Most unreasonable of them not to finish a task, when you come to think about it.

I switch back on, and fight off the urge to say "Look at my board, you, you silly personage, I'm type 2 diabetic".

And with that, the trolley, which at this moment in time, is a breakfast trolley, complete with its urn of now luke-warm tea and bowls of sweetener (which, incidentally, is sweeter than the sweetest sweetener from Sweetsville, Sweetyland), about turns, eventually, and wends its way to the next patient, *Tom,* who is lactose intolerant. I wonder what he has on his cornflakes. He's always the life and soul of the party at about eight in the morning—perhaps its beer?

During the day, the trolley appears and disappears, but in a different guise, with a new operative. These drivers come in all shapes and sizes; some will give you extra *'bourbons'* if you smile nicely, whereas another particular guy, of whom I have fond memories, had developed an uncanny knack of propelling your refreshing liquid of choice in the general direction of your bed-side tray rather than ensuring it remained within the mug!

To conclude, in actual fact, the trolley did *not* have a fringe on top. Also, other than being a county, I have no idea of what a 'surrey' is. Also, there was a visitor to the unit whom I secretly referred to as the 'dolly with the fringe on top', but that is altogether a different story! One that I shall leave to your imagination!

On reflection, I think that it would be just a touch too cruel to have tantalised you in such a way that keeps you hanging on in suspenders, so I *will* describe my personal encounters of the third day; sit back and enjoy the journey.

Well, like all good stories, this one too begins with 'once upon a time'. That's vague, isn't it? I used to wonder as a child just why the author chose not to disclose the time parameters of the story he or she was about to enthral the reader with. Surely, with all that imagination going on in their mind, a rough approximation at least could have been offered. People say that the denial of such vital information by the author is, in fact, a literary device, used to help stimulate the creative sources of the reader. Now, that is fine and dandy of course. But, it could lead to the reader getting hold of the wrong end of the stick by imagining the story was set in an eighteenth-century country manor when in fact it was set in the battle fields of Agincourt! What a peculiar and very surreal interpretation of the author's plot would ensue!

So, for the purposes of clarity, I will define 'once upon a time'. I remember it will. It was a Tuesday. It was the second day of my confinement. I had the fortune of being in a bed that was adjacent to a window at this time, so I spent many an hour just gazing and thinking and gazing again—as you do! As you are probably aware, hospitals are by nature very warm places indeed, dare I suggest it but sometimes 'overheated' in my opinion. That, of course, is a value judgement—one man's (or woman's) 'warm' is another man's (or woman's) 'cold'. I can best exemplify this with my mum and sister as prime examples. I swear that they have cold water running around their circulatory system rather than blood. Their hands are always freezing: in Corfu, they are freezing; in Portugal, they are freezing; on a comparatively mild day in Skegness, they are double freezing!

Anyway, back to the matter in hand. I am staring out of the window. The window is becoming increasingly steamed up; the rain is lashing down, to such an extent to render the view dimmed and distorted. There really wasn't much point to continue with my gazing activities—all the birds had gone to bed (nest) and a state of complete nothingness ensued.

Given that it was fast approaching 'visiting time', when I was able to portray the character of 'Billy No Mates' with considerable success, I decided that, having enjoyed a wholesome midday meal (certainly far better than anything I would prepare for myself at home), I considered that an afternoon siesta was in order. So, I shuffled down the bed, pushed the button to control the angle of the bed to ensure the optimum 'resting' position, pumped up my pillows and prepared to drift away with the fairies, which is not a difficult operation for me, because I can do it quite easily! I use the word 'quite' with some venom, however. My brother-in-law Richard, God bless him and all who sail in him, can fall asleep within seconds—anywhere, anytime, and any place—*completely* by purpose! It's not as if he is sitting through a history lecture on the repeal of *The Corn Laws*, or another repeat of '*The Snowman*' when it's not even Christmas! No, he has this inbuilt ability to drop off just when it suits him. Oh, so very convenient, methinks!

In all fairness, I must inform you that Richard is the best brother-in-law you could wish to have. I didn't think so when we first met, however, but then he was not my brother-in-law then. He was a member of the local scout troop and so was I. He was the Patrol Leader of the 'Swifts'. I was in the 'Swifts' too but with a subtle difference. I was *not* the Patrol leader, he was! Thus, some ancient form of serfdom came into being when we went on the annual scout camp. *I* became designated as being in charge of water collection, which was fine, until you realise that it was a task first done at about five in the morning, involving a quarter of a mile trek up to the farm through soaking-wet grass with just plimsolls on, and then dragging the water carrier all the way back, only for all of the water to be used in one fair swoop, which resulted in a return journey happening at least ten times a day! Thanks Richard—'bitter; moi?' At this point, I had no idea that in years to come he would be sniffing after little Sis, and with some degree of success too, as he turned up to our house in a mauve topless 'MG'! Gulp and double Gulp!

I had no idea that in the years to come, he would spend most of his time 'courting' (now there's a word for the kids!) Sis, and of course, he eventually married her. And, as time progressed, we became the closest of friends. I write him poetry and in return, he unblocks my pipes, so to speak! Exchange is no robbery! Each time we meet up, we go through the *Inspector Crabtree* routine, which involves each of us in turn reciting the phrase '*Good moaning*' and '*Oh...good...moan...ing*' with a variety of differing emphases. Back in time, to the amusement of our very young children, (which we both had by now), we would greet each other by enacting *'Big Belly'*. This involved both of us 'exaggerating' our waist lines (although this became easier over the passing of the years) and then running towards and colliding with each other, shouting '*Big...Belly*' as we each took the impact! We also became very adept at reciting *The Four Candles* sketch, and, particularly at Christmas, we took immense pride in who could set up the other person first to deliver the punch line, by uttering a statement like this:

"Rich...ard," I might say, "...how many candles are there on the table? I can see one, two, three..."

"No, there are four," he would reply knowingly and with a wry smile.

"Four what?" I fed him.

"Four candles!"

We were, and remain, pretty good at '*The Four Yorkshire Men*' exchange too.

And so, our banter has continued over the years. Nowadays, the highlight of our conversations goes something like this:

"You know the trouble about getting old, Chris?"

"No Richard; what's the trouble about getting old?"

"You get stiff Chris!"

"Do you? Where?"

"In all the wrong places!"

"So, there are right places to get stiff."

"Oh yes, Chris, but I can't recall *where!*"

Now: where was I? That's right! I had shuffled down the bed and had curled myself up into a little fluffy bunny ready for a trip to fairyland. That trip indeed happened, but in no way was I in fairyland: I was well and truly awake; I can assure you of that!

Hospitals have strange and unfamiliar smells, don't they! There are some nice aromas, some weird ones and some not too pleasant. But, on this wet, windy, steamed up 'Visiting time' in question, I became aware of the evocative smell of '*4,7,11*'. I am not setting myself up as an expert of perfume: I recognise the great smell of *'Brut'* (a perennial favourite on the University scene because it drowns out any body odour issues that might be on your clothes due to them not being washed until you went home to Mum!) But, I was aware of the unique fragrance of '*4,7,11*' because I can remember my Great Auntie Amy' wearing it, and I have also associated that smell with her. A bit of a Pavlov's dog's situation going on here: I had been conditioned by my childhood sniffing, and now I had a firm impression of what was going on. I put it down to two alternatives:

- My Great Aunt Amy had taken pity on me, having no visitors, so decided to drop in on me from the other side, all unannounced like!
- I was to be in the presence of an Auntie Amy 'lookalike'. You have probably created a mental image, a stereotype now, and I suspect the picture you are seeing is pretty like the image I had created for my own personal use.

Be prepared to have that image shattered into tiny little pieces, but *don't* be afraid! In fact, it was a most pleasant encounter!

Before I describe this 'coming together', I do need to provide some sort of perspective so that you can make sense of it before you judge. I will do this by providing a list of things which aptly describe what I am *not:*

- Homophobic
- Racist
- Sexist
- Elitist
- Atheist

And here is another, smaller, list which encapsulates what I *am:*

- Male
- Heterosexual
- Single

I have stated these simple facts about myself to defer the 'political correctness squad' from descending on me like a ton of bricks and leading me away to a darkened room somewhere so that I can be interrogated and 'reconstructed'.

Why do I feel the need to make that point?

Simply because what I am about to tell you may be deemed as 'sexist', demeaning, or disrespectful to the females of our beloved race. Please accept from me that I tell you this for sincere and truthful reasons, with a purpose, rather than attempting to be-little someone just because they happen to be female.

I say all of that because, on opening my eyes, and attempting to focus on the source of the familiar perfume, I beheld what can only be described as 'perfection' in the female form. She was not a *Great Aunt* type at all. Standing next to the bed in which her Dad, I presume, was recovering, there was the presence of a tall, elegant and shapely lady: she must have stood all of six feet in height. She had long, flaxen hair, which she kept flicking behind her, and her appearance and demeanour was a pleasure to behold, complete with a softly spoken, but Oh so comforting a voice, which I could have listened to for ages. ('Here's a copy of *War and Peace:* would you mind reading it to me, kindly please?') She then took a seat and began chatting away to her Dad, I assumed, and other members of the visiting group, listening attentively at what was being said, and every now and again, laughing at a comment or observation with the sweetest of tone. I suppose the word I am looking for here is 'besotted': I was captured by her grace, elegance, style and beauty.

Now, you know when sometimes you are looking at someone, and they catch you staring: to minimise eye-contact, either the one staring looks away or the person being looked at, likewise. After a while, the inevitable happened and this lady caught me, mesmerised: a bit like a rabbit in the headlights. Her response was not to divert her attention however: instead, she smiled beautifully and mouthed a silent 'hello' to me. I smiled in return. Then, having said her goodbyes to her father, she got up, gathered her things together, and went to leave the ward. On the way out, however, she hesitated, briefly but with purpose, by my bedside, took a brief glimpse at the chart above my bed, and spoke quietly to me: "Goodbye, Chris." And then she was gone, but the perfume lingered.

Fast-forward twenty-four hours, give or take, and this incredible awareness of '4, 7, 11' delighted my nostrils for the second time. And then, she entered the ward. Again, she made herself comfortable by her father's bed-side; made him comfortable, helped him with his drink, filled out the next day's menu for him—all the menial tasks that you just sensed she would relish doing. She was obviously at ease chatting and laughing, this time with a different collection of family and friends. Then, she whispered in her dad's ear, he nodded in agreement, and she shuffled her chair, got out of it and walked towards me.

"Hello, Chris," she spoke quietly and kindly, "how are you today?"

"Feeling fine, er…OK…er…"

"Jasmine, my name's Jasmine," she interjected, fully aware that I was struggling to discover her name.

Then we exchanged pleasantries; I explained to her how I happened to be here, where I lived, that I was retired but used to be a teacher, and items for discussion that are spoken about within a normal conversation between friends.

This encounter lasted five minutes, I suppose, but it felt like hours. It appeared that we had a connection—impossible, I know—I had never met this lady before, but that's what my senses were telling me.

She subsequently rejoined her gathering, said farewell again, but this time as she exited, not only did she say, "Goodbye Chris, nice to have chatted with you," she blew me a kiss via her hand in that familiar gesture. I waved and smiled again.

This daily programme of events appeared to be 'on loop', the only difference being that our conversations became lengthier and deeper on each occasion, as our mutual understanding developed.

Before I knew it, I had received the green light to go home, a topic that I will speak about later in the book. As I was packing my bags, I thought it only right and proper to speak to the chap whose daughter I thought Jasmine was, just to let him know how nice it had been to chat with her and wish him well. Clearly, judging by his drawn looks and sullen features, he was 'in' for the long run.

"Morning," I started. "Just thought I'd come across to say goodbye and wish you well; I'm due home today."

He nodded and proffered an awkward smile.

"Would you mind passing on my thanks to Jasmine; she's been so kind and nice to talk to?"

This time, he looked puzzled; perplexed even.

"Who?" he enquired with a weakened voice.

"Jasmine?" I replied, in the form of a question, followed up by a supplementary statement:

"You're daughter, Jasmine? I'm Chris, from the bed over there."

I thought it necessary to confirm who I was to him, just in case he was a little bit confused or anxious. I had no need to worry on that front however. He simply replied:

"Got no children Chris, no daughter."

Oh dear. I'd got it all wrong. He was not Jasmine's father—what a mistake to make.

I pursued the issue though and described as best I could the lady after whom I was enquiring, who by now was well and truly sketched on my mind's eye. What he then said shook me to the bone.

"Had no visitors like that Chris! Wish I *had!* Elsie, my wife, has visited me, and her sister Florence—they're in their nineties you know; don't look it, do they. No one else, no, no one else. I'm ninety-five myself…"

I asked a few others around the ward to see whether *they* had any recollection of this stunning lady. The answer in each case was in the negative.

Yet I *had* seen her. We had spoken to one another. Not once, but on several occasions. They *must* have seen her, or heard her, or something.

This had become a *Dali* like landscape, so real but so confusingly false. It was so apparent to me, but so surreal to others. What had happened?

I never did see Jasmine again. But I frequently re-live our brief times together through regular re-visitations of '4, 7, 11' even though no one is in the vicinity, it is a most intoxicating of perfumes.

I was drawn back to the trolley, had someone slipped something into my hot chocolate! Of course, they had not. There's health and safety to think about, isn't there?

Sleep well.

Goodnight…

The Interlude

Now, whilst you are actively considering the appearance, the relevance and the health risk that *is* 'Dolly', I think it is a clever idea to contemplate where we started and where we are at present. At this very moment, it is silly o'clock in the morning—not normally a time you are aware of back home. That's the case for me, anyway, because I'm a lazy 'so and so'. Lots has happened to you already; you've been prodded, poked and have probably engaged in many surreal conversations with people you had no idea that you would be meeting. You've been washed, scrubbed, polished and are engaged in the task of eating your breakfast. How did you get here? Two options really—injury or illness, expected or not, in either case, particularly undesirable. Mine, as you know by now, was the latter. I experienced a minor stroke. To be honest, I didn't even know I had one: it's just that my mouth went tingly, when I walked, I was bashing into things on the right of me uncontrollably, and I fell over four times in succession. Next thing I knew was that I had become hospitalised—a unique experience for me, even at my advanced years of sixty! And, who knows, it could be your first admission too, younger or older than myself, a 'hospital virgin' or not—it makes no odds. My sympathies go out to you—that's why I wrote this little book really, to reflect on everything that is going to happen *to* and *with* you over the duration of your stay, from a whimsical, slightly 'off the wall' perspective really. I've talked about ceilings so why not walls? You could describe these days or weeks 'on holiday' as part of a play really (what's your favourite play: mine is *The Crucible* written by Arthur Miller—a gory tale written about witchcraft in Salem, Massachusetts, mirroring the McCarthy trials that happened in the sixties, I believe, in the USA—the fear of communism, 'reds in the beds' and all that. George Orwell's *Animal Farm* springs to mind too—on the surface it is about a farm run by the animals (hence the title presumably) but in effect a direct reference to the Russian Revolution in 1917.

But, let's get back to the 'play' analogy. Most plays have a start, middle and an end. I am excelling myself at astuteness here! Your time in hospital can be regarded in the same fashion—you arrived, you were worked on, and you left. In this book, I have titled one section as 'The Prologue' (the introduction), I will call the last chapter 'The Epilogue' and what goes in between is the middle bit—the plot.

Plays also have an Interlude, so, what is an interlude? One definition says that it is a short dramatic piece played separately or as a part of a longer entertainment. Or, I think, it is a convoluted way of referring to a general break in proceeding, justified by many prime purposes including:

- To stretch one's legs
- To visit the 'necessarium'
- To stuff your face with over-priced ice cream
- To make good your escape from a play that you have no chance of understanding, without drawing attention to yourself as some type of thick theatrical heretic!
- Any combination of the above
- Any other reasonable justification you can arrive at

When I have been to the theatre, the interlude, interval, break (whatever you want to call it really) arrives at just about the appropriate for me personally with reference to the first two points. Being six feet five, my knees and the seat in front of me tend to become very closely associated with one another, the net result being my legs go 'all pins and needles', probably because they are aware that the knees and the chair in front are 'in love, baby!'. Also, it gives the occupant of the chair in front a momentary lapse from being constantly 'kneed' in the back, for which I humbly apologise, but just can't help. Note to theatre planners: give us more leg room, please; please with sugar on top (or artificial sweetener for the type two's out there.). A visit to the loo speaks for itself: just witness the dash to 'the facilities at the interval'. As for the ice cream thing, I refuse point blank to pay a small mortgage for a tub of half-melted excuse of said 'treat', and queue up for the privilege. Bah! Humbug! I say.

My rationale behind the appearance of an interlude in this book is to provide you, my ever so lovely reader, with a well-earned distraction from the main plot, as it were. I think it is only right to give you the opportunity to rest your grey matter for a while or go for a pee. The question crops up though—*how* can I distract you?

There are a few possibilities I suppose:

1. I could strip naked, but there really is no justification for that sort of behaviour.
2. I could attempt to enlist your support in my attempt to become the international leader of *The Natural Law* party—you know, the one where all the world's problems are solved by floating men called 'yogic flyers' (good name for a pop group that think I'll place a copyright on it.).
3. I could perform a solo concert for you. Believe me, you would be begging me to stop if that was to happen!

I tell you what, you insert two distractions of your choice in the space below, and I will see what I can do:

4. ....

5. ....

Sorry, I will not do *either* of those suggestions on the likelihood of them being too painful, rude or embarrassing!

So, ladies and gentlemen, please allow me to introduce, for your literary edification, a short story and a few poems like wot I wrote a while ago. They really *are* quite............!

The Eastbourne Wave

The Eastbourne wave: I sat, and I was hypnotised; I can recall it,
I disrespected the dead peoples' benches: a dictator foresaw it,
There was a crash relenting, accordingly,
Capsizing the waves over six-foot-high but not a monster
Forty feet; I cannot predict the height of waves, but I exaggerate.

Success was D Day France
And we start at Flatford Mill
Or Saint Pauls'

A birth of a wave; an intriguing notion
"You get something for nothing," a real commotion,
"I'll be the wind, I don't require a lot,"
I feel like *The Lady of Shallot.*
Ripples blow over the surface, a restoring force.
It is said that energy of the sun creates the waves,
So how different is the sea to an amount of land?
Water washes by and cogs go up and down,
And the waves reveal what is hidden from view.
A shocking insight as to who or what rules the universe,
But then we've got nothing in our purse (except a card or two)

To Eastbourne then: waves are not made of water but energy,
Man makes them: a synergy;
Like transport and idiocy, like talking to you.
Like the sand in the waves and the waves in the sand,
Who speaks to you, who really speaks to you?
Who makes the noise beyond compromise?
I believe it is an orchestra creating.

There is one perfect band of energy: so, ride the float:
If you don't, it will ride you:
It is the viewers' experience: sitting on a boat,

Up and down, up and down,
You and I occupying a three-dimensional space
Upon a two-dimensional surface, declaring "it is too cold for
summer!"

Waves on the surface of water (others below)
Quote 'talking of Michelangelo'.
The familiar world is one side of reality
Where life is processed; hidden from us in one easy word.

Everlasting flows, but nothing endures;
So difficult it is to get into places
Where they ask: who are you?
And what is that you might do?
The answer; without a feeling of remorse,
Is "I don't know: are waves true?"

Consider this: our lives are in continuous change,
A considered thought of reality, strange,
Where one no man is understood
And everyone else is misunderstood.
The world is but an object of processes,
A collection of processes invisible
To you or me, the in-between,
Or whoever saw the roses.

Eastbourne then.

On a beach; a sandy shore, a listless environment,
There is something I abhor,
Benches that declare "I am dead" to walk past is a criticism,
Looking out to sea.
Create and destroy in equal measure,
Making misty mountains without an argument.
Without a paddolo!

Have you ever seen a mouse?
Have you?
Have you really?
A mouse to model, a natural world?

I saw a mouse once;

It gave me a map,
So, I saw structures and jigsaws and processes and on time
I saw windy days and dynamics in between.
It was not good, so let's not worry.

The consistency of an object must be an illusion,
Surely, doesn't it?
Saint Paul's: not shorter, a constant friend,
Constant in time—sublime.

'Mathematics did not hurt World War Two'.

Strengthen, duration, fetch: three factors
26/27, pick the dates Walter,
See the progress of the ocean waves.
The boat is flipped: The Thunderbirds,
No land to tether though; Antarctica
'Make sure you tell everyone mate',
'Don't bother; it's too late'.

We are going on a seven-thousand-mile journey,
Do you know what we are looking for?
What size will the waves be?
In total anonymity?
Seven thousand miles and nowhere to go.

There is a crest before it breaks,
I look at the sea and I know I should walk,
But what I need to do is talk,
I watch carefully, and I look beyond
The energy, which cannot be destroyed,
I look beyond a surprising number of options.

They say, "Chris, a wave is born just every day"
Seven thousand miles is my guess,
But in all innocence, I'm only dancing.
This is an arrest before it breaks.
No manta, no shape, just a mistake.

I own the atoms I consume,
I chose to vacuum my own room,
I am a poet, philosopher, in flux

A human being in a cup,
And I thank you so very much!

So, the day has arrived,
A question of tawdry rotten stuff.
A day when it is asked 'is there life or dissipation?'
There is life, comes the answer; it is like speaking to a wave.
Mother watches over the waves,
So, there must be life, I'm told.

Take a photo: hold the moment,
Illogical, but I must do it,
There is no sense of form,
There is no sense of feeling;
Music would be no good,
If it goes on forever.
'Tic toc', a begging of an end,
And a structure of closure.

It's not just poetry,
It's not even a metaphor,
It just keeps popping up,
In a most peculiar way,
Whilst,
We are away,
In Eastbourne,
Waving as the waves wave back; thinking.

Laura, the Thinking Person's Lift

'My name is Laura;
I am a lift in the employ of the NHS
I am, by nature, a simple soul
Easy going, laid back;
Easy to please and eager to please.
I would describe myself as steady,
Nothing too intricate;
Capable of carrying out the basic tasks in life.
I generally go un-noticed; I'm just there;
Impeded by a limited vocabulary,
But able to make my point.
I am clear and distinct in tone,
I pride myself that I speak the Queen's English in a weird sort of way.
I don't shout, I won't moan,
I respond to the simple touch.
Sadly, my role in life is limited,
Restricted to 'Going up' and 'Going down',
From 'Doors opening' to 'Doors closing'.
And that would appear to be the sum of my existence
UNLESS; yes, wait for it, have patience prey,
I get confused, or get misused,
And if that happens, all hell's let loose.
I become of two minds; a split personality no less.
My doors will shut
And then will open;
Again, they will shut, shut, shut,
Followed by open, open, open;
I will be going up,
I will be going down,
I will be going up, then down,
Down, then up;

Up, open, down, shut;
Down, no… up, shut… no… open,
Up down shut floor one, no… ground floor, open, shut, basement;
It's all so thoroughly confusing,
BUT,
I won't give up, oh no;
Neither will I accept the blame for my unfortunate predicament.
So, as you walk away, either out of embarrassment or mirth or birth,
And you think you've got away with it
Oh no you haven't!
I will let you know about it in my dulcet tones;
I will inform the whole hospital that YOU are the culprits;
Your howls of laughter will be drowned out by my verbal outburst
And you will be haunted by me as you make good your escape.

Then, of course, the men in white coats will arrive;
They'll sort me out and calm me down,
So that I am capable of logical thought again
And can ponder the more meaningful issues in life,
Like: do I need medication? Do I need hospitalisation?
Is life but a dream?

I rest assured though when I DO gather my senses,
That you won't choose *me* for your next perambulation!
Through pure deduction and procrastination,
I KNOW you will go elsewhere,
Or use the stairs indeed.

Park Bench

You know,
Sitting on a park bench, floundering.
Watching all the leaves go, wondering
Whether it is right or wrong
That all around
Goes on and on.
And on a park bench sit I,
A lie to be told,
A sad person to behold.
The trees, the sighs,
The 'don't know why's?'
The laughs, the shouts,
The hangabouts;
The sun is shining overhead,
But what the hell is in my head?

It is quiet now, so appealing
And I am left with tranquil feeling,
And aloneness, and peace,
Yet they do not understand.

I always told her I write in anger,
And so, it is, but why?
I try, and I try
And I try, and I cry,
But try as I might I'm losing the fight
To hold on to what was meant to be:
My abject curiosity
And the certainty held
That 'I' is 'Me'.

Amongst those gathered, I'm told (advised}
There are those amongst them who are so wise!
But hiding in their awful glare,
Do they know who's *really* there?

I am condemned by such e feeling
That haunts me, reeling;
On my own.
The trees can only whisper,
The leaves can only journey by,
Haunting, jeering,
On my own and more.

Yes, sitting on a park bench
Floundering;
All mis-understood.

Discussion with a Diabetic

Good morning, Metformin,
Another gulp, another day,
So, greetings, Metformin;
I'll soon be on my way.

Felicitations, Type 2
Sorry you're overweight
In every other respect, my friend
You're looking truly great!
And as your GP says,
Adopt more healthy ways
Get on your bike!
Do exercise!
MATE!

In my box, I have some pills
Medication for my ills,
BP, Tension: got the lot,
Like the Lady of Shallot.
8am, in there, sorted, fine
Got them queued up in a line.
Which one first, which one last?
Which the future, which the past?
Glass of water in my hand

Head stuck firmly in the sand.

Hello Buddy, I'm your friend,
And I'll be with you to the end
My dose goes up, but never down
You see: I'll always be around.
I will be in your personal space
I will manufacture your face

I'll put right the errors that you make
When it comes to pie or cake;
MR O. BEECE

So, what am I supposed to do?
Take one now, or later two!
And what if GP says to me
We're going to have to make it three!
Surely there is nothing new
In being Diabetic 2?

Do you like my box, my style?
You've not said so for a while
Keep me safe, and keep me dry
Never worry, never sigh
For all your sins I will atone
And yes, the doctor's on the phone, PIE-FACE!

Oh, for sugars in my tea!
Pints of beer and then a wee!
Melton Mowbray sound to eat
Now it's just a naughty treat
Chocolate bars and creamy cakes
Roasted peanuts were my mates
Diet this, and sugarless that
I'm not thin, but sure aren't fat!
It's now as if I must bat
For the other side.

Look, you're plus sixty, I am free
Can you not my benefits see?
Don't I top you up with glee?
Isn't it all just down to me?
CHUBBY!

Dear Metformin, are we mates?
Do you really guide the fates?
And have you seen my insurance rates?
Aren't you just a dirty word?
Never spoken, never heard?
Making claims just so absurd?

You know, sometimes, when you're in bed
A cursed thought goes through your head.
Well, I'm like that; I'm on repeat
Upon my word, they check your feet,
And once a year, drops in the eye,
Make you squint and make you cry
We are partners, we are grand
Let's go to the promise land!
Together!
Forever!
MUG!

We're not friends, are we?
...Well?...
You're a label...
...You're Type 2!...
Just a con-man
...and you're my conned-man
SADDO!

The Sad Lament of Moby, Probably the Most Immobile Mobile Living in the West

I didn't cost a lot you know; two pounds fifty, maybe three
But now, they hand me out: 'for free'
I'm not hi-tech, I'm no computer
Guess I'm not ready for the future.
I am a mobile phone: old but not a brick
Can't be said I'm very slick.
But I serve my purpose: I make calls
To Stoke or to Niagara Falls!
If you're dining by The Seine
I can reach you (in the main)
Greece, Australia, Pakistan
I will find you: I'm your man!

But it would seem that I am not
I might as well go flat and rot!
I live alone
I never roam
This is my house
But not my home
I am Moby by name, but not by calling
And I can feel my spirits falling
You'll best find me on the top,
Or under the fridge, or beside the mop,
By the shelving, inside the cat!
Behind the hi-fi, under the mat.
Lost with the keys, or within a book
Anywhere you chose to look.
I am forgotten, left on the stairs
Nobody worries, nobody dares;
Easy to discard, no one cares,

And I am left with just one mission:
To contemplate the human condition.

I am a phone; no frills, no fuss
(Don't go and leave me on the bus)
I'm not Version 7, much less Version 8
Comparatively not that very great
My branding is 'one touch'
Which means 'not much'
But I am good for you,
I can tell a lie or two
I spread sadness, I cast doom
I can stun a silenced room
I can be deep with feeling
I can get them reeling
I can ad-lib
I can be anything you want me to be
And tell another fib.
I can put the world to rights,
I can set the place alight!
While you're walking or in bed
I'll speak those words inside your head

OK! I don't take photos, but gladly send texts
I'll message religion; I'll take on the sex!
But in the greatest scheme of things
Where teachers teach, and singers sing
There is nothing I can bring
Demoted to an 'also ran'
In other words, flushed down the pan!
(In which case, I'd be a floater: I'd not sink
Wouldn't escape the ghastly stink!)

So, must conclude I'm not that mobile
I do have worth, but it is futile
I cost you but a pound each week
One hundred pennies let you speak
To all and sundry,
Even on a Sunday
The day of rest
I am a victim of your neglect
I mean nothing, in effect

Not in your ruck-sac, nor in your bag
I guess I'm just that extra drag
There are landlines,
So, what's the point?
Free at weekends; cook the joint!
And by the time it's three
You have forgotten about me.

So, get a contract
Please upgrade
Sign the form
New model displayed
And I can hear you saying
"My phone does all this!"

The trouble is, I'm not your wife
Don't trade me in for a younger life!
Please just set me free,
I beg; DO NOT TOP ME UP
Just to ignore me.

River

Flowing slowly; in meander,
Never searching, seeking answer.
With discussion, full of candour,
And with bullets to add rancour;
Intoxicated with a sigh, and a 'don't know why'
A reason guessed, a knowing sigh,
A time of perfect manipulation.
A space of sordid postulation.

High above the river; do you recall?
The tragic splendour of it all,
The summer's peak, the autumn's fall
The winter's curse, the spring's re-call
A juxtaposing of the mind,
The fear of waiting left behind.
Some guilty pleasure in our head
Without a word, so nothing said.

River splendid, river guessing,
River silent, river messing,
Sun-shit beating on our heads, relentless,
Torment raging, doubts, resentments
Passions flowing into view,
And 'what you know', and 'who is who?'
Passions rising; frailty burning,
Always guessing: never learning.
Careless. Free-less; full of guilt,
It can't be seen beneath the quilt

So, we are here; upon a hill
Looking for a timeless thrill,
With no one to judge, no one to scream
No one to call a total obscene;

No one to deny what they have seen
By the river.

Shall we, shall we not?
No can do!
Experiment beyond the zoo.
Passions soaring without a chance
Of what was said and thought in France!
A risk too far, too many denying
The futile fear, the toll of crying.

Too young, it was said, too young by a year,
The season's not right, so bring out the beer,
Let's celebrate the occasion successfully stopped,
And rejoice in our sobriety!
Tethered sadly by reproach
There can be no approach.

You saw the visage
You saw the view
You said I wondered,
You said I knew,
You felt a kindness
You almost fled
You spoke of trying
You spoke of dread
And you, well you, asked me kindly so
It's time to leave, please let me go.
You called it all a rude investigation
I called it a mindless resignation.

And the river flowed
Beneath us
The torment grew
Within us
The people spoke about us
Until it was no more.

Flavour

She resembled a 'golden girl'; she danced with John,
Pirouetting, shaping, chagrin: wrong,
Feline, sublime, unnecessarily a creature
A lady who said "I'd love to meet you"
Shimmering slightly, a grace beyond her years,
Disguising, kindly, all her fears.
Crowds shouted profanity in her head,
'Off to school' or 'off to bed'.

She seemed like a 'diamond girl'; she sang a song
Mixing, fixing: the action was too long.
Full of good grace, au fait with her teens
Left wondering about the 'in-betweens'
So confused and ill-defined
An ogre in her role sublime,
Talked of 'without', and 'part of the scene':
The charming wretch, the beauty Queen.

This was a 'tired out' existence; old before the date.
A complementary repose to secure a mate.
Such cried out of torture, a life beyond a grief
Absent in its empathy, just beyond belief.
It was called a modern exposure,
Complicit with shouts and sordid disclosure.
The war had just finished, aspects to define;
Who is yours, and that is mine!
What's the rush and now's the time
To liberate, consummate, procrastinate, fine!
With lashings of spirits and passable wine
We'll turn our back on acceptable crime,
And sigh the hour away
So that we can meet it on another day.

There is no doubt she was platinum in appearance,
Bronzed, enlightened; space between us.
But the organ grinder resonated deep in her thoughts,
Evenings were fine, and presents were bought!
Abused by a power, yet 'chill out' she thought,
Just what is it that I've sought?
Is it this; something caught?

Charmed and charming, right but sad
Always noticed, never glad
And she smiled; the countenance on her face
Offered an eternal grace.
This was a force yearning to be free,
Who surfed the waves for you and me?
In all their real complexity
Which ebbed and flowed in dying light,
Emotions dimmed and giving flight.
Tossed and thrown, demeanours just for fun,
The whole damned thing had just begun!

In the end, though, she was blessed
A victim of a putrid mess

Girl was toxic, girl was mule,
Girl was living, livid fuel
Girl was victim of the time
Girl knew nothing of the rhyme.
Girl was crazy, and perplexed,
Girl was lonely, cold and vexed.
Girl said 'Hi' to those who cared
Girl made promise, but was scared
Girl said "I love you" with a gun against her head
Girl said "I love you"
But then was dead

Chillingly, unwillingly, she had sacrificed her soul,
Treasonable, unreasonable, she did not know the toll.
She had fled to an uncompromising state
A vain attempt to recreate
The juxtaposition was scribed upon the all:
'You will sink, and you will fall'
'You'll attend the Maker's ball'.
She danced a wicked dance.

Gorilla

Gorilla, Coachella; words to guess and say,
Gorilla, Priscilla: things to make you stay,
Impacting, contracting, a feast along the way,
A sadness, a brightness. A dark November day.

"What?" I hear you say, "What do you mean?"
"Is something out there: in between
The darkest shadow, and what has been
The dancing of the moonlight Queen?"

I am just one of those guys,
Whose words don't work because of lies
Whose thoughts are simply alibis
And Father weeps, so Mother cries.

"What?" you chance it once again
The utter shrill, the cheap refrain,
Of 'are you sure or just insane?'
Co-incidentally, in the main,
It's not snowing, but it is rain.

Something pours about my frame
Is it just another game?
Where rules don't shout and numbers count
The problems bellow like a fount.
I cannot do it!
Beyond reproach
I might as well
Indulge in toast
With Yorkshire Brew
And mug of tea
Anonymity!
I cry to reason, another quest

Another tale; I'll do my best
To hide my soul, to guess the rest
Within the sullen sea.

I am now upon the hill
The metaphoric ghostly thrill
Where trees are wild, but plants are still
And birds sing forth a culling chill.

On our wedding day, we said
Ably shot by Father Ted,
We would do so well; instead
You and I were filled with dread
So, slept a sleep on irksome bed

Gorilla! Chowchilla! A word ill-defined
A 'chat-up'. A 'focus', a toss of the mind
Some 'home brew', the wrong crew,
The swingers so near,
Instigation, configuration, and someone on the floor
'*The swingers are swinging all next door*'
And this is something I told you all before.
You said less but reasoned more.

In came the drag act; suspenders to the throat!
Then came the P.O,
She just rocked the boat!
And she kept us swimmingly afloat
In a world of resistance
And persistence, wine-fuelled insistence,
Yet we kept our distance,
Us, from just next door

We were a pair once; a couple of losers,
Who wore the pants and who wore the trousers?
Who saw the sun up high in the sky?
Who said: "No thanks," and who said, "Let's try?"
Who said, "I'll laugh," and who said, "I'll cry?"
Who said, "I'll live," and who said, "I'll die?"
Who begged the question of what really: "Why?"
Who said: "I'll swim, and you can just fly!"
Who said: "I will wave you sad goodbye."

And who was left, and who would die?

Gorilla, Gorilla, what have you seen?
Something real or something dreamed?

A Walk in the Woods

We left the party and struggled past the losers; do you remember, those guys who you reckoned were your friends, and perhaps mine too? But they weren't of course; they weren't. They were just: 'hangers on' who fancied a night out at your expense, because you had done so well in the examinations. Do you recall? Well, I do. I had fished you out of a pond in your parent's back garden. You stank of vomit and shit. I remember you uttering slurred words and phrases such as: 'Where am I?' and 'Are my fairies with me?' I replied in the affirmative. It could have been in the negative, but you would not have known. There was a lovely Irish lady present. God knows who she was, but she was there, and kindly words came from her fragile and confused countenance.

"Well, hello; you are at Pete's birthday," she said. "You are looking a little poorly now." I knew it. She knew it. You most certainly knew it. It was your decision to go for a walk. "Just through the Woodland Walk," you said. I asked, "Why?", but you had gone. In the disguise of the cool shrill night, you had pushed me aside— mumbled words like "I must find her, I need to, I must". You in your Caftan and beads, bell bottoms and winkle pickers, reeking of patchouli, and me, with the missing cat, which you had tried so gallantly to locate in my parent's mud. I felt obliged to pursue your sullen footsteps. In shorts, sporting a vest, donning a pair of trainers I had found in the lobby. You colliding with steps on the wall; you with voices in your head; you still reeling with a dread that I knew nothing about, but we left the party and fought off the gentle folk who were questioning our sanity.

"To the woods," you said. "To the woods," I said. "Let's have a walk in the woods." And so, without a moment to reflect or change our minds, we walked. We glanced back almost furtively just the once to re-assure ourselves that we left the party in full-swing. Indeed, it was: the brothers continued to vie for some sort of superiority, we could hear their voices above all others. The atmosphere was crackling; it was alive. The music pounded out a relentless beat that raped the seriousness of the chill air. The vibes provided us with a soundtrack for our solitary perambulation to the woods. Still the purpose was clear to you: "She is out there, and I will find her," you repeated in an eerie, echoic, style. When I asked of her identity and whether I knew her, you just turned to me and smiled in a most peculiar fashion: as if I was to be made aware of some untold revelation.

"We're here," you said. "I know," I said. So, on we went for our walk in the woods. But, I did not know the rationale for this surreal exploration of ours, or, should I say, "Yours?"

Confused; startled by the slightest attempt at a noise. Unsure of our step. Cautious: feeling our way with a petrifying silence. Struggling; laden with a paradoxical fear of what might be. Bravado; an uneasy exalted awareness. The sultry woods signposting our way, but to where, we had no realistic comprehension. It was a violent, unforgiving path we took. You tripped. I slipped. You fell. I flipped. The impossible darkness of that disposal hour had disappeared.

"Is that her?" I asked you, almost accusingly. She was a beautiful vision—flying, swooping, and singing in the sky—the lace of her crimson dress flowing gracefully behind her, as if unattached. She asked us to join her and we did. So, we let ourselves go, abandoning the limitations, boundaries and contradictions of our existence. We flew high—higher and higher—her spectral aura as our guide; smiling a knowing smile, her countenance afresh and her spirit ever knowing. She whispered: "Come with me," and like two love forlorn adolescents, we were under her magical spell: that enigmatic smile which I am sure I had seen before, beguiled us with its intricacy. "Is that *her*?," I repeated with suspended disbelief. And you said: "I am not sure." One moment, flying free. Next second, floating, drifting, all at sea. Then, trying to take off, but failing. Soon to be losing height, losing sense, flying as if a mythical creature. Guided towards the light: re-connecting with our past: a nostalgic journey requiring us to let go of our senses. And then becoming hampered: fierce winds and echoes of that sweetly smell. I asked you one more time: "Was that her?" You turned at me with a languid, almost forgotten expression, and said, "No." In fact, you pleaded: "No."

We could not see. We could not even hear under these circumstances that were not normal. But I was near you all the time. Not loving you but wondering about you: patiently waiting for you to send out a thought to me. I sensed your depression; I empathised with your need of emotional support. I was there in your barren loneliness with the ghosts from your past.

But now, we had entered a peaceful environment. We connected with the space that was attractive and peaceful. You surrounded yourself with flowers and energies and thoughts and emotions. And I was fearful lest I hurt you. Yet, you breathed a golden breath; full of tranquillity and peacefulness. And then, you felt her touch; a heavenly, special touch. You asked her name. "Is that you; are my travails over?" She had no name; the lady with a waft of innocence about her, and her words came as a shock to me and a devastation to you: "I am who you want me to be, and who you do not want me to be. I am your friend. I am your foe. I am by your side. I despise you. I weep tears and yet I celebrate your failings. You are me and I am you." With that, my eyes had been opened: a simple exercise but so full of inner meaning. I was compelled to ask a salutary question: "Do you remember the first time you made a wish as you blew out the candles on your birthday cake? Was it granted?" A pensive, inquisitive, morbid-like expression took hold of your face. "No," you responded. "So, was *that* her?" I further probed. And you were not happy with my line of enquiry and you merely uttered "No" again, so I let it rest.

We persisted with our walk in the woods. You had become delightfully animated by now; beyond 'cruise control' but somewhat tainted in an indefinable manner and meandering without apparent care. Yet it appeared that you were creating a personal space for yourself; apparently an attractive, beautiful, serene place: a venue where you could connect with *her.* Together, we surrounded ourselves with the energies of the night hours, battling with the emotions of rage, fear and pain, which were fighting for our very souls. Slowly, surely, we embraced the glowing aura of knowledge that engulfed us with such a physical sensation: full of love, over-brimming with life, graceful: so graceful. And a sweet aroma anointed the air which permeated the threat of the dark, and wafted gently, silently, about our chilled and bewildered countenances.

I *wanted* to question you. I wanted to help you. I wanted to provide you with the comfort for which you yearned. I wanted to support you, sustain you and encourage you. I could feel your presence and knew we were truly alone. I heard you calling; begging for my assistance, but your lips were motionless, and your eyes were steely and inert. So, *I* became transfixed: bound by a cruel spell content to hinder me. "Was that her?" my words choked for their existence. "Is that her?" I spluttered with a semblance of being. "We

130

have not found her yet," came your apologetic retort. We stood still, re-living the gentle assurances we once held dear. "Now is not the time, not the perfect moment," you whispered with disengagement. It was then I realised you had been waiting for the dawning of success.

We had become unwilling participants in a play within a play. You delivered your lines, I delivered mine. It was as if we were seizing an unforeseen opportunity to write a script according to our own true desires. We were ready and deserving of them. Churlishly, and in accord, we released the challenges that we held so tightly gripped within our hands. It was a moment of serenity and surrender; orchestrated by comfort and structured like a raging catalyst setting the wheels of destiny in motion one more time for the fruition of our intent. "Let us give up the search," I pleaded. Again, you blanked me.

But the decision had been made. Without recourse to analysis, argument or motivation, we turned around. Words were anonymous, redundant, and inappropriate. Actions were stilted, cautious and weary. My mind was like a phantom hitchhiker protecting my wildest thoughts and dreams. The stuffiness of the season remained, squeezing the final fragments of growth out of existence. Yet, the visual beauty of our voyage ruled triumphant. The taste of venture was intoxicating. We had embraced the opportunities; we were cajoled into returning.

The party became increasingly audible as we re-joined the festivities. Everyone was still there. The brothers, the Irish lady and the strangers were still present.

We re-joined the gathering. We mingled for a while but soon became bored. You acquired a Merlot; I secured a whisky and, like we had done before, we withdrew from the throng. In the splendid isolation we were in again, I just *had* to say it:

"We *did* meet her, didn't we?" You fixed me with a stare.

"Oh yes," you replied. And we knew.

Never again did we talk about that walk in the woods, not even when we were re-united for our 60th celebrations. And when I drove past the other day, I noticed how overgrown and neglected the woods had become. I reminisced and almost let a primal scream escape but was pacified when it became apparent to me that the woods were going nowhere.

So, there we are: my humble offerings.

Are you back from the loo yet?

Have you had your fill of ice cream?

Indeed, have you fought off the urge to find the nearest exit door?

Well, if nothing else, it has been a distraction from what you are becoming increasingly aware of: that you are in hospital, where you might be staying for some considerable amount of time and that you well experience periods of extreme boredom. Never mind: put into its correct perspective, there is nothing wrong with boredom, so long as you put it to effective use. I know this may be a contradiction of terms: if you are bored, then it is a sad thing, because there is nothing to do, or nothing you can think of to occupy your time. But, really, that is the kernel of my argument. You may well have been doing too much of a terrible thing and too little of a good thing. Be honest with yourself: have you taken regular exercise? Have you got good control over your diet? Do you open a bottle of wine and adopt a mindset that states "no point in leaving any; it'll go off". In all fairness, that might well be true. I know experts talk about opening a bottle of wine about an hour before you wish to consume it to 'let it breathe'. What the hell does that mean? Wine, as far as I know, is inanimate. It has no need to draw breath. It is not alive. It is a dead parrot; perhaps desperately wishing to visit the Scandinavian countries!

You, on the other hand, *are* animate. You *do* exist. Life *is* precious, and, like me, you may well have experienced a 'wake-up call'. If you are anything like me, and I sincerely hope that you are not, for your sake really, then your line of thought would have been something like this: illness, serious illness, bad injuries; they happen to other people and not me! I am invincible. Nothing of any major consequence will ever possibly happen to me.

Wake up! It has!

Scary, isn't it, in the cold light of day.

But, and this is a big 'but', you are not on your own, so, deal with it and accept that people here are doing their best to aid your recovery from whatever afflicts you. Keep that thought in mind. Anyway, the interlude is over. Resume your seats please for the rest of the show. The lights are being dimmed in the auditorium. It is time for you to clear your throat, adopt the most comfortable pose and adopt sponge-like tendencies for what is to follow!

'Let Us Be A-Bed'

"OMG!" as the kids say; there is a story to this! Are you sitting (or laying: perhaps eggs, who knows?). Yes? Then I'll begin. Stand by for a tricky situation worthy of your empathy.

Cast yourself back to your school days (daze?). I am referring again to those Secondary school days: the happiest days of your life. This is a terrifying cliché but, in my experience, it was totally 100% accurate: they were! It is irrelevant at this juncture whether you passed or failed the 11+. You might not even have the slightest concept of what the 11+ exam was anyway, and therefore have no direct understanding of the trauma that it caused to a delicate soul like me. If this is the case for you, then you were a child dragged up, or down, through the 'comprehensive system'. For the record though, I have to say that I did 'get over' any suffering of the mental type very quickly. The first thing that I did on arriving at 'big school' was to pick a fight with my arch enemy Andrew, in the playground, even before we were ushered into the hall to be allocated to classes: like cattle. Not that cattle attend class. But, that's by the by. We ended up big buddies, by the way. Andrew, if you are there: you can have your elastic band back now: that being the object which caused the 'fisticuffs' anyway. Oh, the joy of the pursuit of attempting to be the 'alpha male' at the age of eleven!

I've drifted away from the main thrust of this discussion however, so, just allow me to re-focus and let out a primal scream of some description:

"AAAHHHH!"

Better? I'd say so. I have now re-aligned my chakras, so to speak.

So, here is the scene.

I am now a pupil in what common parlance now refers to as 'Year Eight'. If you are a teacher, ex or otherwise, you will understand that pupils at this stage of their education can be

133

particularly difficult to control. This is particularly true in a mixed sex school, when the girls are flashing anything they have, along with badly applied and 'over the top' mascara and the boys just can't stop drooling at anything in a skirt so long as it has a breath.

The exact location of this encounter of the fifteenth kind was in an English literature class.

The teacher was instructing us in the nuances of *Romeo and Juliet*—much akin to delivering a sex education class in biology I can only suppose, except that in this instance, cucumbers were not a visual aid: metaphors, characterisation and motives were more than adequate replacements.

As was the norm in these lessons, we, as the pupils were allocated 'parts' to read. This was always the source of much trepidation. 'Please God', don't let it be me!' every boy prayed. 'Please God, let it be me' every girl begged.

Well, to cut a long story short, *I* had the misfortune of being selected to read the part of 'Romeo', much to the obvious thrill and enjoyment of my fellow male classmates. This is because there was an unwritten rule amongst us boys that if one of us had the misfortune to be selected to play a part, then the others would take the opportunity to giggle profusely at any deemed innuendo in the script, hence having the impact of putting the reader 'off his stride' and thus incur the wrath of the teacher. It was a cruel place, the classroom, but, you would seize on any opportunity to cause the maximum embarrassment and awkwardness to the condemned male, which might even result in the reader being placed in detention for failing to read the part with the appropriate seriousness: a major sin indeed.

In normal circumstances, I would have bitten the bullet and resign myself to the fact that it was I who had to undergo this trial by classmates. Next time, it would be someone else. The teacher always marked down in his notebook exactly *who* had undergone the torture and on what date. All's fair in love and war, as they say.

But, these were no normal circumstances, and everyone in the class, both male and female, recognised this to their obvious joy.

And this is why.

I had been selected to read the part of Romeo.

And it was the daughter of the music teacher who had been selected to take the part of Juliet!

Everyone in the immediate vicinity understood I had a crush on said girl: I can't begin to name her for obvious reasons, but, on reflection, she would probably have been flattered: her name was *Jane.*

Oh Jane! The love of my life!

Unrequited love!

The irony of the situation was plain for all to see.

There was Jane sitting in one corner of the room, surrounded by her female counterparts, all preening their hair.

There was I in another corner of the room: acne ridden and battling manfully, or boyfully, to restrain my raging hormones.

And at the front of the classroom, was the teacher, bless him, proudly setting up his new teaching aid: a cassette recorder, complete with a C45 tape, ready to record this tense and dramatic rendition of the balcony scene with the two star-crossed lovers.

Gulp, and double gulp!

So, the teacher pleads for silence for silence, having made sure that everyone knocks exactly where they are in the play. You could sense the nervous anticipation in the air. I, as Romeo, was fully aware that at least 50% of the class, the boys, were urging me, no, willing me, to make one major cock-up, whilst the other 50% cooed in a dream-like state at the prospect of a real romance being played out before their very eyes!

Cue the machine and cue action!

Everything went swimmingly for the first few lines. I would read my part and then scan down to the next bit I had to read. That is when the terrors struck. That was when I just *knew* that I was about to provide the boys with an opportunity to mock me beyond their wildest dreams. There was a speech that required me, as Romeo, to declare 'let us be a-bed', in other words, 'time to climb the wooden hill to Bedfordshire'. However, after having practiced the speech in my head prior to reading it, I mis-pronounced 'a-bed' as '*abed*'.

"Let us be abed!" I declared. There ensued one ghastly pregnant pause, then, in seconds, huge uproar and much merriment in the classroom. Guffaws of uncontrollable laughter permeated the room. The teacher struggled in vain to re-assert some sort of order, but he failed miserably, and so the recording machine was stopped, much to his annoyance. Never mind his annoyance! What about my embarrassment? I had lost any 'street-cred' that I had previously possessed in one moment in time. And in front of Juliet; Jane! Did I go red or did I go red? Yes! Both! I knew that I would never live this episode down, and I never did; often hearing said quotation being repeated to me on any occasion possible to create maximum facial redness!

I vowed at that point: acting was a pointless job; I would not pursue it as a career. Also, judging from the sheer anxiety and stress levels that the teacher went through, I further vowed that I would never ever train to be a teacher. In 1979, I started my career in teaching: I never became an actor though, well, not in the true sense of the word, anyway.

All of which leads me nicely into another discussion. How many times have you thought that Mr X or Mrs Y holds down a secure full-time job, and is therefore able to feed the family, which by definition is:

- Futile
- Exasperating
- Fruitless
- Soul-destroying
- Incredulous
- Frustrating
- Petty
- Worthless, and
- Unnecessary?

There's a member of the home team who surely must meet the above criteria: yes, they can be seen as doing serving a key role, but, I would guess, that at times, a line of self-doubt raises its ugly head within their thought processes which results in them asking that most fundamental question again of themselves: 'WHY?' To whom do I refer? Let me enlighten you! They are, in all their glory, the 'bed-makers'. Their days of employ are dictated by three basic manoeuvres.

1. 'Drag' the victim, (sorry, I must stop saying 'victim', or 'drag' in this example), persuade the patient to get out of bed and into a chair, just at the very point that this unfortunate person has at last acquired an acceptable level comfort and relaxation after a 'long day's night'. Good old Ringo! He was the drummer of 'The Beatles' and essentially a simple soul at heart. The song *'Yellow Submarine'* was his baby essentially, and he did a pretty good attempt at singing the lead vocal on it too. But, the journalists and the critics of the time strangled any

childlike innocence out of the song, by suggesting that the lyrics were rife with deep and heavy meaning. Anyway, back to manoeuvre one. This procedure rates eight out of ten in terms of difficulty or virtual impossibility if, like me, you have been incapacitated by a stroke (nice word 'stroke': I stroke cats, unless they hiss and scratch me like *Marmalade* down the road, in which case, another tactic is required.) I would be inclined to push difficulty rating of this exercise up to a nine or ten if you are suffering with a broken leg, broken *legs* in the plural, or a weak bladder, or both or all, but not necessarily in that order. However, given a few bribery attempts, this goal has been achieved. You are sitting in your chair: completely and totally exhausted.

2.   The second manoeuvre. Whilst you rest in your chair, the players set to work on the specific task of stripping the bed, placing the sheets and pillowcases into a plastic bag, throw that onto another trolley (still without a fringe) ready for the laundry (this being one laundry I would *not* want to work in, given the sheer amount of work and the boring nature of it), putting a clean fitted under sheet on, replace the 'soiled' (Yuck!) pillowcases, putting a top sheet on: *all* within fifteen seconds, and all without the slightest suggestion of a conversation (not even a 'Good morning Christopher, which, given the circumstances, I actually would not mind). They've taken the *Elvis* approach: "A little less conversation, a bit more action." That is their mantra for the day: it must be, when they consider all those beds that lay ahead of them. I wonder how they would rate their job satisfaction after manoeuvre three takes place; this being auctioned not by the home team, but by a vital member of the away team: YOU!

3.   This is the tour de force. The ultimate achievement. The great repost! Bomber command is called into action! One small step (or lunge, or crawl, or climb) for man, one giant leap for mankind (again: ably represented by your goodly self) upon which you launch yourself onto the recently made bed and destroy its immaculate state of beauty by re-establishing yourself in the position you had established for yourself a moment of minutes ago.

In my case, I offer up a huge sigh; then after a few seconds I reflect on how, by this simple act, I have totally wrecked the wonderful accomplishments of the bed-makers in one swoop. I offer a furtive glare in the general direction of the ladies who have seen their labours destroyed. I whisper in their general direction: "Sorry."

"Never mind, Christopher; we'll make it again for you. Just give us time to sort the other beds out, we'll be back then."

I nod in passive agreement, or, more accurately, in grateful acceptance.

And so, their circle is never squared. I occupy one bed. Last time I counted, there were five others? That's a total of six in my Unit. Each one of those six is going to be decimated in the same fashion. Then, there's the corridor each containing further wards and further beds. Then, there's the 'Wing'. Then, there's the whole bloody hospital. Then, there's the return visit to re-make the earlier destroyed beds.

What a job!

What a God-forsaken job!

But, thank you, bed-makers, one and all, for your total commitment in the face of adversity.

Thank you from the heart of my bottom, sorry, the bottom of my heart, and I mean that most sincerely folks, as Hughie Green used to say on *Opportunity Knocks* with Monica. If you understand that reference, I know how old you are! (within parameters, obviously!)

Now, before I close this section, just a word about beds.

Cordial things aren't they: especially your own.

But, be amazed, be very amazed, at the new breed of NHS beds, for these are the 'all-singing, all-dancing' variety of beds.

They're automatic, multifunctional, thinking creations!

You 'operate' them via what can only be described as a remote-control button, which can raise the bed, raise your head, raise your feet, sit you up, lie you down and, if you ask it nicely, it can make you a cup that cheers! Treat it with respect though: do not go pushing all the buttons simultaneously or at the same time because you would confuse it. This would result in the bed folding itself up and having you for dinner. You have been warned!

The Storm Before the Lull

Gentleman: are you all shaved? No? Good! Use my excuse: you are growing a beard! Probably you've never considered an outburst of facial hair before, preferring to cleanse your face of all indication of grey hairs that inevitably shine out like a beacon. However: this excuse will get people of your case. Ladies: this will not be a problem you will encounter, unless you're a Russian athlete who has just competed in the 'hammer throwing' championships or have achieved a world record in the weight lifting ratings!

One thing is for sure: you are washed, had breakfast, are contemplating the day ahead of you, and all seems becalmed: nothing now is happening; a kind of truce has broken out, everything and everyone is chilled and are unknowingly being drawn into a false sense of security. Be afraid, my friends, because your life is about to be impacted by a person who holds the key to your escape.

This is, indeed, the quiet time, as if the eye of a storm is imminent. It surely is the lull before the storm. Strap yourselves in, good people; you are in for one roller-coaster of a ride which will be over before it has begun.

You will be aware of a few warning signs.

Footsteps; approaching at a rapid pace. One set dominant, fast moving, dominant, strutting. Other sets subservient, passive, holding back, reluctant. There is evidence of mumbled conversation taking place. And the footsteps get nearer and more pronounced. Nearer! Nearer! Within the ward, there is a sharp intake of breath: you can cut the atmosphere with a knife. Final attempts at grooming take place: everyone doing their utmost to impress the oncoming entourage.

Because, as every patient knows, and is painfully aware in more ways than one, that the impending visitation is of paramount importance. The chairperson of the escape committee has primed you on how to react under interrogation: maintain a smile always, and appear at peace with yourself, even if you are bricking it. Do not 'fart' under any circumstance. Do not present with a newly undiagnosed complication if this is something you can possibly avoid. It simply is not worth the hassle. Remain cool and unmoved by any of the utterances you are about to witness. You see, this is a test, my friends: a test of your ability to maintain decorum under fire. A judgement is about to be made about you. The fact is that you are 100% under the control of the person who is at the head of this visitation. Yes: you are about to have a meeting, albeit a brief and fleeting moment, with another of God's representatives on Earth: ladies and gentlemen, allow me to introduce you to a bunch of nervous students, each with clipboards and the outward appearance of a fifteen year old. And, at the pinnacle of the procession, is the object of their idolisation and career prospects: I give you, "TRA-LAA," the Consultant; him or her who controls your future!

There is a flurry of posh suits, bow ties, stethoscopes and clipboards. The chief of the tribe approaches each patient in turn, displaying a well-rehearsed regimental bed-side manner, and his minions follow nervously behind him, at what they deem as a respectable distance, hanging on his every utterance and feverishly scribbling down the pearls of wisdom he imparts. Clearly, they are dreading the prospect of having to 'bat away' the 'googly' that the chief is going to bowl at that as a question at some point in the proceedings. To compensate, and by way of an obvious attempt to derail or postpone any imminent enquiry of them, they giggle childishly at any joke their Consultant cracks that neither they, nor indeed I, understand.

"And how is one today, sir?" the consultant booms.

This is wrong on so many levels. Has he not noticed that I have a name? It is written on the board behind my bed.

"This is Mr Moore sir; admission for a stroke," says one of his students. Bearing in mind that I occupy a space in the stroke unit does not really require any major qualification.

Something seems a little false here. It is an unusual meeting. I feel that I am in a position of disadvantage since I am sat in a chair in my pyjamas and he is standing in his tailor-made attire. And what does he mean by 'how is one?'

- Which one?
- What one?
- Suppose there were *two*; would that invalidate his question?
- Or three?
- Or any other number, other than 'one'?

Also, the last time I looked, I had not been elevated by 'Her Majesty' to the ranks of a knighthood. This would be an honour indeed, and of course would be thoroughly deserved for all the 'good works' I have accomplished over the years. But I haven't received anything in the post yet, requesting me not to tell anybody about my recognition until *The Queen's Honours List* is made public.

And, of course, I would have thought it was clearly beyond dispute as to my current state of affairs, and I think to myself, although I wouldn't *dare* say it in the presence of a demi-god:

"Top of the world, Doc! Never felt better! A1! Feeling F-I-N-E, my man, with a capital F!"

What then follows appears to be a rather alarming breakout of 'foreign tongue syndrome', as all those gathered around my bedside exchange technical data about me, who, by the way, actually *is* present in the room. By the time that the chief has exhausted both his quips and his concerns, and his fired off a couple of unfathomable final questions to his increasingly relieved students, it then is the cue for his final shot:

"Good! I'll see you tomorrow, Mr Moore; any questions? No? Well goodbye then: don't do anything I wouldn't do!"

And before I get the chance to reply—"well, just a couple of things Doctor"—he's gone; made an effective withdrawal, and has moved on to Bert, who is asleep, lucky chap, to repeat the entire process. And so on and so on. He progresses through the ward as if on speed! Then, he and his entourage have 'left the building', well, the ward (a bit like Elvis I presume who *also* had left the building, apparently). Thus, with the deafening call of 'Hole nineteen' ringing in his ears and the very minimal dust having settled (metaphorically speaking: there is absolutely no sight of even a speck of dust in here; the place is immaculately clean), he and his cronies are gone: vanished into the ether. Everyone in the ward breathes again and settles down to the further adventures that await today (whatever the day actually is; you may be losing track by now and, let's face it, it holds no real significance for you anyway!)

Now, I have a bit more time to think, and you will too.
This is a resume of what I was contemplating.

1. Why is it that very important doctors are referred to as 'Mr', as a sign of superiority? This one always gets me thinking. I am called 'Mr': a dustman, sorry, a 'R.D.O.', a refuse disposal operative to be politically correct, is called 'Mr'. Somebody detained at Her Majesty's *pleasure,* is a 'Mr', so I fail to comprehend how a Consultant's considerable skills and experience are acknowledged and recognised by plain old 'Mr'.

2. Perversely, a *junior* doctor, who is possibly not fully qualified in terms of examinations et cetera, *does* enjoy the rank of 'Dr', even though he or she might not be one just yet. I would have thought that in this case, 'Mr', 'Mrs', 'Miss' or 'Ms' would be more appropriate

"Aah, Doctor Jones," I call this out because another suit has just entered the unit.

"I'm Mr Jones; yes, Mr Moore, how can I be of assistance to you?"

Whoops! Sorry and all that. Hope I have not compromised my treatment through disrespect. No, I wouldn't have done that: it's a common mistake to make. So long as I get it right next time, no harm has been done. These consultant people are very understanding (the cheque's in the post Mr Jones).

"All's going well Mr Moore; you're making excellent progress, sir. We'll have you on your feet in no time!"

"Thank you, Mr Jones, I'm very grateful for all that you and your team have done for me, Mr Jones."

By saying that, and by re-enforcing the sentiments with emphasis, I consider that I have guaranteed an extension to my own personal life-span, for a while anyway.

"Why?"

This is a good and valid question indeed.

"WHY?"

The question/comment is put from an anonymous voice with greater force.

Why what? I think. No sooner have I thought that thought when the answer is made apparent by an extension of the incomplete sentence.

142

"Why does this happen to me? I've wet myself again. NURSE! Can you help please?"

I feel so sorry for the unfortunate Nurse whose misfortune it is to respond to his plaintive cry.

I bring this situation to your attention because it is likely that you may be asking the 'why' question too. It may relate to 'pee', or the lack of it. Similarly, it may be asked about the 'other thing', 'the devil's dumplings', or lack of them. The latter was my problem. I was putting the food *in,* but I was having severe difficulty in 'getting it out'. Never mind: there is an answer. For me, it came in the form of prunes and a swift gulp of laxative syrup. It's then a case of: well, let's put it this way with a firework analogy: you've lit the blue touch paper, now it's time to retire! Eventually, the relief is out of this world! It is important that you remember one of the unwritten rules which apply to your fellow patients: out of respect for them, offer them as much warning as possible of the impending relief that is coming your way, and suggest that they have ear protection in place and masks on until, and for ten minutes after, your triumphant re-emergence on to the ward, complete with a broad smile on your face and a much easier gait! Do not be embarrassed at all about this. It's a natural function, for goodness sake. It's one of many things that we all have in common. We all piss and we all poo, and sometimes we have trouble with one or the other or both. No, revel in your glory. You may even be granted a round of applause by your chums, as you increasingly consider them now. I was. It felt great. On *both* counts!

As to the question 'why', I bet my mum asked that of herself as she brought me into the world!

And as my Mum was posing herself that most basic but fundamental a question, I made my grand entrance to this mortal coil, accompanied by much screaming, shouting, gasps of pain and profanities. Most of that, of course, emanated from dear, not so old, Mum. In my defence, at the time of birth, I had not quite mastered the skills of vocabulary! Besides which, even at the tender age of two minutes, I was, by all accounts, a most mellow of babies, very passive, placid and content: dare I say it, but even *Dylanesque*in attitude!

I was brought forth into this beautiful planet we call Earth in 1956. Let me be exact: the 30th December 1956; probably the most boring day ever invented in the Gregorian calendar!

I blame Mum for that calamity! (and, to be fair, Dad must accept his share of responsibility himself.) I have often given thought to this one: if I had been born a day later, it would have been New Year's Eve. What a double-whammy that would have been: think of the parties! Similarly, if Mum could *possibly* have held on for two more days, not only would it have been New Year's Day, so I would have appeared in the local rag as a 'beautiful bouncing New Year's Day Birthday boy', I would have had further sets of parties to enjoy in the future along with the bonus of being one entire year younger!

But alas, alack, 'twas not to be. The thirtieth it was! Have you ever tried booking a restaurant on this day? Most of them are closed, or, if you're lucky, partially open with a limited menu and limited hours, as the establishment prepares itself for two of its biggest earning days. If you do find one, there is no atmosphere; there is nobody else there! It is as if the thirtieth of December was an 'add-on': something to be endured and slept through, before the fun *really* begins.

Which leads me on nicely to the next point I wish to make, which indeed, I am prepared to believe that a lot of you will disregard or dismiss as 'utter tosh' (other adjectives are available!) It is this: I *think* that I can remember being born! Honestly! Somewhere in the deep recesses of what I call my psyche, there is an impression of me emerging into the light! Now, I understand walking *towards* a white light is said to be a realisation of passing on, so, yes, I accept your cynicism. And of course, this was my birth, not my death: if the scenario was reversed, I would be a very crazy and messed up person indeed! Besides which, when I eventually 'am no more', I don't know about a *white* light, but I envisage coming across a massive set of traffic lights permanently set on *red*, without even a modicum of a chance of *amber* appearing, let alone *green*!

It is up to you whether you wish to bring my sanity, or lack of it, into question. As one of my lecturers at University used to declare with regular monotony, "That's you're call guys!"

Apart from my birth, of course, 1956 did not have a lot going for it really. What follows is a mini run through of some of the 'highlights' of that particular year.

- January: the possession of Heroin was declared as being totally outside of the law. That implies that before then, most people were 'crack heads!'
- February: *Routemaster*buses became operational in London. Now, this is a fact worthy of note. I used to love these buses. When I stayed with my Nan for a week's

144

summer holiday, as a treat, my sister and I were taken ⟨
day's outing to *Battersea Park,* which back in the day ⟨
an amusement park, complete with the *Caterpillar Ri⟨*
and the *Ghost House.* To get there, required a bus ride on
said mode of transport. It was my main intention in life to
sit in the front seat of the bus, adjacent to the driver, so that
I could pretend to be the driver myself. Sweet! It must have
been something in my blood: the greatest joy I had of all
was pretending to drive the bus when my Uncle Albert
was! I remember it well: his route was the *109.* There was
another 'excitement' about these buses too; there was no
door to go through, just a pole to hold onto, which meant
that one had the thrill of jumping off the bus before it had
stopped! God, I must have been a rebel in those days! Poor
old Nan! In my defence, Nan had a particularly cunning
way of telling me off: she would threaten me with a 'neck
wash!' If you need a reminder of this type of '*Nana's
Revenge',* which has already been alluded to and makes me
come out in goosebumps at the mere thought, washes of
any description at Nan's were not a pleasant activity, even
if on the odd occasion *mauve soap* was used, which for
some unknown reason, amused me. These washes were an
event to behold: they ranged in severity from a '*cat lick'* to
a '*face tickle'*, then came the '*neck wash'* through to the
ultimate 'punishment', the '*body scrub!'* Each of these
procedures required of me, or Bev, to sit on the draining
board of the sink whilst the errand was done. The net result
was I did behave myself quite a lot at Nan's, apart from
rolling my own cigarettes out of discarded butt ends, but
that is altogether another story!

- March: A memorial to Karl Marx was situated in Highgate
  Cemetery. Just one thing to observe here: Why?
- April: Premium bonds were launched. Never won a penny!
  Thought I'd write a letter of complaint about this travesty,
  and sign the letter as being from '*Bond, Basildon Bond;
  Man of letters!'*
- May: John Osborne's play, '*Look Back in Anger'* had its
  premier. I was too young to understand the intellectual
  dimensions of the piece at the time though, which was
  disappointing!
- June: This is a good one! Third class tickets on British Rail
  trains were re-named as Second class! What on earth was

'third class', or 'second', or 'first', come to that? Perhaps *this* is why Karl Marx suddenly had a starring role in Highgate Cemetery! Keep the red flag flying, comrades!

- July: Parliament passed the Clear Air Act, so that at last, the sparrows would stop coughing!
- August: The dubious activities of Dr John Bodkin Adams were investigated by 'The Yard', not too dissimilar to the Shipman debacle.
- September: The *'TAT-1'* transatlantic telephone cable was set in place between 'good old Blighty' and North America.
- October: The RAF retires its last Lancaster Bomber. Now, according to my calculations, that's eleven years after the cessation of the Second World War!
- November: The big event of the year really. The Suez Crisis erupts; people begin to talk about the threat of nuclear war. (Come back Lancaster Bomber; your country needs you...)
- December: *'PG Tips'* (again, other brands of tea *are* available) launches an advertising campaign on ITV featuring chimpanzees drinking said beverage at a tea-party

So, there you have it. I was born under a flurry of possible nuclear Armageddon and tea-drinking, dressed up chimps! No surprise then that I was somewhat confused and vexed! This got me thinking as well though: perhaps my Mum and Dad were 'reds in the bed', and they had been celebrating the erection of Karl Marx's statue way back in March 1956! Who knows? Who cares, Beaky!

I bet that my Mum thinks, with the benefit of hindsight, all of that screaming and shouting and swearing was well worth it though, when she considerers the unbounded and unconditional fun I have brought into her life!

I wonder if she re-calls that at the age of five, I was continually being brought home from school in a right old state because I had adopted a 'martyr-like' approach whenever someone else in the class had committed a minor mis-demeanour, resulting in the whole class being slightly reprimanded by the unfortunate teacher. It was *me* who felt compelled to take the full blame for the offending incident, even though I had absolutely nothing to do with it. You see, I was purer than, and as innocent as the newly driven snow! Yet, it was *I* who cried out of sheer remorse; *I* who was continually being withdrawn from the class so that I would calm down! What a fragile, empathetic and adorable little boy I must have been then: probably the apple of my mother's eye, if that is the right expression!

Move on four years or so, and I suspect the word 'adorable' would have been dropped from my list of virtues!

I didn't like dentists! I still don't! I used to start to panic about the impending visit to *'the Torture House'*, as I had named it, about a week before the appointment. Perspective did not occur to me: the fact that the examination and any subsequent attention would amount to no more than ten minutes, was not something I felt the need to consider. No, my mind would drift, and in moments of sheer dread, several galling images came to memory!

- The waiting room itself, resplendent with a huge Grandfather clock in the corner of the darkened, Victorian room, whose incessant 'tic-toc-tic-toc' seemed to slow up time to an unbearable limit.
- The Gothic-looking Dining Table in the middle of the room, which was the home of several well-thumbed, but not funny under any stretch of the imagination, ancient copies of *'Punch'*.
- The huge and noisy fish-tank, which appeared to bubble as if boiling, used to drive me to distraction as the fish went around and round and round, with no purpose in life whatsoever!
- The long and sweeping stairway that led from the Waiting Room to the home of the 'masked one!'
- The sight of the huge contraption which greeted me, pertaining to be a 'reliever of pain' but, in fact, was the 'donor of pain!' It was the foot-operated implement, lovingly referred to as the *'Road Drill'*. To make it operational, the dentist pushed hard on a foot pedal, which drove a rope which in turn started the drill-bit to rotate and get up to the right speed. Having achieved this status, it was applied to the rotten tooth (I had tried to pretend that there was no pain there when he prodded and poked it previously, but to no avail) and, as ground into the tooth, the drill got slower and slower, the pain got worse and worse, and the smell of burning tooth still haunts me today.

There was absolutely no point in trying to dismiss, or rationalise, these horrific images of what can best be described as a barbaric form of medieval torture, along the lines of the '*Spanish Inquisition',* and nobody enjoyed that!

Thus, on one visit to the dreaded place, I became enlightened! I realised that there was a concept called the 'fight or flight' conundrum. I chose the latter. I went charging down the stairs, out through the entrance door, and on to the High Street at an alarming rate of knots, pursued by an increasingly irate dentist who was shouting:

'Come here quickly, Mrs Moore, Christopher has been very naughty and has run out! Do get him back please and teach him some manners as well!'

I was eventually re-captured. I was pausing for breath outside of *'Woolworth's'.* The rest I will leave to your imagination, suffice to say that the un-loved dentist and I continued to have regular confrontations, right through my adolescence to adulthood. Those were the days: do you remember them Mum? I do; with amusement!

Christmas Comes but 365 Days a Year (366 in a Leap Year)

I don't know about *you,* but I love Christmas and everything that goes with it (except for it arriving in the shops during September: that's just taking liberties and increasing profits. For me, Christmas starts on what my sister and I have always referred to as 'Christmas Eve *Eve*'. The tree is up, artificial or otherwise, the illuminated but tacky LED pictures of a wintry scene are back on the wall temporarily, and all the cards are strung up from the ceiling (that ceiling gets everywhere!). I'm sixty, and I still get excited! I have bought all of my gifts, including the heavily anticipated 'tree presents' and I have wrapped them so that they are notoriously difficult to undo! I just can't wait for the festive period!

I have many happy childhood memories of Christmas too. One occasion sticks permanently and dominantly in my mind as an utter 'hoot'. I must have been nine or so and my sister, seven. On this evening, we were packed off to bed. I can remember that on this one night of the year, I wanted, no, demanded, to go to bed early, working on the assumption that I would go to sleep quicker and therefore the big day would be upon us even faster. Of course, sleep as a general concept, was at a premium on the twenty-fourth of December. I must have grabbed snatches of the commodity periodically during the night but, as far as I can re-call, they were few and far between.

Anyway, during one of these brief experiences of something approaching sleep, my parents, bless their hearts, put into practice a 'cunning plan' they had developed. Creeping silently into my room, they attached a note to a long piece of string which trailed out of my room, along the corridor, down the stairs and into the lounge. The note read:

'Follow me for a massive surprise. Love from Santa xx'

Which, much to my parents' increasing frustration, I did so, or attempted to, on numerous occasions through the night! I would wake my sister from her slumbers and then we would follow Santa's instructions and excitedly follow the string to discover what joy awaited us! I think that my Dad, who was on 'interception' duties, abandoned all hope by about seven in the morning and allowed us to enter the inner sanctum! And there they were in all their glory: a pram for me, and I bike for my sister! Sorry, the other way around: I got the bike! Joy unconfined! *And*, in our pursuit of the Holy Grail, my sister and I had totally bypassed our 'pillowcase' of presents that Santa had left by our bedsides. You see, we had totally outgrown the hanging sock idea for years now, and, as a rule of thumb, we did not really appreciate the lump of coal and an orange we knew that we would find therein. That was a quaint custom gone too far, really!

I expect you are now at least pondering just why I am talking about Christmas. The chances are that you are reading this when it is *not* Christmas Day and are therefore doubting its relevance. Well, let's do some maths, (or 'math' as the Americans would have it). Christmas day is one day out of three hundred and sixty-five, (and yes, before you say it, I *know* that a Leap Year has an additional twenty-four hours, and a bit!)which means that, as a percentage, there is a 0.0027397 chance that you are spending the festive period in hospital. Put that another way: there is a 0.9972602 percentage chance that you are *not* in hospital for Christmas. I present (get it?) this mathematical calculation for your attention for two main reasons:

- If you do happen to be in hospital over Christmas, fear ye not! The efforts that the home team put in to make it a special time for all concerned is an example to us all: they put others first, which surely is the whole idea of Christmas. ('Don't call me Shirley!' Who said that? Answers on a postcard please!)
- It has come to my attention that there is a lovely team member, or members, of the home team who work under the belief that Christmas day is *every* day. By this, I mean they distribute gifts to all and sundry *whatever* the date.

So, let's examine this 'land of plenty', 'the purveyors of plenty' and the 'Mother/Father Christmas's of the wards'.

These kindly folks represent the gift that keeps on giving, and in my experience, they come in the very acceptable form of delightful ladies. Please note that in no way do I mean that in a sexist or patronising way! I mean it in a 'Prince Charming' sort of way: not that I am a woman dressed as a man wearing tights, carrying a stick upon which is attached a screwed up handkerchief for the containment of worldly goods (because pockets weren't invented for these characters), slapping my thighs with boring regularity and dragging a poor, scruffy feline along under the sad misconception that the streets of London were paved with gold! That would be a daft idea: if ever I heard one!

Without any further 'to-do', here is a typical conversation I had with one of these angels who was bringing manner from heaven (the stockroom) to me. They have a generic title: physiotherapists (pronounced 'fizz-e-o-thair-a-pists')

'Hello Chris' (a promising start) 'My name is X, Y or Z'

She didn't literally say her name was X, Y or Z: to the best of my knowledge, no-one is actually called X, Y or Z. Mind you, the singer formally known as 'Prince' once changed his name to 'squiggle squigglesquiggle', or something to that effect, but ultimately changed it back again, having got fed up of people addressing him as 'Mr Squiggle SquiggleSquiggle' rather than 'Mr Prince'. Also, to be considered would be practical issues, like how would you sign 'Mr Squiggle SquiggleSquiggle' on a cheque, and how would you differentiate between one 'Mr Squiggle SquiggleSquiggle' and another 'Mr Squiggle SquiggleSquiggle?' Use an identifying initial, I suppose, like X, Y or Z!

So, for arguments sake, let's assume the lady said:

'Hello Chris, my name is Y'

'Y?'

'Why?'

'R, Y'

'R U Y 2?'

'Y?'

Now, that got me thinking: Yolanda, Yasmine, Yovanna, or Ukulele?'

Can't think of any more names beginning with 'Y', and, of the four I have listed, I am only confident of the actual existence of one of them: plus, the last one doesn't even begin with a 'Y' but it *sounds* like it should. I readily admit, however, that it is highly unlikely that any parent would name their daughter after a musical instrument made infamous by a certain Mr George Formby (that high ranking Consultant) and his innuendo-ridden songs. Here's your next challenge: beg, borrow or steal a sheet or two of A4, along with a suitable writing implement and jot down any names beginning with an X, Y or Z.

Score yourself thus:
0-5: Poor
6-9: OK
10-14: Average
15-20: Good
21-24: Excellent
25+: Bloody brilliant, and 'I don't *believe* it!' (who said that?)
Answer to who said that
is:..no,
not who said *that* but who said THAT!

See, it's not that easy is it?

There you were, thinking this task would be a piece of cake, especially if you are 'nil by mouth' when, in fact, it wasn't!

'I'd just like to see how mobile you are today Chris'

'Y,Y?'

'R; U 2 A?

'I'

Obligingly, and because I have been spoken to so nicely, I lever myself out of the bed, within which I have now become firmly and fondly established again but come across all unnecessary; that is to say, a tad dizzy.

'Oh my God, you won't fall on me Christopher...' (Oh Dear: I've done something wrong!)

'You're *so* tall: I wouldn't be able to catch you!'

Catch me? Catch me? How preposterous! I'm not a ball, or a stick for a dog. I'm a 'man', Betty, as Mr Spencer would say (another eminent Consultant). However, I get her point.

She's right of course. I've been tall since the age of about thirteen when I went through what is known as a 'growth spurt', with accompanying 'growing pains'. In retrospect, the signs of these afflictions were clear for all to see. My long trousers became three-quarter length trousers overnight. The sleeves on my pullovers ended just below the elbow now. The 'pain' of the embarrassment was everywhere. The acne procreated at an alarming rate: very awkward when you are beginning to notice 'girls' for the first time in a favourable light, and again, very excruciating when you begin to apply liberal coatings of *'Brut'* all over, a la Henry Cooper and Barry Sheene!

'Yep! I am six feet five and weigh in at a splendid eighteen stone!'

This is a statement of fact which is re-iterated I would guess up to five or six times when I was being 'mobilised' for whatever reason: be it exercise, practice or the call of nature.

I continued to feel unsteady on my feet and felt myself wobbling a little bit to my right. That was the side that had become weakened by the stoke and, for one split second, I thought I was having another one.

"Hold on to the door frame!" the physiotherapist ordered with a degree of anxiety in her voice.

Which I did, without further instruction, and regained my balance, breath and confidence.

"We'll really *have* to get you something for that. I couldn't catch you if you fell."

That had been previously agreed, I thought. Lovely!

Present time, I thought further.

"You have been lucky with your stroke, haven't you Christopher?" she suggested.

"Y?" I considered replying, but discretion was the better part of valour in this respect. Instead of taking that route of enquiry, two possible answers to her question came to mind, in no particular order.

- Thought number one. Had I won the lottery? This was not such an unlikely event as far as I was concerned. I did win the lottery: once. It was on the first ever lottery draw. I got three numbers up and therefore won £10. Easy-peasy, I crowed, and went down to the local garage from whence I had bought this golden ticket some hours before. That £10 was going towards a Chinese take-away for dinner that evening. I presented the ticket to the garage attendant who looked at it, scratched his head and informed me that he didn't know the procedure for paying it out and that I should come back tomorrow, and everything would be sorted. Well, I never did make the return journey: apparently I had lost, or mislaid, the ticket. I enquired of my ex if she had seen the ticket: her reply was that she had 'tidied away' some scraps of paper. 'Tidying away' was a euphemism for disposing, binning: call it what you want, but the net result was the same. 'Bother', I may have muttered under my breath in her general direction. Years later, she was to quote this as an example of my 'unreasonable behaviour' in her divorce petition! This was *my* unreasonable behaviour! I don't believe that her behaviour had been 100% exemplary in her carefree attitude to what, potentially and theoretically at least, could have been a very big win! It *wasn't*, granted, but that was not the point: it could have been! As a supplementary to this, when people talk about 'their amicable divorce', don't believe it. They are talking total and utter bullshit! This concept never made it on board 'The Ark' at the time of the biblical flood. Incidentally, was Noah married?

- Thought number two: has Carole Vorderman, at last, agreed to 'tie the knot' with me? She would be a perfectly adequate replacement for Mrs Moore version one, and she looks good in uniform! That image is replaced by a comedy-routine!

'You *would* though, wouldn't you? This is a joke my brother-in-law cracks at any available opportunity. Then, he embarks on another example of his comedic repertoire: this time being the *'Dead Parrot'* scenario.

Finally, Richard embarks on his interpretation of the punchline, the climax, to his performance, which goes something like this:

'Your wife, Chris', does she *go*? Know what I mean sir, nudge nudge, wink wink: a nod's as good as a wink to a blind bat?'

'Yes, she *goes;* she goes to Purley!' I feed him the requisite line for him to complete the gag which I have heard on numerous occasions:

'I bet she does, I bet she does, say no more, Squire; say no more. Does she like sport?'

'Yes, she likes cricket!'

This exchange is all very reminiscent of one of the hilarious *Monty Python* sketches. If you want a good belly laugh, when you get out, treat yourself to a box set, or put it onto your Christmas 'wish list'.

One for the record: Dick is not the Messiah, but he is a very mischievous young lad!

'Earth calling Chris, earth calling Chris!' I am back to reality with a thump. No, not an actual fall, but a metaphorical thump: the type that stops you daydreaming and brings the unpaid utility bills into focus.

'Think we'll try you with a stick', Y says.

'But, but, I'm afraid of water! I declare, as the boys from *The Village People'* sing, but this jolly joke falls (get it?) on deaf ears.

Undeterred, Y continues:

'Actually, I think a Zimmer would be good for you too!'

This suggests another great advertisement on the TV, for a certain 'spectacle makers' company. In this ad, we see a short-sighted vet about to perform an operation on a cat, but in actual fact, the cat is a hat: the vet discovers this as his puzzled assistant removes it from the operating table and places it on her head. Meanwhile, a cat in the room lets out a silent 'GULP'. Very funny, and very astute, and very akin to my situation now.

'On second thoughts', Y is in her prime now, 'we'll order a Zimmer, a walking stick, a raised stool, a 'tall boy' seat, home visits, a raised step a couple of grab rails and a Mowbray'

'What's a Mowbray?', I ask, 'I thought it was a pork pie and I'm not feeling peckish now!'

That's another wise crack confined to the death-bed of comedy one-liners. Y has ignored it.

Y?

I don't know.

For your information, you will become aware of a lot of unfamiliar words during your stay in hospital. A 'Mowbray' is one of those novel words. It is a raised (everything appears to be raised for stroke sufferers it seems) toilet seat which sits (SITS!) over the top of your existing one, with grab rails either side, which, in theory, make it easier to get yourself on, and subsequently off, the John.

'Is there anything else, Chris, you can possibly think of, that you would be likely to need when you get home Chris, we can arrange it for you?' Y declares. Now, that really *is* asking for trouble! My mind goes into warp factor three:

'Carole Vorderman please, she'll give me firm support and something to grab onto!' (I've got a 'thing' for Carole, you know!)

Not a whimper of a titter. Nothing! Zilch! Nil! Joke number three has suffered a similar fate as jokes numbered one and two.

The round trip is completed. I am escorted back to bed. Y writes a new instruction on the board behind my bed which reads 'Self mobile + 2'. That translates as 'Chris can get out of his bed but needs the assistance of two able bodied people for support or catching duties as he goes to the loo'.

So, what's to look forward to? At least five trips to the toilet, along with a Zimmer or a stick, a drip on wheels (if I am hooked up to one at the point of urgency) and two assistants. Actually, I found the best-case scenario was to make this journey with the stick (in the loo, with the candlestick, for you *Cluedo*fans: I wonder if the Reverend Green, or is it White, or whatever colour, will be in there too?' This would be useful for divine intervention as well because, ironically enough, I continued to experience some trouble on the 'number two' front! However, I was calmed by the thought that 'Mother Nature' would take the appropriate action given time, thus averting the necessity for a dose of the 'liquid that cheers' or, for more radical action, a none too overtly pleasant placement of an enema up my posterior!

As I gathered my thoughts whilst laying on, rather than in, my bed, I concentrated on the number of distress calls being uttered by fellow patients in the unit and through the entire wing:

'Nurse, Nurse, can you come here please?'

'I'm in pain, someone help me!'

'Quickly, quickly!'

And, always following up at the rear:

'Why?'

Why? Why indeed? I had been lucky: I had only suffered a minor stroke. As I surveyed the scene, there were many others far worse off than me. I had benefitted from a stroke of luck.

The Night Shift or to Sleep, Perchance to Dream

Just for one minute, assume that I am Professor Brian Cox: yes, he of the continuous smile, boyish good looks, and ex boy-band member. The Moon, as we know, is a celestial body. It has no real light of its own: it reflects that of the Sun. It changes shape, transforming as if by magic, from a crescent to the whole nine yards. Thing is though: it doesn't change shape at all. It's just that at times, distinct parts of it are in shadow, thus giving it the outward appearance of being a shape-shifter. As young children, we are told that there is one solitary man who lives on the moon. Poor sod! What can he possibly do with his days? He could play golf, I suppose: there are plenty of bunkers up there, but what would he use as a club (a walking stick perhaps) and more importantly, what would he use as a ball? Mind you; the whole thing's pointless anyway. Apparently, there is minimal gravity on the moon. This would result in, once having hit whatever you are using as a ball, it would float far away into the outer reaches of the universe with absolutely no chance of 'a hole in one'. Just for the hell of it, list here six things that the man on the moon *could* do in theory, with all things being equal (which, alas, they are not!)

1. ....

2. ....

3. ....

4. ....

5. ....

6. ....

Crazy theories are boundless about the moon as well. Can it be true that it is made of cheese? Do vampires and other ghoulish apparitions come out to play on the event of a whole moon? Why did people way back when get described as 'lunatics'; lunar as such being the root of 'moon'? I will leave that you for to decide at your leisure. But, one thing is for sure: it *does* guarantee the emergence of the 'night-shift' and hours of refreshing sleep.

Is that, in your opinion, a cast-iron guarantee? Do you *really* think so? Is it worth the disproportionate amount of money you pay when you buy a washing machine, with the peace of mind that an 'extended warranty' supposedly brings with it?

In the grim light of day, or, more specifically here, in the gloomy darkness of night, the answer is a big, fat 'not really!' Well, certainly to the last part of the guarantee. I can assure you of this: sleep will be a precious commodity whilst you are in hospital. You might even be of a mind to request a sleeping tablet: something to help you 'drop-off'. Be wary of these sleep-inducing miracles of science: in my experience, they do help, or indeed *make,* you go to sleep, but is an un-natural sleep. It's as if one minute, one minute, you are fully aware and the next minute you are comatose! When, finally, the medication permits your metabolism to rouse itself from the slumbers of the night, it feels like you have been punched in the gut by *Giant Haystacks.* I didn't feel rested at all: I felt exhausted. My advice to you on this one is to avoid using 'the sleeping draft' if at all possible. Mother Nature will take care of your 'shut-eye' requirements in due course. When you absolutely *must* enter dreamland, you will, quite naturally, and without any form of chemical enhancement.

So, let's deal with the sleep issue first. It is usually quoted that as human beings, we spend approximately one third of our lives asleep! To put that into context: if you are seventy-five years young, twenty-five of those have been spent 'away with the fairies!' As Ian Dury once commented: what a complete and utter betrayal of good sense; however, he was not too concerned. A waste, maybe, but don't we just love it! (unless, as a curious child, you ask: why do we have to go to bed when we don't want to and then have to get up when we don't want to?') All part of life's great tapestry, I suggest!

Any, one third of any given day equates to eight hours. This is a figure you may ideally aim at when at home, or thereabouts, but have you noticed that when you are away from home, staying at a relative's home or in holiday, you never *quite* achieve your optimum? It's a mystery. It's the same process involved, which might include counting sheep, or counting the number of goals your favourite football team have conceded recently (and for all 'Palace' fans, this is a painful process indeed!), or attempting to ascertain the real dimensions of the Universe. Whatever helps you to drift off, it's not as easy as being at home.

I have to assure you of one thing: all things being equal, you are NOT going to get much sleep in hospital, to start with at least, that is until your body tells your brain: "I have had *enough!* See you in the morning." I would suggest that in your first night's stay, you may be able to grab 'pockets' of the commodity; sporadic 'on and off' episodes of something resembling sleep. The second night will be much of a muchness, but, by this time, sleep will be approaching a necessity and you might well have a 'cat-wink' during daylight hours. However, you will become used to this form of deprivation: as I said earlier, you *will* sleep when you absolutely need to. You would do well to accept this mind-set. It just is not worth the bother to become tetchy with people who are trying to help you. It is just something that *happens* in an unfamiliar bed within unfamiliar surroundings.

There are reasons for this:

- This is not your bed. They are not your sheets, your blankets, and your mattress with the lump situated in just the right place for your ultimate sleeping pleasure. This is the hospital's bed. Immaculately fresh and sterile. Clean bedding at least once a day. No lumps or bumps just as you like. Also, if you lean inadvertently onto the operating switch (the remote control if you like), you may well find that your feet begin to elevate, or you are persuaded to adopt an upright seating position, or, even worse, both at the same time! You see: NHS beds have a mind of their own. Your bed at home, probably, just occupies its own space in your bedroom, and does as you want it to do, in the main.
- Neither is this bed you are currently occupying within your usual environment. That is unless you sleep in a hospital ward at home, which somehow, I doubt.
- I would also presume that your bedroom at home is a sanctuary from the trials and tribulations of the day. I bet when you lie down, an audible sound of 'AAAHHHH!' springs forth from your lips. You are now in a splendid

state of what Queen Victoria described as 'splendid isolation': immune from the sights and sounds of the world. This is not true of your present location! Here, you will be witnessing monitors monitoring and bleep-bleep-bleeping, disembodied voices either pleading for something (usually a 'bottle': not for the drinking from, which may well be desired right now; but for the peeing into purpose!) or pontificating on a current hallucination they are experiencing, along with the general racket of the ward: patients being wheeled out, other patients being wheeled in (very much reminiscent of a game of 'musical chairs' but with beds.) It seems that fun is being had by all, except you!

- A fourth thing to bear in mind is that, at home, you may, or may not; share your bed with a partner. I don't, but that's not without trying, since my divorce (as if I 'own' it, which I do not and have no desire to!) Well, in hospital, you are sharing your room with at least five people who are totally strangers. A 'swinger's party' it most certainly is not! If someone *has* managed to drop off, invariably, this is the guy with the loudest, deepest, most bloody annoying snore anywhere in existence, and of all the hospital joints in the entire world, he lands up in the bed next to yours! Typical! And he's well and truly 'taking the pigs to market: no holds barred!'

Yes: the sooner you accept that the concept of sleep, or a sleep-like state, is going to be hard to achieve, the better it will be for you, in terms of your sanity! There's only one way out of it: suddenly, abandon any socialist principles you previously ruled your life by, and go 'private'. It will cost you thousands mind: and surely you wouldn't rest easily with the fact that you are 'queue jumping' and getting a supposedly better level of care (and sleep), would you?

Would you?

Oh, you would!

Let's not get all political now! Take that red flag down: at once! STOP DREAMING!

Shall we assume that you are not sleeping as well as you might normally do then? Shall we further assume that, since you are not asleep, you are not dreaming (unless it is day-time, where possibly, you might be day-dreaming?) Well, that might not be such a tough time in a way. You have been granted a time for considerable thought. You can develop some marvellous ideas that you develop into a fortune-making invention after your release. If you have the pleasure of having a window seat (you don't have to pre-book this type of window seat, and it doesn't cost more), you can stare out of the window to your heart's content, and witness the beauty and awe of the stars in all their majesty, just like in the illustration above, and utter silent, peaceful and calming words to yourself such as: "damn it, I can't sleep," "bugger this for a game of soldiers," and other such sweet sentiments!

Let's face up to things here. The chances are that if you were at home, slumbering deeply in your pit, you would probably be having a nice dream (let's call that a 'nice dream' for originalities sake) or indeed a nasty one, often referred to as a nightmare. My brother-in-law says he has never had a dream. I don't believe him! The brain needs to dream to make sense of the events that are lodged in your mind. In my case, that requires an awful lot of dreaming time, and I have occurrences of both phenomena.

Yes: my nice dreams *are* nice; very nice indeed! To the extent that I am unable to talk about them publicly, suffice to say they are nice!

But my bad dreams are terrible, and usually focus on several repeated themes which, to you, bring a whole new meaning to the word 'random', but to me, strike terror into my heart. I can categorise them thus:

- Dreams in which I sprout wings and fly, but I am not *Superman* despite any stretch of the imagination!
- Dreams in which I am in a lift which is 'going down', but at such a rate, that my feet become separated from the floor and I fail to keep up with the descent!
- Dreams in which it appears as though I am moving to a new house and, despite every effort, I cannot stop packing more and more items away into boxes, and this eventually becomes an overwhelming, frightening and an impossible task to complete!

Cue the men in white coats Chris: they're coming to take you away, ha ha!

Given, therefore, that it's a fifty/ fifty chance of being a nightmare, compounded by the fact that one is in an unusual environment which allows for strange thought processes to enter your sub-consciousness, it might not be a terrible thing that you are having trouble with 'the kip' anyway!

Contemplate the meaning of life! Calculate the value of *Pi* to its ultimate value! Read the unedited version of *Lady Chatterley's Lover,* or, if that is not available because there is a queue of people on a waiting list for it to be delivered to your bedside by the hospital library, get a copy of *Fifty Shades of Grey*: I am sure it is fifty, or it could be forty or thirty I suppose: I can't be totally honest in my declaration of the actual number of shades because I have never read the book! *Honestly!* But, I have been *told* that it is similar in plot to the D H Lawrence 'masterpiece' I have just referred to!

So, here is another fun-filled activity for you to engage with! I will give you six spaces to jot down six books you would like to read given the opportunity. When you reflect on this, it is possible to put a convincing case forward that argues you will not get a better opportunity than your predicament right now!

1. ....

2. ....

3. ....

4. ....

5. ....

6. ....

My list would include *'Alice in Wonderland',* the authorised Crystal Palace FC Story, any book written by *Le Carre*, along with *'The Beano'* annual and the collected works of T.S. Eliot, which must include *'The Wasteland'* because after getting on for fifty years of reading it, I still haven't got a clue as to what it's going on about. Same thing happens when I read Browning's *Chide Rolande to the Dark Tower Came.* Put Browning and Eliot as extras onto your list, and when you get out, I defy you to read them and understand what the hell is being described! Then, send me your conclusions in a plain envelope: I would be most grateful!

Right: we have ascertained that you are not sleeping and not dreaming, with or without your permission! This begs an obvious

question therefore: what can I do to occupy my mind through the wee small hours? I always used to wonder why the word *'wee'* was associated with say one to four in the morning! As I have got older, and my bladder has become weaker, I am now fully enlightened!

The answer, my friends, is surfing the breeze, as Mr Bob Dylan would have us believe. No, I would not suggest anything to do with 'blowing' or 'in the wind': there is enough of that activity anyway! No, my suggestion is 'people watching'. Study the behaviour and utterances and nuances of a rather specialised breed of team member: the night shift! This is a very strange cast of people indeed: they would rather come out at night to work and sleep during the day, a bit like ghosts and vampires, and wibbly-wobbly skeletons! They are the angels of the night-watch. And a vital service they provide too. Their aim is to get people asleep: as we have already discussed, for one reason or another that is virtually impossible to achieve. However, I stress 'virtually'. There *must* be a time when every single patient in their charge is asleep! Task accomplished! *Then,* and only then, their fun begins! They now take it in turns to wake people up for their observations, or 'obs' as they are called in hospital. Thus, the circle begins again! In-between times, the night shift amuse themselves with juicy gossip that you strain yourself to hear: it can be like an episode of *'EastEnders'* except that you never quite hear the outcome! Or, they complete copious amounts of *Sudoku* puzzles, or they fix themselves a lovely fry-up (a 'full-English, no doubt) at around about four in the morning, the smell of which permeates your senses and leaves you saturated in dribble! As an aside, when my sister and I were kids (not the goat variety; little kiddy winks!), every Friday night Mum and Dad would pack us off to bed, having had a jam sandwich and a glass of milk. Then, of course, along came the fish and chips van from which they purchased two portions of said delicacy for their own personal consumption, whilst we were confined to barracks! The pervading smell was torture! Never mind: we survived! But, I've digressed again: back to the night shift and how they pass their time! Another personal favourite of theirs was to have a: 'who can arouse a patient the most noisily to ensure that everyone else on the ward is awake too' competition: very annoying, that one!

I Am Jesting!

The night shift performs a key role. I couldn't personally do their job at all. It calls for a dedication beyond the call of duty, and they must put up with a lot of totally unwarranted abuse. I know. I heard it. And I was amazed at the way they did not react to it.

The abuse and general disrespect that one human can willingly throw at another, with such apparent relish, both amazes and dismays me; or, to put it bluntly, absolutely p...... me off. It's that question of 'why?' again. Why do individuals appear to harvest such joy and enjoyment by either verbally or physically attacking someone? What's to be gained from it? According to Darwin, we are the most highly evolved of the various species which inhabit our planet. We have been gifted with a functioning brain, of which we only use two per-cent according to 'the experts', capable of expressing motions and human kindness. So, why do we bother wasting that precious two per-cent on negative traits which can inflict so much pain onto our kindred beings? Animals don't, unless they have a 'need' to: it's not something they choose to do to maximise their personal enjoyment.

I am going off on a tangent here, but did you know that you need to use less face muscles to smile rather than to express anger. There's a moral in there somewhere: it appears that you are required to use up less effort and energy by being nice than being nasty. Thus, being considerate is far more energy efficient than being cruel. Anything which reduces the effort I personally must expend on *any* activity is good by me!

And have you ever had the misfortune to watch those dreadful day-time television programmes which salute and pay homage to bad behaviour and victimisation? These programmes get high ratings apparently, so what does that say about the watching public and even more incredulously, the countless number of people who go out of their way to be a member of the studio audience.

I don't 'get it'. I just do not 'compute'.

During my stay in hospital, I can report with much confidence that such boorish behaviour is only expressed by a minimal number of people: unfortunately, they represent a dis-proportionally significant and vocal minority though; whose impact clearly has a devastating effect on the target.

People say that "no news is good news". Thus, to turn that expression on its head "some news is sad news". How true that is: why is it that we celebrate sad news over good? Similarly, in the hospital situation, are you more likely to hear someone say:

"Bloody hell; what are you trying to do with that bloody thing; kill me!" thus leaving the nurse or whoever in a state of anxiety and guilt.

Or, is it likely that a comment such as:

"Thank you so much for all that you are doing for me; I really appreciate your efforts," is going to be heard? I will leave you to decide on that one, but I would guess that for every ten abuses heard or seen, only one positive re-enforcement would be apparent. Why? I am ashamed to say it, but as humans we have an inert sense to get pleasure out of somebody else's pain and distress.

Don't for one moment think I am away in *La-la Land* or that I have forgotten to take my medications today. And, No! the men in white jackets are not coming to drag me away right now! I am aware that as humans, we are irrational beings, blessed (if that is the correct word) with a whole array of emotions which, in the main, do not affect the everyday life of the Tortoise or the Sloth, for example!

Here is a situation I found myself in a few years ago. I was painting the eaves of my house, requiring me to balance precariously on a not too steady set of ladders. You've got it—I lost my balance and fell. The ladder subsequently followed me. The impact with the ground and the effect of the falling ladder upon my personage ensured that I was in a considerable degree of pain. Apparently, the air went blue at that point, and that was not down to the colour of the paint because it was white! You see, I was 'caused' to 'involuntarily' (and these are the key words here) let a few expletives go! Given the circumstance, it was not as if statements like:

'Oh, my golly gosh; Oh dear, how dreadfully unfortunate: I appear to have sustained a fall and at this moment appear to be in a considerable amount of self-inflicted pain', would be a suitable replacement for the more succinct:

'F... it!'

But, here's the rub. This comment was aimed fairly and squarely at *me*. At no point was I seeking to upset anyone else, by blaming them for not holding the ladder for example (I couldn't anyway, because nobody *was* holding the ladder!) Even if somebody *had* been tasked to hold the ladder, in what sense would it be appropriate for me to abuse the ladder-holder? Falling off a ladder is an accident; you do not normally *plan* to fall off a ladder: your defence mechanisms kick in and suggest that pursuing such an activity would not be in any way advantageous to oneself!

Let's get back to the hospital scenario again. As humans, we have irrational fears. The fear of spiders comes to mind, I believe it is called acrophobia, when fully grown humans get petrified at the mere sight of one of God's smaller creatures, scuttling across the floor. It's a ridiculous state of mind: have you considered the human: spider size ratio, for example, and whose fear of being splattered by a slipper is greatest, would you think? Of course, you won't find a single spider in a hospital; the cleaning staff are meticulous and by all accounts are required to attend 'spider-awareness' courses anyway!

I am aware that a lot of people are similarly scared of 'needles'. Not the knitting variety I would suspect, but the medical ones which, in hospital, play a vital role in your recovery and are therefore best tolerated. I don't particularly *like* the procedure: it is not something that I would actively select to *do* on a wet and windy afternoon! However, it must be done. So: look away! The person charged with administering the needle will always pre-empt it by saying 'just a small scratch' and, if you are anything like me, you must fight the urge to respond with 'so long as it's not a big prick!' But there is absolutely no point whatsoever in chastising or abusing the practitioner administering the needle. Unfortunately, I witnessed more than once a tirade of foul-mouthed objections being aimed directly at the medical staff, blaming them directly for all the faults in the world. I was embarrassed to hear it.

There is a similar 'needle-based' procedure called 'inserting a canola'. For the faint-hearted, squeamish or easily upset, skip to the next paragraph now!

Gone?

OK! I'll continue. This is something they put into the top of your hand. I won't go into too much detail, but it allows for various drips to enter your blood supply without the need for continually piercing you. To put it 'in-situ', a good vein is located along which a needle is inserted horizontally. If you are a Doctor or a Nurse reading this, sorry if that detail is not entirely accurate, but that, in layman's terms, is what happens. Again, this would be not at the top of my fun priorities, and admittedly, it is something more than 'a little scratch' this time, but nowhere near the size of a big prick! I would describe it as a 'fractionally disturbing' experience, but again, not worthy of some of the vile comments I heard being yelled by some when this procedure was taking place. I am not 'holier than thou', by any stretch of the imagination, but when it was done to me, I said "thank you" and I was rewarded by a smile. And, of course, there was the bonus that I had used up less energy being nice. It was a 'win-win' situation all round.

I think it is probably fair to say that it is the night shift workers who bear the brunt of any abuse, but not exclusively so. Why this is

I have no idea. Perhaps it's the 'full moon', meaning that the patients turn into werewolves. Or perhaps it is because of the setting of the sun, whereby each patient is transformed into a Vampire, and thus feels that it is quite alright to complain about the lack of sleep one is getting!

Joking aside, I thought long and hard about including this next section in the book. Put simply, it is a sad reflection of society today. I could have pulled cotton wool over it and forgot what happened. I could have ignored it as a 'one-off'. I could have decided that it did not fit the tone of the book and was therefore 'superfluous' to my needs. I could have thought any of those things; it seemed perfectly reasonable to do so. But in the end, I concluded that I had a duty to bring a disturbing matter to the public attention, for no other reason that we do not find ourselves acting in this atrocious way during our hospitalisation.

What follows is an account of a discussion I had with a nurse during my hospitalisation. The ward was empty, even though it was about two in the morning. If needs be, procedures such as X-Rays and other common place procedures are operated on a twenty-four seven basis, such are the demands on the Health Service.

I whispered 'good evening' to her, secure in the knowledge that I was not going to wake anyone up and incur their wrath.

'Ah, Good evening Chris: having trouble sleeping…?' she enquired.

'No, I'm OK; just 'come to', but thanks for asking!' followed by '…what's your night been like then?'

The Nurse, a lovely lady who was, I guess, in 'middle age', replied by saying:

'Awful!': she looked around the ward furtively to ensure that no-one could possibly overhear us. She then started to cry. I know this Nurse's name, but obviously I will maintain her anonymity: I will not even use a pseudonym for her: it is irrelevant.

The next three minutes, which seemed like an eternity, shook me to the bone.

With a broken and choked voice, with tears streaming down her face, she told me many things that would surely break the will of *any* caring and reasonable person, let alone a nurse.

- That over the duration of her career, she had lost count of the number of times she had been sworn at, spat at, or threatened with dire consequences.

167

- There had been a few occasions when she had felt 'unsafe' at work.
- That she had been accused of directly causing a patients' death through neglect and error.
- That she thought her health was beginning to deteriorate
- That she felt she was nearing the end of her tether and that she was being pushed out of the profession she dreamed of entering as a child, through no other reason than abuse in all its forms.

I was dumfounded. I could not believe me ears. One of the most caring people you could ever hope to have looking after you, felt like a piece of s…

All that I could say was something pathetic like 'I am so sorry to hear that', which I genuinely was.

And there she was the next evening:

'Good evening Chris: how have you been today?', asked with such obvious concern and caring, with a smile that seemed to go on forever.

Again, I stress that this appears to be the actions of a minority, but a minority whose words, actions and deeds, can have terrifying and long-lasting consequences

Do me a favour, will you: if *you* encounter one of these bigots, ignoramuses and idiots amongst the guests when you are in hospital, would you very politely ask them to 'do one, and shut the f… up!' We, as humans, are better than that: rise above it and feel good!

Things Best Advised
to Avoid Really

Of all the horrific events in all of history, including:

- The Fire of London
- The Plague
- All wars: why was the First World War called 'The Great' War: that has always perplexed me?
- Nazism
- The Spanish Inquisition
- I'm sure you could add more, but, in this instance, frivolity is not the order of the day, so I shall not give you a list to complete on this occasion

Which would I rank as the worst? The pits? The dregs of humanity? My answer to that is the subject of the above illustration. It was a terrifying ordeal for all of those involved, and so were the other abominations I have listed. Indeed, it could be argued that by ranking world events in order of 'badness' is a disrespectful act. How can you possibly define the extent to which one event was more destructive and soul destroying than the other? This is a task that, over my career as a history teacher, I used to stress to my pupils that ranking 'evil' is impossible and bears no relevance to anyone. Another thing that I used to 'push' with some determination was a quality that humans possess which no other animal does: and that splendidly unique skill was the power of humour, which seems to overcome any adversity that is thrown in our general direction as a species. This is why 'The Spanish Inquisition' always comes to mind first when I am pondering such things. Why? Because I re-call another *Monty Python* sketch simply entitled 'the Spanish inquisition', whereby fun is had at the expense of a dreadful episode in history. Similarly, Rowan Atkinson's portrayal of life as '*Captain Blackadder*' during the First World War, is a cynical, yet funny interpretation of life in the trenches. Material of this nature is not disrespectful, I would suggest: rather, informative and educational: bringing horrific issues to a whole new generation which can only be a good thing.

Blimey: it's as if I was back in the classroom then, trying to engage the Year Nine bottom set on a wet Friday afternoon with an enthralling examination of the Corn Laws of 1815 and their impact on rural society in England. Not the most entertaining of subjects, I would tend to agree with the students on this one! Now, if only Rowan Atkinson had tackled *that* subject via the *'Blackadder'* series: that would have made for a much more interesting lesson!

So, how can I justify *this* digression?

Quite easily actually!

There are events that happen in hospital which, out of preference, you may prefer not to have seen. I saw a few things like that, which were potentially distressing but, if viewed with a sense of humour, put the whole matter into a true perspective.

Are you a glass half full person, or a glass half empty person? In other words, are you an optimist or a pessimist? I am the former, even though I suffered with diagnosed acute depression for several years. I could pop the pills, yes, to lift my mood, but, even though I was eternally grateful for the help they provided chemically, I found that the ultimate release came through humour. Somehow, it felt good and right to laugh at a situation rather than fall into the depths of despair.

I adopted this philosophy during my stay in hospital.

Don't get me wrong: I did not collapse into fits of uncontrollable laughter when, on one occasion, I witnessed a patient whom I had briefly got to know, being covered with a blanket, and very respectfully, wheeled out of the ward. He had passed on. 'Gone to meet his maker.' The *Dead Parrot* sketch came to my mind resulting in me inwardly smiling: I got to thinking, I wonder what he would have said right now to all around him if he was afforded the opportunity to make a final comment? I bet it would have been something very witty. He was that sort of chap. I don't think he was 'pining for the fjords', but my guess would be that he might have spoken those memorable words of Spike Milligan's, to the effect of: 'I *told* you I wasn't feeling well!' Or perhaps the line delivered in my favourite funny film of all time, called *Airplane*, in which one of the air controllers says something akin to: "Seems like I chose the wrong day to give up sniffing glue," after which he plunges out of the tower to his ultimate demise.

What terrible events. Again, I am not denying the agonising effect they have on the family who are left and must grieve. I am trying to express the idea that out of adversity comes success, and *that* can be achieved by humour. What follows then is a light-hearted discussion about things and events that, given a choice, you might choose to avoid, but ultimately, if unavoidable, some enjoyment can be harvested from the most unlikely of situations, hence improving the speed of your recovery and thereby reducing the time you spend in this incredible place called 'hospital'.

So, here we go! Yes: it's number one; it's top of the flops! Brace yourself!

1. Grapes! What is the point of grapes? White ones, which are green or red ones, which are purple. What is the justification for their very existence and prominence in a hospital ward? Are they God's gift to patients in hospital, or is God having a laugh! 'Eat these blighters!' I can hear God saying, 'you chose to eat from the apple tree, so have some of this!' They are pesky unimportant things: similar in so many ways to gooseberries, but without the spikes! Some are called 'pip less', but I'd be wary of this claim! Many is the time that I have started eating one of these so-called pip less fruits, only to chip a tooth which, under any other circumstance, would indeed be regarded as a pip! You will be delivered truckloads of this commodity by all and sundry. They'll be piling up on your bedside, and, despite your efforts to share these delights with your guests, they will kindly decline the offer and say to you: 'tuck in, eat them up. You'll feel better!' Feel better? Feel better! *You* consume the buggers then; *prove* to me that they make you feel better! In my very humble opinion, grapes of whatever colour were placed on this earth with one intention and purpose in mind: to produce red or white wine! That's their place: not here! They are duty bound to be crushed under somebody's stinking feet: not to aid my recovery! I can't stand grapes you know: I have nightmares about them, whereby I am forced to eat buckets of them, complete with pips, and I become a grape tree; a vine I suppose. Not nice: not nice at all.

2. Coming in at number two, and just missing the number one slot, are those tiny packets of margarine, jam or marmalade which accompany your breakfast, or the packets of

individual portions of cheese that are served at lunch. I can't bloody open them! I might use a utensil such as a knife, but this is as much use as a chocolate tea-pot! I don't have delicate little fingers, vital in the pursuance of opening said containers. I try ripping them open with my teeth, but to no avail. If I have visitors, and one politely enquires of you: 'can I do that for you?' I immediately say, 'would you be so kind?', knowing full well that they will fail in their endeavours as well. The cheese, or whatever, will then be passed from pillar to post without anyone being successful in the apparently simple task of opening the wrapper, by which time, I think: *Sod it; I've lost my appetite.* We've asked this question before, but it needs asking again: 'WHY?' We've landed on the moon; we've split the atom! Why can't we invent a wrapper that can be opened easily? Or is it all part of a cunning plot? Goodness knows! My advice is, for the sake of your sanity, either get an expert of opening these packets to your aid, of which you will find *one* in the hospital, or forego the pleasures contained within. I believe this to be sound advice.

3. Dropping down two places to this week's number three is the plain old window. You might be wondering why such an inanimate object is the subject for so much 'pain' (get it? Am I a wordsmith or not!) As the Meerkats say: 'simples!' Are you, like me, a fan of fresh air? Do you like to have the windows wide open at night, even during the winter, so that you can feel 'at one' with nature? I love to. It has even been known for me, on a night when a thunderstorm is raging, to get up, put on some form of waterproof clothing, and sit outside in the garden, complete with an umbrella, to witness and enjoy the event! Try it sometime: don't worry what the neighbours are thinking: they've probably already established that thought about you, without this event being needed to re-enforce it! No, I am not raving bonkers, but I shall continue to extol the virtues of fresh air: a free, basic commodity readily obtained by opening a window! Now, as I have mentioned before, I felt privileged to have a window position for my bed and chair, so I could blissfully while away many an hour watching the birds, the trees swaying, and the rubbish flying about! So, I thought, rather than having to listen to the constant droning of the air conditioning system located

near to me as well (it *had* to be, because it had a long tube protruding about the back of it, going out of a tiny gap in the window; looking every bit like an overgrown 'vented' tumble-dryer!), what I would do was turn off said machine and open the window fully so that the ward could be filled with fresh, natural air, rather than stale, recycled air. It would be much healthier. Now, I supposed, and you too would logically arrive at the same conclusion, that opening the window is a relatively easy task to perform: we have accomplished it countless time without giving it much thought. But, in hospital? No! Forget it! I pushed, and shoved and rattled and forced the window, which was already open ajar: I even let out a little expletive on my failure to perform this act. However, would it move; what it budge just a millimetre, the little bugger? Would it heck as like! Whilst I was getting increasingly 'worked up' out of sheer frustration, a nurse came up to me and we had this terse conversation:

"Christopher, what are you doing?"

I looked at her, thought of saying "trying to make good an escape route for the committee" but didn't, and opted for the obvious "I am *trying* to open the window!" I thought that this was self-apparent, but clearly not.

"You can't," she sighed. "These windows are only designed to open a few centimetres."

"A few centimetres: that's a bit of an exaggeration isn't it?" I replied with a touch of irony and incredulity.

"No, all the windows are designed like this so one can't fall out." I was situated on the ground floor.

As I climbed back into my bed again, suitably chastised, that blooming question that I had heard so many times during my stay, came back to haunt me: *why?* Why have a window that hardly opens? My tip for you here is, don't question it, and just accept!

4.   At number four and having reached the number two slot but failing to pip the grapes to the top of the pile, we have 'Get Well cards'. So lovingly given; they stand proudly on your bedside cabinet. You start counting them and comparing the number *you* have against the amount *they* have! *I'm more popular than you!* you may think. Alternatively, you might think that "I'm nearer to kicking the bucket than you" is more apposite! My next piece of

advice to you all is this: for God's sake, don't read them! They are patronising in the extreme and if anything is going to put your blood pressure up to unbearable levels, these little blighters are, for expressing sentiments like:

"8,257 people want you to get well soon; they're in the queue for your bed!"

Charmed, I'm sure!

"While you're in hospital, don't worry about your work, the dishes or the cleaning. It'll all still be there for you when you get home!"

Thanks a bunch: *Mate!*

"Heard you had an accident, here's hoping you're OK, know that we are here for you, every step of the way. We'll bring you Grapes (Oh! *Please,* no more: I beg you! Here: you have them!) and sandwiches, until you're well and fit, you'll get the Royal Treatment, just don't get used to it!"

Nothing like kicking a bloke in the privates when he's down!

Invariably, they are signed off with 'Lots of Love' or 'Speedy recovery'.

Lots of love? Lots of what? Love? Really? 'Speedy recovery? On a diet of grapes?

If it was down to me, I would ban the sales of such grounds claiming they cause much offence. Either that or persuade *Hallmark* (other greetings cards publishers are available) to give me a job writing the sentiments in these things. I'd get my own back then!

5.   OK. I assume that when you were taken in to hospital, it was not for elective surgery. 'Oh yes, *please* admit me; I so much want you to rip out one of my kidneys and sew me back together again: preferably without anaesthetic!' Such a ridiculous use of the language; you don't *elect* to have this procedure; you've bloody well *got* to have it! However, it this *is* the case, whereby your admission is planned well in advance, you pack yourself a travelling bag, as if you are going on holiday, including pyjamas! So, this week at number five, a non-mover this week is: bed attire! The best advice I can give you here is perhaps create a mental note of what items you must take with you in an emergency: money, phone (complete with charger), a change of clothes, and your favourite pairs of pyjamas. Otherwise, you will be subjected to the NHS 'one size fits

174

all unisex pyjamas, along with not buttons, but press-studs! On more than one occasion did I lose all dignity and subjected myself to wolf whistles and unrestrained laughter from my fellow patients as I inadvertently 'burst open' one of the poppers! Pretty bad these items of clothing and a poor pattern and colour scheme on them. Very 1970s! But, they do have one saving grace: they get you acclimatised to the real horror of horrors: the hospital 'operation gown'; the joys of which I shall regale to you in later pages. You have been warned!

6. To complete our run down of the six top things to avoid whilst in hospital is the simple pleasure gained from the TV. I congratulate Mr Baird (another senior consultant I suppose, but these titles showing superiority are beginning to confuse me somewhat) on his invention of the one-eyed monster that sits in the corner of the room. Gone have the days of flickering black and white pictures, posh BBC voices, and the white dot that appeared and then disappeared when the set was turned off for the evening. It used to be a choice of two providers: *Auntie Beeb* and the new kid on the block, ITV, paid for by adverts which were often better than the programmes (nothing's changed there, though!) Nowadays, we have a world of colour (how *did* they make sense of snooker, back in the black and white days; similarly, why was colour wasted on '*The Black and White Minstrels*' show?), hi-definition, hundreds of channels, and, if you will excuse the pun and titters, no doubt, everything is measured in inches! We have gone from the days of saying:

"Mine is nine inches, you know," to:

"Mine is 32 inches."

"Mine is 47 inches."

"Mine is 60 inches."

"I have a cinema room for mine."

However big or small your one, or more, is, we still derive the same basic pleasures from it, don't we? Life would be unbearable without the thrice weekly joys of *Corrie,* the disasters that frequently befall the *EastEnders,* and the whole myriad of favourite films, features, documentaries, comedies and sports that appear on our screens. So, it only makes sense, that to make somebody's stay as comfortable as possible, a TV set should be provided in each ward, perhaps even two: one at each end of the ward. This might have caused arguments as to which channel to watch, but, in the good old days, it was Matron who had the final say, and you would not argue with Matron!

But, nowadays: FORGET IT! TV in hospital has become a roaring business. Let me explain. An individual set is suspended above your bed for your own personal televisual experience. You just pull it down to the required eye level. However, all is not a bed of roses. You must buy a card, requiring a mortgage, to pay for the facility for several days. Say you pay for a seven-day package but are allowed home after three. Tough luck as far as the TV is concerned. No refund is possible. This results in you being left with a card which has credit on it, so, what can you do? Answer: create a 'black market' in non-expired cards! It goes something like this:

"Here, mate, do you wanna TV card?"

"Yeah mate, how many days credit you got on it?"

"Four days mate!"

"Four?"

"Yeah, four mate!"

"I'll give you a fiver for it, mate."

"No mate, need more than that: call it nine pounds."

"Split the difference; give you seven mate: in cash."

"Deal!"

"Deal!"

And the transaction is complete with money and card changing hands appropriately. You have become a participant in the murky world of the black market: you feel sort of guilty and naughty. You sense that all eyes are upon you and that, in a later day, someone will pursue you for what they regard as 'payback' for being ripped off in the first place.

My advice: Don't bother! Occupy yourself! Buy *The Sun,* or, if you are middle class, *The Daily Mail.*

"I *love* a daily male!"

"Ooh, Matron no…"

Well, there you have it: my top six list of things best avoided if possible. It's all 'tongue-in-cheek' stuff, as I am sure you will appreciate, but I offer to you as an earnest consideration. You will encounter incidents and events, words spoken in anger, and other such oddities which will incur your wrath.

Don't let it get to you. You will be home soon! Best just to take a deep breath, count to three, and perhaps see the funny side of it. Most occurrences do have a funny side: it's just seeing it that can cause problems.

And, as my Nan used to say, 'laughter is the best medicine'. She *would* though; she had the mauve soap and the ultimate sanctions at her behest!

My Nan passed away one night sat in front of her old black and white TV, rented in those days. When her body was found the next day, she was sat in her favourite chair, with a half-consumed cup of tea on the table by her side, complete with the crumbs of a *Digestive* biscuit, and a burnt-out cigarette stub in a glass tray. Next to her chair was a copy of *The News of the World*. Her next-door neighbour used to work for the company that published this, and other titles, and, regularly as clockwork, he would drop a free copy of it through her door. The paper lay on the floor, folded, as papers often are, so that the TV listings were apparent. With a scratchy old biro, she had circled *The Val Doonican Show* and *The Morecambe and Wise Show*.

She had died of laughter.

Not a bad way to go. Not bad at all.

Things That Might Give You 'the Wobbles', but Don't Let Them!

So, what scares you? Does the possibility of the existence of ghosts spook you out? Is it perhaps the thud of a brown envelope that drops through your letter box with the words 'final demand' plastered all over it for all and sundry to see? Perhaps it is that North Korean newsreader who appears on the BBC news; no doubt a lovely lady in a weird sort of way, but she does tend to get over-excited at the prospect of her mother country 'nuking' the entire world: *how* she bounces about on her seat with an enthusiasm for bouncing which seems to surpass all expectations of the act! Is it your birthday that 'does it' for you, particularly when you receive cards that you are only 'x' number of years *young*! Who are they trying to kid? With every year that goes by, you are older: not younger. Up to a point, that is fun, but after that point has been circumnavigated, shall we say, it becomes less amusing and more of an annoyance. Does your 'tax return' bother you: do you feel an overwhelming urge to ignore it, but then reconsider because it is only Mr and Mrs Average who incur the full wrath of the law: not the rich who have accountants and lawyers to sort things, and not the poor who receive government support and handouts!

Perhaps you are scared of yourself? Perhaps, you fear others? Perhaps you have a morbid fear of cats? Perhaps you don't like the dark? Perhaps you would prefer not to get out of bed in the morning? Do you think that the world will end pretty damn soon? Do you pray to a God whom you are not totally sure exists, because if he or she did, then there would be no suffering in the world: would there? Have you freaked out over philosophical considerations which push your mind to the furthest extremity it can get to, like, if God *does* exist, and therefore is omnipotent and the creator of all; well, where was he when he created it?

I reckon that everybody is scared by something all the time. I further believe that you may well be 'bricking it' during your stay in hospital. Trivial things will play on your mind, and you may well develop irrational fears. Irrational? "No way, McShay!" There are things which occur in this environment that could potentially 'scare you', but I would encourage you *not* to let them. Here is a list of twelve possible things that potentially, could rank quite highly on the scariness front. But, in all honesty, they are not as bad as you may think. Believe me, I speak from experience. These are the things, in reverse order, which had a slightly unsettling effect on me: that is wrong; had me 'shitting myself' metaphorically speaking. And was there a logical rationale for this reaction? Answer: I don't really know, but I *do* know that at certain times of the day, or night, seemingly insignificant events or actions did cause me varying degrees of discomfort, either physical, psychological or downright pathetically. When you get to read and reflect on the following, I guess that your mindset will be something like this: "Pull yourself together, man; you're talking utter tripe." My response to that would be: "No, I am not." You see, during my stay in hospital, I witnessed seemingly trivial occurrences, in my opinion, putting fellow patients, because I regarded them as 'fellow patients', comrades, brothers in arms, however you want to describe them, seriously upsetting these lovely people. These were eventualities that had no impact on *me,* but I was able to empathise with their distress. I implore you, do not dismiss my selection of twelve 'wobble-inducing' scenarios. To me, these were real fears in a very unreal situation. Some of them are quite funny though, I must admit that!

So, what are these pearls of wisdom I wish to impart?

Let me—no—pray indulgence, whilst I inform you. Let's do this as a 'top twelve', as they do on all good radio shows, and even on radio shows that *I* present!

At number twelve then, and very much a surprise for many (including myself at the outset) is:

- Visiting time; especially when every other patient on the ward has a gaggle of visitors around their bedside from two in the afternoon and you have none! You might start to think: 'why does nobody love me?' and 'am I *really* so unpopular?' Yes; there's no escaping the inevitability of your loneliness on these occasions. A time when the family are gathered, chatting away, discussing the meaning of life and hernias. All that you can do is 'eves drop' into their deliberations and try to work out just why it is that Julia's cooker just 'packed in', or Tom's decided to re-locate to the Isle of Man, or the next-door neighbour has bought a parrot to keep his cat company! The way to avoid such futile thoughts is to make some adaptations to the scenario before your eyes. It *could* be a 'wake' whereby the vultures are circling to pick up any scraps going. It *could* turn into a massive family argument, and the poor patient is tactfully ignored as the bullets fly overhead! It *could* be that, in theory, the family have come to see you, but, they refer to you in the third person, as if you are not there, in which case the best strategy is to fake a sleep like posture to reduce the risk of you having to make any sort of reply for the duration of the visit. Finally; take time to study your fellow patient's face: is there a fixed grin on it, or is it a painful grimace? In either case, lay back, smile to yourself, and think, *Thank God that's not me!*

Going up the chart then, this time to number eleven, we arrive at another 'wobble inducer' which many of you may ask of me: "What on earth are you going on about?" Ladies and gentlemen let me introduce you to:

- The bedside table which is on wheels! Potentially, this could be a very useful object. The idea of it is that you can manoeuvre this table so that it gives you a surface from which to eat your meals, read the papers, pile all your grapes on and any other use you can think of. Similarly, you can use it for the same purpose if you are sat out of bed on your armchair. Sounds delightful, doesn't it? You can adjust its height to match your requirements and, because it is on wheels, it is easy to move around, even if you've got a broken arm, because it is light, versatile, and simple to use, as it glides effortlessly around your limited personal space. RUBBISH! Don't believe a word of that! Heaven help you if you suffer from hypertension, raised blood pressure or have a short fuse: this innocent little contraption is going to test your endurance to the very limits! Why? Let me tell you! Like a supermarket trolley, this table, because it is on wheels, has a mind of its own and refuses point-blank to be put into a position that suits you! Therefore, it gets stuck: you then try to release the blockage, but in doing so, you pull out wires, muscles and knock things over. Neither does it adjust its height without a struggle. Hence, your knees get crushed underneath it or you need to be a giant as the surface occupies the space above your head! My tip for you: firstly, ascertain whether the table is going to play nicely with you; if not, concede defeat from the outset and risk getting the sheets dirty! You're not on laundry duty, after all!

At number ten, we find a contender which is certain to hit the number one spot at some point. It is:

- The hospital gown; not to be confused with hospital pyjamas! These are charming items of clothing you are required to wear if you are about to go to the theatre: the operating theatre, not the one in town to see the Opera! This apparel too enjoys 'one size fits all' status, so when I put one on, it resembled something like a Roman toga on me, whereas, when one of the poor chaps on the ward donned said clothing, he seemed to drown in the thing! Always bear in mind that reassuring adage: "Size doesn't matter." The trouble is: yes, it *does,* in so many ways; most of which I am not prepared to articulate within the confines of this book! Anyway, that aside, you will be asked to put the garment on. The first question that comes to mind is: how? (*'HOW!'* for all the Fred Dineage fans out there!) Apparently, back to front, so that you, in theory, tie bows behind you to protect your dignity. Who in their right mind invented a garment, which was to be used in a highly stressed situation, that had to be secured by hand-tied bows (Knots will not suffice) behind your back? Unless you are a lady, who seem to have a natural talent for performing this task apparently, be prepared to lose any remaining dignity you may still have! Shall we say that wearing this garment, even if it is a perfect fit, leaves little to the imagination! I know that we've all got the same bits, to a certain extent, but PLEASE! You can survive this predicament, of course, by realising that, for a moment in time; you are a rich source of entertainment for your fellow troops. As such, you are making a positive impact on their psychological well-being which must be a good thing, isn't

181

it? No? Never mind; their time will come, and payback will be yours!

So, breaking into the 'top ten', 'pop-pickers', we have your next inter-active exercise. Yes, at number nine, we have:

- Your very own embarrassing moments! What embarrasses you? Is it having your credit card declined whilst a massive queue starts 'tutting' you in the supermarket? What about if your team are on the wrong side of a twelve-nil thrashing? Perhaps you farted in the middle of a minute's silence. We all have our moments, don't we? Your task now is to jot down the six most embarrassing episodes that you have had the misfortune to encounter 'any place, anytime, anywhere', just like the *Black Magic* man again! Be worried: be very worried!

1..

2..

3..

4..

5..

6..

Are you cringing at the very thought of these situations? Has it been fun to re-live them in all their glory? Did you *really* say that? OMG! All I ask of you now is to bring all those associated feelings of embarrassment, bewilderment, hole opening up in front of you, 'head in the sand' moments, to the forefront of you mind, and rank them on a scale of one to five, thus:

1. Not a problem
2. Mildly distressing
3. Yes; had an impact on me, for the worse
4. Bloody terrified at the thought of them

5. The word 'embarrassment' was invented for me and me alone!

Done it? Good!

Now, here's the rub! Being in hospital provides an ideal scenario for embarrassing situations to raise their ugly heads. Whatever ranking you have arrived at in the above exercise, it is quite possible that you could double, or even triple, your embarrassment factor so that, in effect, you are way off the scale! However, consider this: something is only a source of embarrassment if you deem it as such. Try to adopt a way of thinking along the lines of: *I'm not on my own in here, we're all in the same boat; each and every one of the patients has the potential to really embarrass themselves in here, but only if we let it. Let's make it amusing; let's laugh in the face of adversity!* This is good for the soul, good for your survival, and extremely good health wise: did you know that one uses less muscles if one smiles rather than frowns? True! Apparently. Try it and see if you are less exhausted at the end of the day!

At number eight, there is a situation which occurs at least three times a day, which can make you feel most uneasy. I give you:

• Eating a meal or drinking a drink directly in front of another patient who is 'NBM'. This will be clear for all to see. It will be written on the board above him. It means he is 'nil by mouth'. This means that he is not allowed to eat or drink *anything.* He may be awaiting surgery, or he may be being fed through a tube. Either way, as you tuck into your Sunday Roast, which, you are offered, and in my experience, it was very nice indeed, you can't help but feel in some way guilty as you tuck into your 'meat and three veg', preceded by the 'soup of the day' and followed by apple pie and custard. Just the aroma would 'do it' for me if I was NBM, but the actual sight of seeing somebody actively munching away and enjoying it would *not* aid my recovery, shall we say? And it is not only at formal meal times that you can be wracked with guilt. For example, it throws the expression "I'm just *dying* for a cup of tea" into a whole new light and the drinks trolley appears at very regular intervals throughout the day. In my case, I caught myself thinking: *Poor bugger. I wonder if I could smuggle a handful of grapes across to him because I've got more than enough (definitely!) and it wouldn't do him any harm; he'd probably be grapeful, sorry, grateful.* Of course, this way of thinking is as wrong as it is illogical, so get rid of it right away. The way to deal with this 'guilt complex' is to think that he is NBM for a purpose, and that purpose is to get the guy back to full strength eventually. It might not seem to be happening too quickly, but believe me, it is: everyone involved with his treatment has his interests at mind. That should help ease your feelings of guilt, but, if you are still finding it difficult to rid yourself of this temporary affliction, then avoid eye contact with him 'mid-munch': that way, you will avoid his glare of jealousy and longing, projected in your general direction, or more accurately, in the specific direction of the meal or drink in question! You must be cruel to be kind, you know! Who developed such a preposterous idea?

Number seven is easy to deal with:

- It is YOU that has been designated as nil by mouth, and not someone else. 'Oh bottoms!' you may well exclaim, or even worse. The coping mechanism in this instance is to accept the scenario just described and reverse it! Plus, see it as a chance to lose some weight; something you have been promising yourself to do for years, and now, you have the ideal chance to accomplish it. Nonetheless, it is still perfectly justifiable to experience a passing thought of: 'damn it', or 'I won't be rude about grapes ever again: I love them, and I want to have their babies!'

We've arrived at number six, my friends, and what do we find lurking in this position? Oh! They can be so useful, and yet so annoying! They shift things about. They shift dead bodies about. They shift live people about; taking them to places that, if the truth be known, they'd rather not go at all. These people attempt to humour you at the most awkward of times when, quite frankly, you're not really up' for a laugh. They are, (drum-roll):

- The Porters. Just picture the scene. You have been told your operation (if, indeed you are having one: on this hospital stay, I was not, but, I have had the joy on another occasion) is happening today. You ask: "How soon will it be?" and the chances are that you will be told something like "today, at some point"! Great! An hour goes by; you continuously look towards your chosen clock. Then another hour, then another: your visits to the loo become more frequent and your stomach starts to churn. You progressively work yourself up into a frenzy, and there isn't anything anyone can say or do to alleviate this ghastly feeling. Then, suddenly, and out of the blue, unexpected and unannounced, arrives a jovial chappy in green trying manfully to steer your mode of transportation for your theatre outing.

"Come to collect a Mr Moore," he announces proudly.

"Ah, Christopher; he's over there in bed three; he's prepped and ready to go," says the nearest nurse.

This, in itself, makes you question your existence.

"Excuse me, I am here you know, I am *not* an 'a'! Furthermore, I am not a homework assignment, and I am certainly not *ready* to go."

Of course, you don't actually say that. Instead, you might raise your hand to confirm exactly where you are on the ward; you adopt an uneasy smile and try to appear all nonchalant like! You might even wave to your fellow patients on the ward who appear to be wallowing under the misconception that you are off to the gallows! And, as you traverse the long and not so windy route to theatre, your very own porter takes time to introduce himself, crack a joke or two, like, as we pass the X-Ray department, he declares "frying tonight"! which, under normal circumstances, would be vaguely amusing, but not right now! You may even make the error of laughing at this guy's dark sense of humour, which is fatal because that guarantees the delivery of his entire back-catalogue of unwarranted and irrelevant jokes.

In the true light of day, porters perform a vital role: would you *really* prefer to walk to your operation. No? Me neither. There sudden arrival on the scene is a tangible warning that your time has arrived! This can be a scary revelation. And the porter is the person who is personally going to take you to the place you utterly dread. In these circumstances, you can avoid a serious outbreak of 'the wobbles' by thinking to yourself that the porter is a friendly, happy human being who is taking time to get to the place on time and for your benefit (bit like a wedding I suppose!) and your benefit only. Would you really appreciate it if you were being pushed along by a silent person, dressed in black, holding a sickle, who responded only to the name of *The Grim Reaper*? Because of the porter, despite your trepidation, the operation that is going to 'fix you good and proper' is imminent: it will soon be over, and from there, the only way is up! Also, if you can recall some of the more onerous duties these porters have to perform just to feed their families that will bring a wry smile to your face. It's not all glamour in the porter's life, you know!

Coming in at number five, and destined to go higher in the 'wobble-inducing' charts comes:

- Being called names! What did school sworn enemies call you when you were engaged in a verbal or physical confrontation over a game of marbles? Was it 'you twit', 'you idiot', 'you blooming cretin', or something with more force and affect, like 'piss off', '**** off' or 'you ******* ******' or 'Go **** ********!' As children, we were so charming to each other, weren't we? Peace, love and understanding ruled in the days of the old school yard, for sure.

  You will soon realise that not a lot has changed over the years! I think that you would be wise to accept that, at some point during your stay, you will be called different names and described as various things which, in all honesty, are not 100% true! Certain elements of the description may ring a bell, but rest assured, this will be pure coincidence. Please do treat it as such, and do not take any of the names or accusations to heart! They are probably drug-induced, or it's a full moon, as we've mentioned before!

  Each of the examples quoted above, or variants of them, were muttered in my general direction, and then some! Clearly, my parentage was being questioned at times with greetings such as 'you ******* ba*****' Then, it might be my sexuality that was being questioned: 'you're a bender!' was a typical expression. Or, I was being perceived as an elderly female relative: on more than one occasion, I was somebody's 'Auntie Joan'. I wouldn't have minded really: clearly, this chap thought I was his beloved Auntie: trouble is though; I was informed that Joan had passed on years ago. This was a bit disconcerting, I must admit.

You will survive any verbal insults coming your way by realising that it is not *them* talking at all: it is the medication, confusion, or a dream: they could be asleep, the lucky *******! Most of the time, your fellow patient's will be charming, polite and genuinely concerned at your plight. Just by understanding that another person is going through the same as they are, could well put them at ease.

Never mind, if on an unguarded moment, they call you 'a ******** **** who doesn't give a **** about anyone ******* else!' Just smile sweetly or tell him to "politely refrain from using such crude phraseology". If that doesn't work, you too could consider the '**** *** yourself' strategy!

Number four can be a real shocker, but it is usually down to a malfunction, so really, even though this may cause you a minor problem at the time, just needs putting into perspective, hence, it is tumbling down the chart at the moment. It is:

- The blood pressure machine that indicates you are dead! You know, the contraption that strangles your arm, pressurizes one of your digits, coughs and splutters a bit, churns out a few meaningless statistics, which, obviously mean a lot to the nurse, and then proceeds to let out a prolonged 'peeeeeeep' and shows a straight line on a graph, in common parlance known as 'flat-lining', which, in turn, is a general indication of deadness! Now: try not to be alarmed! You are not extinct! You are not in heaven/purgatory/hell (delete as necessary!) The nurse will be very quick to allay your fears by saying that: "This machine's been playing me up all day; you'll never believe how many people it reckons have died today! It needs re-booting!" It does, of course, beg the question: "Why are you using it then?" But you probably don't make this enquiry because you are so pleased and relieved at being alive! She then promptly 're-boots' it: that is to say, she unplugs it and plugs it in again. I personally am of the mind that suggests a literal interpretation of the term 're-boot' would be a more appropriate course of action. You would also be surprised at how many of the patients would happily perform this task as well. You see, it turns out that the machine has told every patient in the ward that they 'are no more'! Technology? 'Sheckmology!' I spit in the face of all things technical! To avoid the wobbles on this one, give yourself a quick rub-down with a damp edition of *The Radio Times.* This will prove to you, beyond any element of a doubt, that you are indeed 'alive!' Hold on to that thought and rejoice with gleeful joy. Tone your celebrations down to reasonable levels though, or else you might be described as a '******* ****' by the person in the next bed!

Top three time! It gets *really* exciting now. Here is a potential source of a great deal of wobbliness! At number three, and a very strong contender for the number one position, is:

- The Brain Scanner. This always raises concerns of a very serious nature, because in all probability, you are about to discover for the very first time whether you are the proud possessor of one or not! Let's skip to the good bit! You have been delivered to the room where this almighty beast is located. You are in awe at its sheer presence and majesty; it is massive, you think, and so is the scanner! To cut a long story short, you are transferred onto another bed, and this bed feeds you slowly into the tunnel (or mouth) and rotates you slightly to take pictures of your head. Everybody else has scarpered now and oversee proceedings from behind the relative safety of a glazed window in the adjoining room. They have all gone! Why? 'I'm in here, so why aren't they?' Then, the machine starts to whirring into action and, believe me, your scalp starts to tingle. Gulp and double gulp! This *really is* an actual case of 'frying tonight' in action, whereby you are the subject of the frying! *Cod this!* you may well think, *the chips really are down here!* But, no sooner has it started, and then it ends. In an act of apparently total disgust, the scanner belches you out as if it's ingested something very unsavoury and undesirable. You are free from the jaws of the beast. You are now joined by the gang who had abandoned you, saying things like: "Well done, Mr Andrews…sorry, Mr Moore" and "it's all over now" to which I feel like responding: "In reality, it is not electricity (think about it!). Good old Mick; *The Strolling Bones* have still got it, you know, whatever *it* is."

"We'll get the results to you as soon as we can, Christopher, OK? Any questions?"

"Just one, if you don't mind. Can you confirm whether or not…?"

I am interrupted, "…you have a brain?" they retort without delay! Spooky that: how did they know I was going to ask that question? Anyway, after some deliberation, which was a trifle worrying; the answer was "Yes". My transportation was arranged back to the ward. I met up with my favourite porter again; he told me some more joke-type things, and, before I knew it, I was delivered back to the ward and the 'comfort' of my newly adopted 'own' bed, waving gracefully as I passed my fellow patients. They looked surprised to see me; I have no idea why!

So, let's have a run-down of the top twelve to date.
   12. Visiting time (at the zoo)
   11. The bed-side table
   10. Hospital gowns
   09. Your own embarrassing moments
   08. Eating and drinking in front of NBM patients
   07. *You* being NBM
   06. The Porters
   05. Name calling
   04. Malfunctioning machines
   03. The brain scanner

The quick amongst you will have realised that only numbers two and one are left to be revealed: can you make any guesses as to what's coming; realistic or otherwise? Have a go!

Guess one…………………………………………………………

Guess two…………………………………………………………

Well, I have had a long time to deliberate and reflect on this dilemma, and after you discover what I have put down as numbers two and one, might make you consider whether I have lost my marbles! But no; I am of sound mind and judgement as I write (as 'sound' as I will ever be I suppose!) and this represents my considered opinion. As my good buddy, Rene (Rene Descartes; also known as the 'father of modern philosophy') famously said 'I think, therefore I am'. Most wise, sir. A very apt observation, if I may say so. Just missing out on the top spot then, but only just, is:

- The operating theatre. Indeed, every aspect of it: the waiting, the journey to it and your expectations of it. Let's be frank, or Simon or Geoff or Mary or Liz; whatever. Your name doesn't make the slightest difference in your hour of need! We've discussed the issue of time and the way in which you are taken to the hallowed ground of the operating theatre. It's the sheer shock of what you behold behind its doors which is likely to give you the wobbles! First thing that hits you is a hammer over the head (only joking!): no; is the brightness of the light! It appears *so intensely* bright, like you've never witnessed before. You will be greeted with a whole host of medics who announce themselves one by one. "I'm operating on you today," one voice behind a mask will pronounce. Another voice behind another mask will say: "I'm looking after your anaesthetic during the procedure; you'll be out for an hour or so." Or so! Or so? Don't they know? Shouldn't this 'procedure', as they like to call it, be meticulously planned to the second? Calm yourself: these are highly paid and very experienced experts in their own particular specialism.

  You are bound to notice a vast array of equipment around you. If the blood monitor machine on the ward spooked you a bit, be prepared to be spooked a lot now! I couldn't count the number of machines in this space; mind you, I'm not very good at Maths having just scraped a bare pass at 'O' level. As an aside here, I always thought that the term 'O' level was patronising at the time: how very *dare* you describe me as 'ordinary'? And what implication is drawn if I failed the exam: am I considered 'sub-ordinary'?

  Anyway, back to the matter in hand. You will instinctively know when the exact time for your operation is upon you. There will be a sudden increase in the activities around you. Remember, you are now attached to a couple of these instruments; and, if like me, you will not be aware as to the moment *when* the union between man and machine came into being! Nonetheless, another masked voice will ask a weird question: "Can you count from ten downwards, please?"

"Yes."

"*Will* you count from ten downwards please, out loud, right now?"

"Ten, nine, eeiigghhtt…"

Next thing you are aware of is being somewhere else; somewhere else being known as 'the recovery suite'.

"Mr Moore, Mr Moore, wake up darling, the operation's over love," a husky, bronzed Adonis like, 'well-ripped' young male nurse asks of me. (Actually, it was a particularly nice looking female nurse who delivered the line, but I don't want to be considered sexist, do I? Certainly not: perish the thought sir!)

I had experienced my own *Bobby Ewing* moment from *Dallas*! Had the whole thing been a dream?

Let me assure you on this one: if you are having a general anaesthetic, you genuinely will know absolutely nothing and feel absolutely nothing as they slice you open and play with your internal bits! The sensation *is* like waking up from a dream, in the morning, feeling just a wee bit groggy. And before you know it, you will be sipping from a cup of tea, and being re-acquainted with your fellow chums on the ward. So, in summary: to avoid that 'sinking feeling' in this instance, you can do one of three things. Firstly, you can pray for your safety with more vigour and sincerity than ever before! Secondly, you can align your chakra's (whatever that means, but it's a phrase which is becoming increasingly popular now; I believe that it refers to 'getting your head positively around an issue!' Thirdly, you can politely request a 'pre-med': a dose of God knows what which will definitely 'get you away with the fairies', and all the cares of your world will disappear into fits of insane giggling! You might not be offered this though, so perhaps the 'hammer over the head' treatment would be a realistic alternative after all! Either that, or imagine you are sinking a double scotch at your local pub! That would do the trick: in theory!

So, now we have arrived at the pinnacle; we are about to tackle our personal Everest (not the double-glazing company, but the mountain, in a metaphorical way!) This is it! My biggest fear; the fear of all fears, the mother of fears! The one thing that could reduce this fine figure of a man, weighing in at eighteen stone and standing six feet five inches tall in socks, to a quivering wreck: as one of my teachers used to call me "a miserable specimen of humanity". Bit harsh, I thought, but that's of no consequence here. Have a go at predicting six 'things' which you imagine *could* be at the summit of my list of 'wobble inducing' scenarios:

1. ....

2. ....

3. ....

4. ....

5. ....

6. ....

I wonder, I just wonder, whether anyone has hit the nail on the head, so to speak!

Well; prepare yourselves; be afraid, be very afraid!

At the top of the pile, we have: (Drum roll and pregnant pause to build up the tension…)

- The CANNULA!!! Or, more specifically, the cannula insertion!

  Before we start, let me tell you what a cannula is! For the uninitiated, it is a needle. Its purpose, and I know, because I have looked it up. It is 'to give medical personnel access to a patient's veins for the administration of medication or other fluids'. I let out a huge sigh of relief when I realise that only medics have access to my veins: I would hate *Count Dracula* to have a free meal ticket. And what about the 'other fluids?' Gin, OK; beer, fine, Vodka, at a push, a nice glass of red or white (not fussy), perfectly acceptable!

But, left-over slops, cyanide orange juice: I'd have to draw the line there!

Furthermore, let's get over the obvious joke surrounding the matter of needles and injections. Once upon a time, in an age when 'isms' didn't exist, it was quite alright for the nurse, when giving you the injection, to confidently declare: "Only a small prick!" Nowadays, of course, she is not allowed to make that comment, innocent as it is, and this is because of 'political correctness': a notion whereby one has to ensure that any words spoken or actions taken, cannot be wilfully misconstrued. Thus, to avoid the obvious reply of "how do you know?" or "judged against what?" along with guffaws of laughter and further innuendos which are not funny because they have been heard a million times before, the phrase must be re-constructed thus: "Just a sharp scratch!" There is no room for humour there! Well, on reflection, there is, but only a very minor one!

Now, back to business. We have ascertained that a cannula is basically a needle. I for one am not unduly bothered by needles as a whole. It is the actual *insertion* of the cannula's needle which I am not a fan of: actually, it is vomit inducing!

So, what is this horrific process? Well, first of all, one of your arms will have a tourniquet applied. This is a wraparound which temporarily holds the blood in place. You will then find that the top of the relevant hand will be cleaned ready for the insertion. This is when the fun begins! It is not so much put *into* a vein; rather, it is *pushed along* a vein! There is no disguising it. I know that men have a lower pain threshold than women, which is just as well because giving birth doesn't actually seem like a bed of roses to me, but this process bloody hurts! The worst thing about it is that you *anticipate* the pain and that makes it all the more unbearable.

Call me a 'wimp' if you want! Oh, you already have! I can take it. I have broad shoulders! I'm a man!

But, and it is a big but, so let's make it big: BUT; that is not the end of the trial by cannula though. If there is something to be found that it can catch on, and thus 'irritate' the cannula (poor thing, bless it!), believe me, it will, resulting in the needle being slowly and painfully

193

withdrawn from the hand. Lovely Jubbly! My top tip to avoid the wobbles is: 'don't look!' This is an unavoidable invasion of your body which has to take place. Enjoy!

There you have it then. My personal top twelve! Yours maybe totally different! Enjoy!

'D-Day'

'D-Day', what was 'D-Day'? If you are of a certain vintage, like a fine wine, you will know. You will also know if you have been a history teacher. I have been a history teacher so I know. But, I wasn't there. I wasn't born then. In reality, I do not have a clue; about warfare, about the suffering, about the politics at the time. But my forefathers must have known, and perhaps experienced it. I have not fully researched my family tree. Perhaps I should: I don't know whether I should or should not. There is something within me that says: "No, let bygones be bygones: do not delve." There is also a voice that tells me: "Do it Chris, find out: you owe it to yourself." I do not know which way to turn just yet.

'D day' was the code word designating June the sixth, 1944; the day for the invasion of the Cotentin Peninsular, in Nazi-occupied Normandy, by the allied forces during World War Two. It was a massive invasion; codename 'Overlord'; its aim was to overthrow Mr Hitler. The letter 'D' in 'D-Day' did not stand for anything. It was just a name used by the military when planning an attack.

It's funny how history chucks up words, isn't it?

Some words have meaning; others don't. Some words affect the soul; others are superfluous. Some want to make you stay, some want to make you run. Some are positive, some are negative. In some cases, you want to say 'bugger it'; in others you say 'what the hell?' It is all down to perspective, and, so is your stay in hospital.

Being in this place, the expression 'D-Day' takes on a whole new meaning.

What can 'D' possibly stand for now?

Well; 'D' can stand for 'discharge'. That word, in itself, has a variety of meanings. Let's examine them!

Discharge can refer to 'releasing, or letting go'. Or, it can mean 'to pour forth, or to cause to pour forth, as in 'the boil discharges pus!' Nice! There are other definitions too. But, shall we settle on the definition of 'letting go'? This seems an entirely reasonable supposition for us to make at this juncture. You have whiled away the days in hospital. One day has merged into the next. You have no recollection as to whether it is Tuesday, Wednesday or Thursday. Frankly, you are beyond caring. It is the same old routine; day after day, week after week. You watch patients come and go. You dream of Michelangelo! You try to find out the football scores, but, unless someone brings in an up to date newspaper, this ambition is thwarted too. You have become a number; a statistic. You are in the system. You are a cog in the machine; a malfunctioning cog, maybe, but a cog nonetheless.

Perhaps, you lie awake at night. You listen to the constant wailing of people suffering agonies far worse than you can imagine, but all you want to do is yell out: 'Shut up!' You feel that you are losing your dignity and your self-respect. You despise yourself for having such self-centred thoughts. You think to yourself: 'surely I am a better person than this?'

You *know* the answer to that one: of course you are! But that leads on to another thought: why am I putting myself first; why am I considering my welfare when I am surrounded by fellow human beings who are in a far worse predicament than I am?

This is the time when a gut-wrenching enlightenment comes into play. You are concerned about number one. Yourself! It's all very well saying "I hope so and so is OK", but do you really mean that? Do you? Aren't you just a little more interested in your own welfare?

There really is no point in denying it: this reaction is called 'the human condition'. We are programmed to 'self defend'. It's what we do as humans. Sad, isn't it? Pathetic, even?

There might well be a God, but we can't help it; despite protestations to the contrary, when it comes down to it, we put ourselves first.

So, here it is! Our very own 'D-day' has arrived. 'D' can stand for an awful lot of things! Your next exercise is to name them: in your experience, what does 'D' stand for? I'll give you six chances to elucidate:

1. ....

2. ....

3. ....

4. ....

5. ....

6. ....

I don't know how you have answered that, but let's settle on 'departure day' shall we?

How you have waited for this! The Consultants have consulted, the light is on green, the escape committee have agreed that it is *your* turn to do a runner. As the Meerkats say: "Simples!" Oh no it isn't: think again!

In actual fact, it's quite realistic to keep the war analogy going. Not that you've been through anything approaching the horrors of human combat whilst residing in hospital: far from it. As I have pointed out earlier, for my sins, I entered the 'noble profession' as a young history teacher. I accompanied many a group of students around the sites of warfare during the two world wars, and, when I was alone, amongst the graves and memorials, I shed a tear or two. It was at times like this that I would argue a very strong case that history was the most important subject on the curriculum, even if the science teacher at the time retorted by saying that 'history is about dead things!'

Oh, how we debated the point at many an 'INSET' day or in the pub afterwards. Any teacher out there will be able to guide you in the delights of 'in-service education and training days!' What were they? Let me enlighten you. They were five days of additional enforced periods of professional reflection basically 'knicked' from the teachers' holiday entitlement, introduced by the then Secretary of State for Education, Mr (now 'Lord') Kenneth Baker. They were not accepted with much enthusiasm by the army of teachers who were forced to give up days of their holidays to be 'spoken at' by so called 'experts' in the field, who tended to be failed teachers who had been 'promoted' or 'persuaded' to leave the chalk face. There is a saying amongst teachers: 'those who can, do; those who can't, teach; and those who can't teach, teach teachers!'

As I am sure you can imagine, these 'days' were referred to amongst teachers as a variety of things. My personal favourite was to call them 'B-days', written as 'bidets', which is an object used in France, amongst other places, for two roughly similar purposes:

1. To wash their genitals in, or
2. To 'pee' into, if they're short in stature, male, caught short, or acting out of sheer devilment!

Sort of appropriate, actually!

It is very easy to spot a teacher who is in the process of benefitting from an inset day! They turn up at school in the tattiest attire possible; pen and paper in hand to pretend to take 'academic notes' relating to the similarities of educating a dolphin with a low ability mathematics set, or other such influential thoughts on the educational processes! Generally, a brief perusal of these 'notes' would reveal a vast array of jottings which do not have the slightest relevance whatsoever to what the expert is saying: shopping lists being a firm favourite. As for planning for the ensuing academic year—PAH!—I spit on the grave of short, medium and long-term planning, targets, attainments, and God knows what else! Back in the day, teachers even had to write up their own class registers: for goodness sake, what was the secretarial staff paid to do? And, this was in addition to writing up full lesson plans and evaluations for each and every class taught and lesson delivered. Not to mention actually 'teaching' or 'crowd control' as it morphed into over the years! Teachers at this particular time of the year would have a fixed scowl on their faces, whereas the parents of the returning children would be on the verge of ecstasy; not the pill, but unrestrained happiness, or possibly both!

Me: Bitter? Cynical?

Yes! Definitely! Without a shadow of a doubt! Spot on! Correct! Affirmative! 100% true!

Anyway, I appeared to have digressed again; let's get back to the important matter in hand! Your very own *Great Escape* is about to happen! You've been told that you can go home today; there's just a little bit of paper work and administration to do: it shouldn't take too long.

Correct: it *shouldn't*, but it *does*!

Let me supply with some pointers that you would do well to internalise and prepare yourself for. If you decide to take the advice I am about to offer, you will have a 'sporting chance' of not pulling out your hair (if you have any) or not drowning in the deep and murky waters of total and utter frustration. Be like a 'flower power' child of the 1960s—turn on, tune in and drop out!

- The first priority for you right now, is not too get too excited, or over excited, at the prospect of an imminent departure. You have been made aware that today is the day! Do not take this at face value! 'Today' is a term used by the medics to cover a multitude of time scales, ranging from six in the morning to one minute before midnight! In my case, for example, I politely requested if I could be given a very rough approximation of the time for my departure. I was told: "We'll aim for midday."

  Aim? I thought. How good is your aim? I further pondered. With any time offered to you by way of calming you down, I would take it with a massive pinch of salt! This is, of course, if you have not been denied the pleasure of salt, in which case, sugar would suffice. This applies unless you have been denied that pleasure too, in which case pepper would do. Actually, think of the chaos you could cause if you threw a pinch (a generous one, admittedly) over your shoulder for good luck; you could bring the whole ward to its knees in a massive sneezing fit! Given that a good proportion of your fellow patients, with whom you've established life-long and deep and meaningful friendships by now, have got pipes rammed up their nostrils, on reflection, this might not be advisable, but it would be funny! Get a mental image in your head! No, you want to leave on good terms, don't you? Ignore the little imp sitting on your shoulder! It is not a good idea to upset anyone on your departure: you never know when you might meet them again. They might be useful people like builders. They might be GP's, or Magistrates, or Police Officers, or, God help them: teachers: people you really don't need to mess with. You don't want to be tapped on the shoulder a year or two later and be greeted with: "I remember you: you are the person who made me sneeze uncontrollably and brought on a particularly nasty nose-bleed!"

  In summary: with regard to timings. Attempt to ascertain a time of departure. Then add six hours onto that, and a further six hours to cover all contingencies. This should cover some of the eventualities!

- Point of advice number two. Get your brain into gear. You are about to be bombarded with facts, figures and your very own paperwork! "Don't panic, Mr Mainwaring!" Take nice deep breaths, think of England, and take it all in your stride: it's worth it, ultimately!

- Be prepared to repeat your name, rank, and number (well, at least your name, address and date of birth; although they may present you with the ultimate test of recalling your NHS number, which is not really cricket, because they have it anyway!)
- If, like me, there is a distinct possibility that you will lose all sense of reality through sheer boredom, exhaustion and exasperation, I have provided a space for you to enter your details, so you can just flash this page in the general direction of the unfortunate person whose duty it has been to request this information from you for the umpteenth time:

My name is...

My date of birth is...

My address is..

My current state of mind is...................................

Any other comment..

- Point Number Three. Try to be sociable. Remember, patience is a virtue. Don't let anyone see that you are internally seething at the delay. Say "Yes, Doctor; thank you Nurse" and other such pleasantries to anyone who is donning a uniform. It will pay dividends! The tea-lady might sympathise with your plight, and keep you regularly topped up with a beverage of your choice. Be ultra-nice, and you might get a packet of biscuits thrown in. Actually, going for the sympathy vote is a useful strategy. People will do all sorts of nice things for you if you are seen as being a tiny bit stressed but manfully (or womanly) coping! And here's a thing: don't patronise the medics. As Graham Taylor used to say: "Do they not like that!" So fight the urge to pass comments like 'is there *any* chance, however miniscule, of you fulfilling your pledge to let me go home today rather than at some indeterminate time in the future?'

Despite it being an ever so slightly sarcastic but truthful and well-intentioned enquiry!

Just to put everything into perspective, I thought it might be useful to share with you, my reader, my fellow hospitalisation candidate, and, I would like to think of you as my best friend by now, the 'social calendar', or the diary, of my personal *Escape from Alcatraz*! Even though I say it myself, it is a stunning read! Well; a good read: an OK read, a barely passable read, a **** read. Just read it; that's all! You've bought the book and got so far with it before chucking it in the nearest bin, you might just as well continue! What else have you got to do, anyway? You're going home today, aren't you! Ah! But at exactly what point are you going home? Do you know that for a fact? Do you really think it is going to happen? Is it a forlorn expectation? I don't want to be the harbinger of all things doom and gloom, but you really would be well advised *not* to repeatedly ask of the receptionist, or one of the nurses, or anyone else come to that "any news of when I can go?" Because the answer will be the same: "We're not quite sure yet; nothing has changed since you last inquired about five minutes ago. We're doing our best, but there are *other* people to consider, other than you Christopher."

Oh dear! I'm being called Christopher again! I must have done something wrong, or said something inappropriate. It seems like people are getting just a little bit fed up with me; a tiny bit ****** off!

The day when I was finally able to cast off my shackles was characterised by a number of visitations. It was quite a regular occurrence actually: never before had I seemed so important and at the centre of attention. It was very nice actually: I could get used to it! So, after the morning wash, (not shave, note: I am now the possessor of a silvery white beard thing on my face which I detest, but at least it has got me out of doing one daily chore!) breakfast, and the early morning moans from other patients (because I *never* moaned: I was a good boy, on the whole, and on those odd occasions when I wasn't being perfect, I got called 'Christopher', so I was suitably chastised!), the first visit took place. Because it was the first visit, I will call it 'visit number one'. The logic behind this train of thought will soon become apparent!

1. It was a visit from a nurse:
    "Mr Moore?" she enquired of me.

"Yes, the last time I looked!" I quipped.

"Just to confirm that you are leaving us today."

Hurrah! I thought.

2. The next visit was from the 'pharmacy team', or, to be more precise, a member of staff from the pharmacy team. This gentleman had come along to gain access to my *Pandora's Box,* otherwise known as my medicine drawer, which was under lock and key for all of the time. He needed to ascertain whether I had a week's worth of each medication to go home with. OMG! I had come in with nine pre-existing medications, and I am leaving with twelve: that is plus three! I'll be rattling at this rate; I'll probably need a JCB to collect my drugs from the chemist. I imagined the scene in my local '*Lloyds'* :

'Ahh! Mr Moore. Here is your truckload! Will you need any help getting those home with you?'

Sooo embarrassing!

Wasn't it Michael Hanrahan, the journalist, who, during the Gulf War (I think) said?

"I counted them all out, and I counted them back in again." He was being diplomatic and clever with words too. He didn't have to attach a suffix to the above stating:

'I also counted an extra three as well!'

It transpired that indeed I did have in excess of a week's worth of pills, so all was in order in this respect. It did cross my mind whether I would be able to generate big enough an appetite in the mornings to take all these damn pills. Would I line them up? Would I take them individually or two at a time? Would I swallow them in colour, shape or size? Quite frankly, my dear, I soon realised that such dilemmas were neither here nor there. They had to be taken and that was that! No argument! Just get on with it! Don't bother thinking about it: just get your glass of water, shove them in your gob, and swallow; if you'll excuse the expression! At least they are keeping me functioning as something approaching a normal human being!

As I mulled over the trials and tribulations that lie ahead of me on the medication front, my mental anguish was interrupted by another nurse: this time bringing an all-important document. It was visit number three.

3. 'Here is your discharge letter, Chris'
    'Thank you' I replied
    'You can let your GP have sight of it, but don't let him have it! If I was you, I'd get his secretary to take a photocopy of it, or it'll never be seen again!'
    Now, there are two pieces of useful advice here. Peruse it if you must, but don't attempt to read it in detail. It is full of incomprehensible phraseology and a random description of your good self, written in the third person, like this:
    "Dear Doctor. Allow me to introduce this sixty-year-old gentleman to you." My GP knows who I am, so a formal introduction is not really called for. Also, is that *me* being described? I don't recognise myself: 'me' is no more! The second bit of advice is to 'file' the said document when you get home, and not in the grey receptacle in your study used for homing 'final demands'. Note to self: do as you preach, Christopher. I've lost mine

You see, this 'interregnum', between being *told* you are going home and when you finally *achieve* it, can be a potential source of fun and frolics. The reverse might also equally well apply which brings me nicely to visit number four:

4. This was a visit from my consultant. I must remember to call him 'Mr' and not 'Doctor', even though he is a doctor but prefers not be called one. He had come to deliver his final words of encouragement and wisdom:
    "Mr Moore," he started, "at the age of forty-five, we have reached our allotted life-span. That is the amount of time nature says we should live. From then on in, it's up to the whims of your body and circumstance."
    "Well, thanks, doc! It's so good to know that."
    Then, I burst into floods of tears!
    "Nurse, can I have a tissue please?"
    "It's up to the whims of my body?" I repeat to myself in-between massive sobs! "What about *me*? Can I, as a body, really be bothered today?"
    NAH!
    FLAT LINE
    BEEEEEEEEPPP!
    Only joking!

Now, at some point in proceedings, the law of averages suggests that you *will,* eventually, be given the first indication of when you are likely to be released! Cue visit number five!

5. "Hello, Chris; how are you darling?"
    No chance to answer!
    "Just to let you know, sweetie, that your transport home has been booked in for midday."
    I instantly fall in love with this wonderful nurse; the bearer of good tidings! I stumble over my words, and my thoughts get all muddled!
    "Shall I get ready then?" I ask.
    "I would love, yes…" the nurse replies, "you don't want to be caught out, do you?"
    Another random thought presents itself. Caught out? It's not cricket! And, being 'caught out' much actually be a blessing in disguise, because 'getting ready' is a euphemism for putting the same smelly clothes I arrived in, which have since been festering nicely in a plastic bag about ten days ago.
    "Shame, really!" I then blurt out.
    "What's a shame, Chris?"
    "I'll miss dinner!"
    At which point, the nurse withdraws, pulls the curtain around me for privacy, and I pull on my clothing, with some difficulty I may add, because it appears to have got a bit stiff!
    And she's gone. I do hope that I have not upset her. That got me thinking too. Had I upset anyone during my stay? On reflection, there was a possible exception that came to mind: the tea man/janitor/cleaning man/Mr Mop/ window fixer/ general dogsbody chap who was always as miserable as sin. I could immediately see that he was happy and content in his work! He would never say 'morning' in the morning, 'afternoon' in the afternoon, or 'evening' in the evening.
    I have got to give him his due though: he did remember that I was a type two diabetic, and he would always put sweetener in my tea, rather than the devil's own sugar! On the downside however: he did have the propensity to assume that I was some sort of a 'tea-aholic', and that I needed a constant and regular fix of Yorkshire Brew every

other hour. I asked for coffee on a number of occasions, but got tea: great big mugs of the stuff. Once, I actually remonstrated with him, stating, firmly, but kindly, and with much empathy, that I had requested coffee and not tea! His response was the equivalent of *Manuel's* 'Que?' (pronounced 'K') in *Fawlty Towers*. I decided there and then it was just not worth the bother to argue: it was a waste of breath; something of which I have been left with a short supply of it would seem. Also, I would not go thirsty!

In a blink of an eye, which could have been no more than, well, a blink of an eye (or both), my beloved Nurse, yes, the purveyor of good news, made a return visit. This was visit number six.

6. "Christopher, love..."
   Oh oh! It's a Christopher job! *And* followed by the word 'love'. The warning bells rung; I do not like the combination of Christopher and love!
   "I've told the catering staff to put your dinner right at the top of the delivery list, so you will get yours before you go home; is that alright love?"
   Alright?
   Alright!
   I could kiss her!
   Passionately!
   With tongues!
   I felt like I could kiss everyone right now; even the newly arrived bloke in the adjacent bed to mine who incessantly moaned about the toilet seat being down, and 'following through' in his pants.

I knew it was going to happen at some point, but, ahead of schedule? Surely not! Things don't happen sooner than they should! And, I would miss my dinner! Don't ever listen to the moans about hospital food: I found it to be delicious, and far more elaborate than I would have at home. I mean: starters, main, pudding and a drink! However, having weighed things up in my mind, this was a sacrifice I was prepared to make. Hence, the dialogue that comprised visit number seven.

7. "Morning! We're here to collect a Mr Moore?" *'A'* Mr Moore? Only me here! I raise my hand.

"Here I am; you're quick, aren't you?"

At this point, the kind nurse, who I now want to marry and have three children with, disappears, and subsequently re-appears, with a bag containing: two orange drinks, a pack of sandwiches, a slice of cake (good for type two-ers) and yoghurt.

"There you are darling, seeing as you're missing dinner, have these instead!"

Bless her, I think.

"Bless you!" I say.

"That's alright, lovey, sweet! Can't have a man missing his food can we!"

She was either 'chatting me up' or 'mothering me'. I suspect the latter, but wished it had been the former.

"Ready, Mr Moore?" one of the drivers enquires.

"Erm, yes, yes," I gabble in a state of disbelief, "ready and raring to go! Don't forget my stuff, will you?"

By 'stuff', I mean all of the medical equipment I had been given over my stay, consisting of a perching stool, a raised toilet seat and a walking stick.

"Ah! We don't take equipment, Mr Moore."

"Oh!" I say.

"Ah!" says a new visitor.

Yes, without further delay, let's move on to visit number eight.

8. This time, another nurse enters the scene. She appears to be a senior nurse, (do they call them 'staff nurses; I'm not sure?) Anyway, she speaks with gravitas; there is an aura around her.

"You are from (a company's name is mentioned but I cannot recall it either). I think that you will find that we cancelled your service yesterday for the very reason that you don't take equipment."

"Oh!" one of the drivers said, as his colleague contacted head office, only to be re-assured that was this nurse was saying was indeed correct.

"Yes: you are right nurse: nice of them to let us know, (this is a classic example of 'passing the buck' syndrome, seems like you're not going home after all, Mr Moore."

Did I complain? No. Did I kick up a fuss? No. Did I create merry hell? No!

In fact, I smiled; wryly.

It had now dawned on me that I would get dinner after all, and, I had been given my supper to take home as well! *Peace and goodwill to all men, women, and nurses,* I thought, and smiled again.

Visit number nine is something I can gloss over very quickly. It was the return of the 'tea-man'.

9. Here he was again; the mind-reader who said nothing, but who had total undisputed awareness of what type of liquid refreshment I would like this time. It was pointless ordering a change to what he knew I wanted, so I accepted the Tea gratefully, and then, he was gone, without so much as an acknowledgement that I was there, breathing, and ready to go!

In actual fact, the tea was nice: it was hot, not lukewarm this time, containing the right amount of sweetener and just a dash of milk. Most of it had arrived in the mug as well, which was an added bonus, and therefore I was not required to lick up the over-spill from my table! Well-played sir; very well played! Minutes had now elapsed: surely my presentation of visitors had not dried up at this point: I was beginning to enjoy the fame and notoriety. I was not to be disappointed, because along came visit number ten: yes, we had reached the milestone of double figures. I considered whether there was any likelihood that I would achieve triple figure status, but quickly dismissed this as being a fantasy. That couldn't possibly happen, could it?

10. This visit perplexed me. It was another charming nurse, but this lady's ultimate task was to record my final 'obs'. Obs is a word I had come to know and love over my stay in hospital. It is a shortened version of the word 'observations' which were readings of your vital life signs; blood pressure, temperature, heart-beat and so on. If none of these signs existed, it would be problematical because it would tend to indicate that you dead! I didn't really see the point of carrying out this task for two reasons: firstly, I was going home and secondly, I had just consumed a hot mug of tea which may have the knock-on effect of artificially raising my body temperature to such an extent that it would

be deemed unwise to release me! This was panic inducing, as I nervously awaited the machine to belch forth its figures. But, joy of joys again, the readings were well within acceptable limits so all was still 'go, go, go' for my great escape plans.

It was now twelve-thirty in the afternoon. Given that I had been told that I would be on my way by midday, I took to military terminology. "It's now ETD plus thirty," I considered, whereby 'ETD' stood for 'estimated time of departure' and 'plus thirty' meant thirty minutes late. *Never mind,* I thought, because visit number eleven would be a delight!

11. Here is a joke for you to enjoy:
    Question: How does Mrs Batman call her son for lunch?
    Answer:-Dinner   dinnerdinnerdinnerdinnerdinnerdinner-dinner, Batman!
    That's one to think about and re-cycle over Christmas dinner!
    It was dinner time, and the meal was, as my Auntie Muriel used to say: "Delicious and nutritious."
    Visit eleven was the deliverance of a veritable feast, comprising baked gammon and pineapple, gravy, roasted potatoes, broccoli and sweet corn, followed by golden syrup sponge and custard, but not *necessarily* in that order!

'ETD' now plus forty-five. I was in the process of wiping my mouth with the medical face wipe, so thoughtfully supplied, when I was visited by *another* nurse. This was becoming a habit, you know: an enjoyable habit:
Visit number twelve.

12. "Here's your menu card for tomorrow Chris," she said in all innocence.
    "Actually, I won't be requiring that today; I'm leaving today," I replied triumphantly. It was her reply that disconcerted me a tad though:
    "I'd fill it in if I was you Chris. You never know, do you?"
    Was this a rhetorical question, I wondered? For those of you not too au fait with the intricacies of English grammar, a rhetorical question is one that does not require an answer. The great John Motson, or 'Motty' as his many admirers

call him (a well-respected football commentator of many years standing) reputedly once said that "there were a lot of rhetorical questions that needed answering". This is, of course, is nonsensical: the whole concept of a rhetorical question is that it does *not* need answering! Thus, I did not answer the "you never know, do you" question. And, I didn't know; I really *didn't* know! And, because of that, I began to experience that 'sinking feeling' again. Hindsight is a marvellous thing, but, at the time, an acorn of doubt had planted itself within me, and I just had an inkling of an idea that perhaps I might not be going home today after all. I consoled myself by looking at the next day's menu: beef curry. Nice! Wouldn't mind if I did!

So, manfully on to the next visit: number thirteen. This one timed at 'ETD plus sixty'.

13. It was the drug trolley. I should have been gone an hour since, but, since I was still present and correct, I was treated to my medication again.
"It's only your *Metformin*, sir."
"That's OK then," I replied.

Strictly speaking, the next visit, being number fourteen, was not really a visit at all. It was a conversation that I overheard between the senior nurse who had spoken to me earlier if you remember, and good old Danny. I like to refer to it as a 'visitation of the mind!

14. "Danny, have you had any discharge today?"
Danny did not reply but pointed in my general direction. I waived, sheepishly like, (not that sheep are able to wave, to the best of my knowledge) and then nervously raised my hand and smiled. I had made a connection with Danny's mind: I realised what he was getting at. It was a play on the word 'discharge'. Yes: he had been suffering with perforated ulcers, which resulted in discharge being used in one particular way. However, within this context, he was pointing at me because he was aware that I was due for discharge today! A funny chap, our Danny. This was timed at ETD plus seventy five. I felt like crying again, or at least letting go a primal scream!

At the community radio station where I work; no, not 'work' as such, we are all volunteers, but where I am allowed to access the radio waves and present my show, well: let's put it this way: there are a number of personalities and egos to accommodate. This is no bad thing. I have always maintained that we all have our own unique personalities, of which we should be proud, and celebrate. Anyway, that aside; every presenter has their own way of talking to his or her audience. Each DJ has a way of projecting the persona. I do. Others do! It would sound awful if we all sounded the same and I, for one, love to hear the nuances and individuality of people: it is what makes us human; we are not robotic. We have souls, feelings, quirks and oddities which make us what we are. This applies in life as well: presenting on a radio station, fun though it is, does not represent a microcosm of human existence.

Why am I going down another philosophical route, this time akin to the debate as to whether God exists and the applicability or otherwise of religious debate?

Good question: I don't know!

In a roundabout sort of way, I do understand what I am trying to impart, which is a good thing, because if I didn't know, no-one else would, that's for sure!

No, we have a guy at the radio station who answers to the name of Wallcot. Wallcot X, to be precise. He presents a reggae show, and very good it is too! He has a particular catch-phrase which is inspired. In his banter, he will say: "In the meantime, between tea-time…" How I love that expression. "One love, my man! Dub the nation with explanation!" And how apposite now! Because, in the meantime, I am getting increasingly more irritated by another new bloke in the bed opposite, who is basically 'doing my head in', with expletive this and expletive that! I really am not of the opinion that I need to be aware of his toiletry requirements, and the relative pros and cons between adult nappies or wipes! Nonetheless: it is now ETD plus one hundred and twenty. Time for visit number fifteen, I think: I am losing the will to keep a tally now.

15. Another nurse introduces herself, and opens up the venetian blinds next to my bed.
"Hello," I say.
"Hello," she replies, "you don't mind me letting some light in?"
"Not in the slightest: go ahead. I'm going home today."
"Are you? That's nice; bet you can't wait, can you?"

"No, but I have done, and will continue to do so!"

"Are you sure you are going home today?"

"Oh yes!" I reply, but am I? Am I bloody certain?

My mood of despondency is rudely interrupted by another conversation that enters my psyche. With the blinds drawn back, I was enjoying watching a blackbird hop around in the grounds outside, with twigs and grass and God knows what, in his beak; ready for a nest, I surmise. Cancel that blissful image forthwith!

"That's a cracker of a poo you've done there Danny; constipated you are not!"

"Bloody hurt though."

I am very confused. There is Danny the patient, Danny the son, and Danny the medic, gathered around his bed. Why don't they call everyone Danny, to avoid confusion? And, if Danny, the patient, or indeed the son or the medic, have done something wrong, does their mother address them as Daniel? I reckon so!

One thing is for sure though: this is not 'the holy trinity'. Not as I understand it anyway.

Apparently, one of the Danny's is 'dripping', from his posterior. I wonder which one?

"Wow! That'll sort you out Danny!" I hear, almost by way of celebration.

Sort him out? Sort him out! Oh, please, pass the air-freshener!

I held my breath for ages. It was now 'ETD' plus three hundred and sixty. It was high-time for visit number sixteen.

16. This was a flying visit from the physiotherapy unit; well, not the unit as such, but a representative from it.

"Just thought we'd better check that you can get up the step you say is at your front door."

I do re-call mentioning this in passing, but now I had a test to negotiate, because I was presented with a wooden block, resembling a step up to my front door. I did it: I passed.

"You off home now then?" the therapist enquired.

"I think so," I replied, with a certain degree of trepidation and angst in my voice.

Time progressed. I got to thinking again.

I actually like using a walking stick. There is something dignified about it. I make another mental note to myself: buy a wooden stick as a fashion accessory. I've got a panama hat; I've got tinted glasses. I will look very cool indeed: a veritable 'babe magnet' (in my dreams!) Also, I like the loo flush here! There is no lever, no chain. All you need to do is flap your hand in the general direction of the toilet and, hey presto, it flushes. Wonder if I can get one installed at home on health grounds?

That thought is interrupted. Why? Because, at 'ETD' plus four hundred and twenty, an apparition appeared before my very eyes: a massive 'exit' sign! Can it be, I thought, am I hallucinating? No, there it was; in all of its splendid glory. It had a mystical quality about it: it seemed true, but was it? I rubbed my eyes and put it down to an over-active imagination, fuelled by copious amounts of tea. But, I dared to look again, and there it was:

It was green, it said 'fire exit', but that didn't bother me. I would pretend there was a fire. It showed me a way out, a way home. I laughed: like a madman!

Run, fat-boy, run, I thought, but there was no need for that reaction. A new transport company had shown up, and this organisation was more than happy to take me, and my equipment, home. Final comments were passed between the drivers and the medics. The nurses seemed to queue up to wave me goodbye. I quickly scribbled a note on a scruffy sheet of A4, which thanked everyone on the Stroke unit for everything they had done for me. It was a short expression of my gratitude, but seemed to be well appreciated because the lady on the reception desk had to wipe away a tear or two.

"I didn't mean to make you cry," I said, "I just wanted to say thank you."

She smiled, and tried to disguise that another tear was welling up.

At this point, I had been transferred onto the chair which would be the facilitator of my 'final push'.

I said goodbye. It was a very emotional experience. I shed a tear too.

I journeyed through corridor after corridor. I could still hear the plaintive pleas of 'why?' as we passed different wards for different specialities.

Then I saw the automatic door. We went through it. We moved through the army of smokers just outside. Then, I breathed. Breathed the air I had missed for so long. It was beautiful; gloriously intoxicating. The next thing I was aware of was looking out the window of the designated vehicle, and thinking, *You're going home, Chris; you are going home…*

Home, Home Again

To continue with the above sentiment: *'I love to be here when I can.'* *Pink Floyd* wrote that lyric too. It is a very simple sentiment, isn't it? 'Home is where the heart is' and so on! I never did truly understand that idea. The heart is in your chest! It can only be where its owner is, or I am wrong there? However, I *do* get the idea, the notion, which is a comforting one, without any element of a doubt. We love our home, don't we? The space that is ours and ours alone; our refuge from the day, our escape from all of the problems that are out there; either locally, nationally or internationally. In the summer, we get out into the garden and have a BBQ; in the winter, we pull the blinds, draw the curtains, and switch on the TV. Whatever the season, there is a feeling which curses through our veins to the effect of: World: I don't want to know! Do one: take a running jump! Leave me alone! I have often wondered just why it is that the concept of 'home' has such a comforting feeling, because, to someone who lives on the street, where 'home' is represented by a cardboard box and people's charity: how can *that* be comforting? And what about the poor people who are affected by floods, famine, drought and disease: that can be abroad, or in good old 'Blighty'. It really does not matter, does it?—not in the great scheme of things, whereby one man's loss is another man's gain. We look to our conscience at times like this and think, *Look, I buy a poppy every year, even though I have a supply of them in my drawer; I have a direct debit set up for this charity and that charity. I am doing my bit.* That makes us feel alright, doesn't it?

Whatever 'home' is, however we choose to define it, is undeniably re-assuring. I think that whatever circumstance one finds oneself in, shelter is a pre-requisite, and, by inference, that shelter can be called home. Is it *really* important that you feel obliged to mow your front lawn if a neighbour has mown there's? Not really, is it? But, guess what: oh yes, we are out with the Flymo's! We pray for the last mow in October! Been there, done that, got the pullover! Our home is our 'bubble': our place, no one else's; our universe: our locked out, locked in piece of sanity. Our disguise: the 'fancy dress' we wear. And, when you have been away from your sanctuary: my God, how you yearn for it. It makes the home-coming that much sweeter. It makes you appreciate just what you have. Money doesn't enter the equation: not in the truest sense. Home is home is home: I am relieved that I am heading in its general direction!

It is truly happening! With a bit of an effort, admittedly, I was transferred from one chair to another, and then one of the poor chaps had the arduous task of pushing up me up a forty five degree angled slope into the back of the ambulance. I was then strapped in: something in the past I had done automatically but, on this occasion, it felt right and proper for someone else to do it for me. It was just then a final case of confirming name, rank and number, along with my intended destination, to which I can recall saying: "Home, please!" The 'sat-nav' was set; the ambulance sprung into life, and we slowly manoeuvred around the illegally parked cars, the delivery vans, other ambulances and further groups of smokers and approached the exit gate. There was no mistaking it. There was a big sign confirming its status. I will never forget it: it simply read:

"EXIT"

It did not say:

"ENTRANCE"

To re-iterate, it proudly proclaimed:

"EXIT, EXIT, EXIT: YOU, MY FRIEND, ARE GOING HOME!
YOU ARE NOT COMING IN, THAT'S WHAT HAPPENS AT
THE OTHER PLACE, AND YOU ARE LEAVING THE
BUILDING, JUST LIKE ELVIS! FEELS GOOD WITH A
CAPITAL G DOESN'T IT?"

In all of my considerable experience, never before have I been spoken to, in such a manner, by a road sign, and very surreal it was too. I put it down to the medication temporarily failing to cope with my levels of excitement!

We turned 'left' out of the hospital grounds. When you are in hospital, one day seems to merge in to the next and, apart from all the care you are receiving and other various entertainments, nothing really happens. You tend to forget that outside of your Ward, life goes on as normal. I gazed out of the window. There were people milling about, going about their daily business. Some were just chatting; some were taking their dogs for a walk, some had clearly been shopping but all was in its right place at the right time. The sensation of re-entering the human race struck me, and that felt good.

I knew a little bit about Lincoln. However, I was not particularly au fait with the exact location of 'The County Hospital'. So, the first few minutes of the journey involved me looking out for anything I recognised at all, be it a building, a park or a shop. And, after about five minutes, that happened. I suddenly recognised the road we were on: we had joined the main road to Boston from the city, but at a different point than I usually did in my travails. It was the 'eureka' moment:

"I know the route from here mate!" I declared with pride.

'How long have you been in mate?' the guy sitting next to me asked.

This one I had to work out:

"What's the date today, mate?" I enquired.

I was informed.

"Does that form you've got give my date of admission?"

He perused the document. After a few seconds, I was told when I was admitted. It was then a case of basic maths. Just as well it was only basic because mathematics was never my strong point. Actually, on reflection, I don't think I *possess* such a thing. If I do, it is beautifully summed up by my brother-in-law, who once said, with great originality, but has subsequently repeated to the point of absurdness: 'You write poems and I sort the plumbing!' So, yes: when strong points are defined by actual usefulness, I do not possess anything near approaching one!

"That means," I started to reply in a very hesitant manner in order to buy myself thinking time, "that means I've been in here for ten days. Ten days? It can't be?"

I attempted a couple of quick re-calculations, but the same answer resulted each time, this in itself being rather calming because I hadn't gone totally 'do-lally' just yet. Ten days. That took some consideration. An awful lot of stuff could have happened in ten days, of which I had been cloistered from. North Korea might have 'nuked' the USA by now; Palace might have scored a goal; who knows? I didn't. In order to remedy this, I asked my travelling companion, a thoroughly pleasant bloke, whether anything big had happened in the news recently. He proceeded to give me a very acceptable resume of the latest news, and I felt suitably up-to-date with world affairs.

There was still something niggling away at the back of my mind which was causing me a degree of frustration. Are you aware of that feeling when, you get up to do something or go somewhere, and then immediately forget what it was you got up to do or where you had intended to go? Bloody annoying, isn't it! And so was this scenario until, at last, it came to me:

"What *day* is it today mate, please?"

"Thursday; all day!" he replied, kindly and sympathetically enough.

You see, losing track of the days is a side-effect of being in hospital. In normality, we are dictated to by the clock, the day, the week, the month. In hospital, days are such are a meaningless concept: Tuesday is no different to Wednesday which in turn is no different to Thursday, and so on. The expression 'ignorant bliss' comes to mind. There is a lot to be said for not fretting over the issue of normal (whatever that is) day to day life. Our lives are rushed too much: the stresses and strains build up invisibly. It really is no wonder that our bodies require a 'time out' once in a while. Let's get back to the hippy days: far out man, peace love and understanding: wear flowers in our hair (if we have any!) Hair, that is; not flowers! Mind you, flowers are at a premium in my garden: in estate agents talk: 'it is mostly laid to lawn and is complemented by a sizeable patio to make this an effective low maintenance space'. In other words, it is boring and suitable for lazy sods like me!

Anyway, the journey continued. I now knew exactly where we were, and I had the added bonus of knowing what day it was too, which helped with the contextual side of things.

The route between Lincoln and Boston (or Boston and Lincoln, if you are going in the other direction) is very straightforward, once you leave the confines of the towns. Lincolnshire is a beautiful county, and on this journey, you pass an RAF base, rolling countryside, vast open fields filled with crops and you can't help but notice the massive and awe-inspiring sky. Very inspirational indeed: I found myself just staring out of the window, mentally feasting on the sights and sounds of the journey which, as driver, you are not fully able to appreciate.

"I see you were in for a stroke, mate?" my thoughts had been interrupted and my attention drawn towards my travelling companion's question.

"Well, I wasn't admitted *for* a stroke, mate," I quipped, "anyone could have done that for me at home, if I had asked politely enough!"

He laughed. I laughed. The driver laughed. I continued:

"I was admitted *because* of a stroke, mate, even though I didn't even know I'd had one: I just kept falling over!"

I didn't elaborate on all of the other symptoms.

"It was only a very small stroke, though," I added in all seriousness, which was entirely true, judging by what I had witnessed over ten days, apparently, in the stroke unit; 'I've been very lucky indeed!'

"Guess you could say you'd had a stroke of luck then?"

He delivered this line with a mixture of empathy, humour and awareness.

This phrase has cropped up before, and right now, it means more to me than any of those other 'off-the -cuff remarks that people say to you out of politeness, like: 'how are you today? OK? Good!' and never wait for a reply, even if it is plain to see that you are writhing in agony with a broken leg, or even 'unclear' to see if you are enduring a bout of depression.

Yes, I accept it: a stroke of luck. It had been a stroke of luck indeed.

We exchanged pleasantries for the rest of the journey, discussing topics like how busy the ambulance service had been over the recent months, how it appears to him that strokes occur in the summer months, how having a stroke is not an 'old person's disease' anymore, and what he was going to buy his wife for her upcoming 'special' birthday. By the way, I didn't ask, working on the premise that a gentlemen never tells! Then, I heard the driver say:

"This one on the right mate?"

Without me being aware of it, we had arrived. I can't remember going through the traffic of town. I can't even remember spying *The Stump* as we approached town. I *was* aware of the curtains twitching in other homes which comprised the cul-de-sac I live in, nicknamed 'GWR': God's Waiting Room! For all they knew, I had been carted off ten days ago potentially to meet my maker! But no; I had not been claimed: far from it! How shocked they must have been: somebody *returning*: surely not! (Please don't call me Shirley…I no like…no likey, no lighty!' Actually, talking of lights, in my haste ten days ago, I must have forgotten to turn off the external light, which was shining like a beacon at midday, almost as if to say: 'come on burglars, here's your chance: there's clearly no one in residence; what pillock would leave his light on twenty four seven?'

That did cross my mind.

Something else crossed my mind too.

The driver suddenly said:

"You're popular mate; there are two people in two separate cars parked up in your drive-way! Are you expecting visitors mate?"

Was I expecting visitors? A quick bit of thinking on my part, and then I came out with the definitive answer:

"Errr, no mate; not that I'm aware of, anyway."

And therein was the problem. Who were these people so keen to see me? I had no idea. This brings me very nicely onto another joke:

Q: What do you call a blind stag?

A: No idea! (Think about it!)

Anyway, the ambulance backed up into the best possible position to aid my exit from the vehicle. I dug down to the very depths of my hospital bag in order to find my house keys, which, gratefully, I accomplished. I said: 'thank you and good bye' to the driver and his assistant, and: 'hello, I am Chris; how can I help you?' to the two ladies who had now got out of their cars. That answer was to come, but first, I had to do it: turn the lock and get in!

It's funny the sort of thoughts that pass through your head at a time like this, isn't it? It's like coming back from holidays, when you wonder whether you left the house in a bad state, and if you put things away. If you're anything like me, a nasty idea crops up along the lines of: have I been done over?

Under normal circumstances when I return home after a period away, there is one feeling I do *not* suffer from: embarrassment. Usually, almost exclusively, it is only me who is going to re-cross the threshold, and I have grown up as a re-born singleton where shocks do not hit me concerning the internal state of the property or how I left it. I tend to get more excited about the mountain of post which generally awaits me, but I have no idea why as it comprises junk post and bills in the main. Somehow or other, I get a kick from picking it up in one lump, re-arranging it in date order, and methodically working my way through it, complete with the re-cycling box at my side and a comforting drink from the 'cup that cheers'.

However, at this precise moment in time, I was *not* experiencing normal circumstances, for one unique reason: previously, I had not really had an opportunity to ask a nice looking lady into my home, (with the possible exception of the lady representative from *The Jehovah's Witnesses,* who seems to be on an insatiable mission to save my soul, which, in itself, is weird, because I am pretty sure that it has been saved by the *Church Of England* up the road anyway!) But now, I have *two* ladies waiting to be ushered in! They have both introduced themselves to me, and each is from a different support agency that has been provided with the details of my admission into hospital; their specific role being to ensure that in the early days, post-stroke, I am able to look after myself at home and cope with the everyday chores, seeing that I live on my own. I used to be married, you know. After twenty-three years, my ex filed for divorce. There is no need to go into that particular story now; it is well and truly in the past. But, during the good times, of which I can remember many, it was the mutual support that was so beneficial and, at times like this, it would have made things a lot easier.

Don't despair if you, like me, live alone though. I can count a number of very real positives that emerge because of living alone, not the least amongst them being the twenty-five percent discount on the community charge! Also, it elevates you to a comparatively advantageous position on the after-care services provisions list. You are not alone, and I will speak more about this concern in the final chapter.

Right now, though, I *was* on my own! I was about to experience two professional ladies (I know that sounds wrong, so don't let your thoughts run away with you at this point: I could not afford what you are probably thinking anyway!) entering my home: my bachelor pad, my crash-pad, which, at the best of times, was not meticulously clean and tidy: it would be 'man-clean' as a general rule. When my Mum comes up to visit me from Kent, I have a blitz on it which can take up to two days to complete: even then, I have a mild panic attack, wondering whether I've missed something or left something else 'inappropriate', shall we say, in full view. Anyway: all I can say is that Mum had not been up for a while now, and when I left the property all those days ago, I exited in great haste! I was dreading what lie behind the confines of the front door: what *had* I left the place like? As I fumbled to find the right key, I came over 'all unnecessary, like' as a turned the lock, pushed the door over the blockage being caused by the accumulation of post, and thought, *'No turning back now Chris!*

Problem number one presented itself. To get into my home, which is a bungalow, you have to take quite a big step upwards to get in. I'd done this as a matter of routine thousands of times before without even thinking about it: I suspect that if I had been asked whether there was a step to take in order to access the place, I would have to have given that enquiry serious thought. It's like driving a car, isn't it? Can you honestly tell me *which* pedal is the brake, the clutch or the accelerator, without thinking about it?

Anyway, I could not physically perform this task right now.

"That's a big step!" one of these ladies said, "I'll make a note of that: you'll be needing a grab rail out here."

"Just use your stick now Chris," the other lady interjected.

Even that caused me a problem. Where should I position the stick? What leg shall I lever myself up on? The answer was obvious really: I was told how to use the stick to support my weak side, which I did. The resulting manoeuvre was as satisfying as it was simple.

So, I was in: so too were the ladies. I had a very quick perusal of what I had imagined would be something to a war-zone, but it was not that bad. Filled with newly emerging confidence, I said:

"I really fancy a nice cup of tea," (well, I wouldn't fancy a nasty one, would I, and I have had a few of those in my time: haven't I Lorraine?)

'Can I get you ladies a cup too?

They agreed, and accompanied me to the kitchen.

Bad move!

It was filthy!

Unpacked shopping on the floor, unwashed dishes and utensils in what was now a cold, putrid, bowl of washing up water, and, I suddenly realised, there was worse to come. I had to admit to this, so I bit the bullet and said sheepishly:

"BBBAAAAAAAAAA!"

No, I did not bleet. I said:

"If you open the oven up, I think that you might well discover the dinner I was about to eat when I was taken to *The Pilgrim.*"

Slowly, surely, one of the poor ladies, who appeared to have drawn the short straw for this unenviable task, opened the other door. A nasty smell was omitted, followed by a tentatively held oven tin of something unrecognisable, which was doing a fine job at fermenting mould all over it!

"Sorry about that," I said.

"That's alright love; we've seen worse! This was going to be your dinner was it Chris?"

The answer to that was in the affirmative, but *not* in the sad condition it now found itself in.

Embarrassing or what?

Embarrassing!

Somehow or other, we located a suitable receptacle for the offending item, and the de-composing meal and oven tray thrown in it for good measure. I think that it must have been at this point in proceedings, when the mothering instincts of both ladies took over. This was weird, since these ladies were young enough to have been my daughters. Perhaps they had kids of their own at home. Perhaps they saw me in a whole new light as an overgrown kid: a *very* overgrown kid! Who knows! However, I was suddenly 'under instruction'.

"You sit down Chris; we'll just do a little bit of tidying up in here," one of the ladies said.

"Now, where do you keep your tea, Chris?" I indicated the location.

"Mugs, milk, sugar?"

"Mugs are in that cupboard, sugar, I don't have: I'm type two, but sweeteners are up there, and the milk is in the fridge over there!"

Problem number two presented itself!

Well, it *was* milk ten days ago: now, it was doing a very passable imitation of something else far more solid and stinky; a bit like your favourite cheese that has gone off! The contents therein were shaken out down the sink, followed by copious amounts of disinfectant. We improvised by using *Coffee-Mate* in our tea, but, boy, did that taste good! Being suitably refreshed, and me being ordered to remain seated, the ladies went about the business of cleaning up the kitchen and generally sorting things out for me. This was clearly well beyond their remit; their job-description. Yet they went about this task, for which I was very grateful, with a smile and a joke. There really are great people out there!

Finally, they ascertained that I would be able to get in and out of bed, and carry out basic functions. I was re-assured that someone would visit me at ten in the morning. And then they were gone. I was at home, alone (good films, those) with this new addition to my life: post-stroke existence. I determined there and then that it would not get the better of me. Yes: it had been an eye-opener. Yes, I needed to make a few lifestyle changes. Yes, having had one, I was a prime candidate for another, which could be ten times worse in its effect on me.

At tea-time, I had the meal given to me by the nurse at Lincoln County, which was supposed to be my dinner for that day but, as you know, I had dinner anyway as it happened: very nice it was too.

After that, I watched the TV for a while.

Then I listened to some music.

Then, I went to bed.

That night's sleep was beautiful. There is nothing like your own bed, is there? It was if it was welcoming me home again. I positioned myself in it, lie still for a minute, did not bother to set the alarm but made sure that the time being shown was sort of right, and let out a huge sigh. I could have let out something else as well; I have no re-collection of anything else being let out other than aforementioned sigh!

The next thing I knew was being greeted by Alan Brazil's Scottish tones on *'Talksport'*; my radio station of choice, except for the community radio station that I work for, which the radio on the other side of the bed was tuned into, but I was just too comfortable to roll over towards that one, where I would have heard Dylan's dulcet voice, greeting 'the good folk of Boston'. Actually, *he* doesn't use that phrase: *I* do! I had forgotten that!

I lied in bed for a few moments, so that I could update myself with all matters football.

I also took the opportunity to reflect:

- I had suffered a stroke: accept it.
- I have been lucky
- Remain positive
- Do not give in
- Make those necessary changes
- Do not put things off
- Accept the help I will be given
- Do not judge
- Be grateful
- I *have passed* 'Go!'
- I *can* collect the metaphorical two hundred pounds
- I can, and will, beat the stroke: it will be 'a work in process' a whole new me!

The Epilogue

This book started with a prologue, it had an intermission, so it's only right that it has an epilogue as well.

But what actually is an epilogue? Does it serve any specific purpose?

Actually, yes: on both counts.

It can be a speech addressed to the audience by an actor at the end of a play. It can also be a short post-script to any literary work, such as a brief description of the fates of the characters in the story. That's what *Collins* says anyway, and I, for one, am not going to dispute the authority that *is* Collins.

I suppose that in some way, what I have described has been 'play': I have been an actor in it, and you have been the audience. Similarly, the idea of 'fate' has been a constant throughout.

And, of course, the roles could be reversed. You may well be the actor in your particular play. But, have you learnt your lines; do you recognise your cue?

Is it a case of 'that's all folks?' That is for you, the reader to decide.

For my part, I am going to conclude this offering by reflecting on the whole process I went through having been discharged, let go, allowed to escape: whatever you want to call it. In my opinion, the post-hospital period played a vitally important role in the totality of my recovery which needs to be acknowledged as well.

So, I want to say a massive thank you for all of the input made by the various external agencies that I have listed in the front of the book.

I have benefited from physiotherapists, for example, who were marvellous in hospital and terrific in my own home too, even if they made me contort into positions I had previously considered unattainable or unnatural, or indeed, both! So, thank you to the ladies who visited me on various occasions, greeting me with the invite:

"Shall we do some exercises in bed now, Chris?" the innuendo being as clear as day!

Also, thanks to the lady who walked tirelessly around the estate with me, in order to develop my balance, strength and co-ordination skills. We walked slowly to start with: at a snail's pace; it must have been desperately tedious for her, but she persevered with me, and every day, when a further lamp post was reached, she would say to me:

"Have a rest now, Chris: you've done brilliantly, but you've got to get back, haven't you, *and* up that step."

So kind, so re-assuring, so human.

Day by day, we went a little bit further; then, up to the bus-stop, so she could see that I could catch a bus if I needed to. That made both her, and I, happy in equal measures.

Then, I had visits from the health and well-being team, whose task it was to make sure that mentally I was in the right frame of mind, and whether I had been cognitively impaired in any way. This would be checked by a selection of 'tests', for the want of a better word, designed to check my 'reasoning and logistical skills'. Don't be put off by these: it's not a pass/fail situation. I'd suffered enough with that, at the hands of the eleven plus! One test bothered me slightly though. This was when I was read a list of random information; simple facts about names, colours, jobs, dates and the like, and then other tests were administered in order, I suppose, to distract my attention. I knew what was coming: about five minutes later, I was asked questions about what I had been asked before! How well did I do? Not very well! In fact, it took several prompts to recall all of the information, almost to the extent that she was 'spoon-feeding' me the answers!

"Ah, yes: that's it, I remember now!" I can distinctly remember saying.

Trouble was that I couldn't distinctly remember anything about the names she had mentioned, or the colours or the jobs: nothing, if the truth be told.

"Don't worry about that Chris," I was informed, "most people have difficulty with that one, and you've done extremely well on the other indicators, so very well done!"

'Thank goodness for that', I thought to myself, but then again realised that these were exercises to aid my recovery in every single way possible. I, for one, barely knew what a stroke was prior to having one. I certainly did not know the extent to which individuals who suffer them can be affected in so many different ways. I was being cared for and looked after in ways I had not imagined: I was not just being 'dumped' back home with a 'get on with it now' approach.

Further visits ensued. There was a lady who was inquiring after my financial situation. On one occasion, I mentioned in passing that I was aiming at going into town by bus, but that I would not be well received by the driver because I did not have the exact change for the fair. That evening, as an extra visit, she came back with a bag of fifty pence and pound coins which I could exchange my twenty pound note for. She didn't *have* to do that for me: she did it out of human kindness. There was another lady who got me to do a 'getting in and out of the bath' exercise (without water, I should add, and fully clad!) The result of that was that she was going to arrange for me to have a grab rail installed, at no cost to myself. There was one slight hiccup here though. Neither of us had taken into account that the rail would have to be attached to a stud wall. As the installation chap said to me:

"With every respect, Mr Moore…"

I just love it when somebody starts off their sentence in that way, because you inherently know something not so nice is going to follow:

"…there is no way that stud wall will take your weight pulling on the rail; and for health and safety reasons, I *could* fit it, but I am not prepared to."

Fair enough. I didn't particularly cherish the idea of ending up in a dishevelled heap whilst attempting to exit the tub!

"I fully agree mate," I replied, having brought that most undesirable outcome to mind, "I don't blame you at all."

To which he responded:

"Do you want to keep it though mate? It might come in handy for someone's Christmas present this year!"

How true: how true indeed! Brother-in-law Richard: you know what you are getting this year!

I had practiced walking without a stick around the home, and I found that with patience, this was something I could reasonably do. I had also practiced it during my short forays outside, safe in the knowledge that should I fall, then the kindly lady, with her petite stature, had the responsibility of breaking my fall by putting herself between me and the ground. Ah! The age of chivalry is alive and kicking! Let's face it: she wouldn't have stood a chance, bless her!

However: I had targeted one special day. It was a Friday. I was going to do it! I was going to walk to the bus-stop, get on it, be dropped off in town, and do a few necessary chores. And this was going to be done without a stick.

I started walking: ever so slowly to start with, looking downwards most of the time, just making sure that my feet were firmly grounded. Then, as my confidence grew, I picked up the pace a bit. I then became aware that I was not looking down any more; I was looking forward, and walking with a purpose.

I subsequently informed each of the agencies of how I was doing, both in walking and in everyday activities, which I had once taken for granted. I can remember commenting to them, again, in passing, that I would never take anything for granted again. This comment, to which I had given no forethought whatsoever, appeared to be the catalyst: the undeniable sign that I was indeed ready to be discharged from their very considerable care too. Thus, the forms were signed, and there would be no more visits. I had grown to like these people who had worked so tirelessly on my behalf: we established a very good rapport and I was sad to see them go. I shed a tear or so after the final 'good byes': I'm a lot of things, but never thought of myself as a 'big softy'. But, as I wiped the tears out of my eyes, it seemed to be the perfect encapsulation of my journey. It was over, but strangely enough, I felt that it would never totally end.

So, back to my first walk, without the stick. I had come to actually *like* using it! In fact, I ordered a wooden one from a mail order company. It soon arrived and very dapper it looked as well: a veritable fashion accessory which afforded me a certain style and grace, particularly when I donned my panama hat! I felt like I could parade around town greeting everyone with a pronounced 'hello, darling!' I didn't actually do that at all, but the point is, I *could* have done, if I really wanted to!

The point I want to end on is this: when I was ready, I stopped looking down and started looking forward, both physically and, more importantly, spiritually. There *is* a life out there, just waiting to be enjoyed again, after your illness or injury. Rejoice in that fact. Set yourself small but ultimately achievable targets: they might have been thoroughly insignificant before, but now, they take on an entirely new meaning. Accept the help you will be given with open arms. Take into account that, as humans, we are all different in our make-up: do not condemn somebody for saying something inappropriate or down-right disgusting: celebrate the fact that we are all free to say and do things as we wish. It is called 'the human condition'.

If you have been in hospital, either as a 'virgin', never having experienced it, or as a seasoned attendee, I hope this book has helped by putting matters into perspective, and I wish you a speedy recovery. If, on the other hand, you have just read this book out of sheer curiosity and you intend to visit someone who is in hospital, please do not break wind and try to pass it off as someone else's! That's not playing the game!

Yes; of course it is great to make somebody else's day: not only does the recipient of your kind attentions benefit from your actions, but as a result, you get a warm, tingling feeling as well, in the knowledge that you have helped another person.

But, let's be clear about this: it is of vital importance that you make your *own* day too. In other words, you need to take responsibility for your future welfare, probably to a far greater extent than you ever have done in the past. This may well be a scary realisation: it was for me. In my particular case, I was told that my stroke, albeit a mini one, was a warning: bells had started to ring telling me that I had to make some lifestyle adjustments for my own good. In some instances, these alterations to things I had done for years and years without question, and indeed had afforded me with a great amount of enjoyment, were not easy to palate. It is so easy to accept the mindset that says: "Well, you've had a rough time, but you've been in hospital; they've sorted it, so life can go back to what it used to be now!" That, my friends, is a totally incorrect assumption to make. You've got a stark choice to make: you can either take the easy route (like a motorway, I suppose, which will get you from Point 'A' to Point 'B' with the minimum of fuss,) or you can select the minor country lane, which serves the same purpose but takes things a little bit slowly and in a more considered way. In my situation, a quick fix is not the answer for me: I would rather take my health seriously and thus progress small steps at a time, rather than risking all in the fast lane of the motorway.

Thus, to conclude this book, I just want to spend a little time talking about the aftermath of your hospitalisation: the awkward time when you realise that you have lost your virginity and you now stand alone: yourself versus the big wide world.

To be fair: in actual fact, you are *not* alone. You have joined the countless number of others who have suffered from the same ailment that put you into hospital in the first place. These people will *know* what you have gone through; they will be sympathetic about any issues which you will now face and they will be happy to offer good, honest, practical advice, which you will come to regard as a life-line and 'godsend'. So, tip number one:

- Go out of your way to join any support networks that are made available to you. Do not let your pride, or embarrassment, get in the way of accepting help. There is absolutely no shame in accepting human kindness. Avail yourself of the many support Agencies that will, I can assure you, make themselves known to you.

And here's another stark warning: just because you have left the confines of the hospital, largely because the experts deem it appropriate for you to be discharged, do not, for one minute, think 'that's it!' Hopefully it is, but possibly, or probably, it is not. Let me tell you of what happened to me in this respect. It must have been about two months after I was sent home. I had come to realise that in terms of stroke, I had indeed, been very lucky indeed. Have you seen the 'F.A.S.T'. TV advertising campaign which brings the symptoms of a stroke to the public's attention, and what to do if you happen across an unfortunate person in the throes of one? Well, all strokes are different, and have varying degrees of outward manifestation. I, for one, did not appear to have been anything like so badly affected: I was just aware of a residual weakness in my right leg and the occasional trouble with maintaining my balance. One evening, I decided I want a bath: and this presented a conundrum. I had previously been informed that it would be easier for me to 'shower' rather than 'bath'. To most people, this would not be a problem at all but, by preference, I am a 'wallowing' sort of guy: rather than a quick 'in and out' that a shower facilitates, which is very time efficient, I just love to have a long, hot soak, lasting at least thirty minutes, complete with the radio on and a book in hand! The temptation was just too much: I 'ran' (or 'drew' the bath: where does that expression derive from: I thought that 'drawing' a bath would necessitate pens, pencils and paper!) the bath, put in my favourite luxuriant, got in and relaxed! The problem arose as I attempted to get out. For no apparent reason, my right leg gave way under me; as a result, I lost my balance and fell backwards, crashing through the shower enclosure behind me and shattering the glass, some of which lacerated my head. After regaining composure, I thought it would be advisable to call the '111' service and an ambulance duly arrived and checked me over.

It was then a case of 'deja-vous'. You know what's coming, don't you!

"Think we need to take you back in again, Mr Moore, just to have you checked over as a precaution, like."

It was those two words: 'back in', which put my mind into overdrive again: 'what if this, and what if that…?

'OK, thanks', I replied, in a vain attempt not to look stupid! History, I thought, was about to repeat itself!

In actual fact, after the very thorough examination, I was discharged again, only suffering from minor lacerations and bruises, and I arrived home at about four o'clock in the morning, and surveyed the scene of smashed up glass and pockets of blood which had covered the floor of the bathroom (not the blood; the glass, in case you are worried!)

Anyway, tip number two is this:

- Do not assume than now you are back home, everything will go swimmingly and be one hundred percent fine! It might be. It might *not* be. Do not take chances with your recovery: if somebody has told you not to take a bath, then damn well *don't* take a bath, as much as this might irk you! As I used to say as a scout: 'be prepared' for the odd blip or two along the way!

And here's a final few points to consider. If you have been given a fitness regime to follow, you must make an informed choice. Choice number one says: 'sod it, I am *not* doing this!' Fair enough; that is your right. Or you can adopt choice number two which states: 'I might not like doing this, and I might not have done anything like this before, but I'm going to give it a 'go', at least!' If you choose the latter, then, good on you, but *don't* expect the impossible in terms of your recovery: set realistic and achievable goals.

My first goal when I was at home was to walk to the first lamppost and back, along with the walking stick, and accompanied by a support worker. This must have been a distance of twenty metres on the round trip and I was exhausted afterwards: I am sure that there was a snail that lapped me on the circuit, and, as to what the neighbours must have thought, (and yes, I could sense the twitching of the net curtains: suburbia at its finest') I hate to think! The next time I did it, we went that little bit further; and again and again. I'm not really one for proverbs: for example, cows do *not* sit down to reserve themselves a dry space before it rains, but it is reasonable to assume the validity of the proverb which states: 'from tiny acorns do mighty Oaks grow' because it is inherently true! This was the case for my walking exercises.

It was also suggested that I went swimming more often. Swim more often? I had *never* gone swimming. I can't swim. I don't see the point in swimming! If we were meant to swim, we would have been born with fins and other fishy necessities! So that idea was a non-starter!

So too was the idea that I joined a Gym. I attended a gym for a period of eight weeks, having been referred by my doctor in order to achieve a weight loss. I knew this was to be of no avail too when I first stepped on to the treadmill only to be unceremoniously dumped off the other end because I couldn't keep up with it. How I sweated over the course of my membership (or, if you prefer, perspired gently), rigorously working the weights, the rowing machine, the bicep machines, the static bike and other associated forms of torture! Finally, it was time for the big 'weigh in' at the end. I stood on the scales, in trepidation of the result.

"How much have I lost then; one pound, two pound, five pound fifty?" I quipped.

The instructor looked, and then said to me:

"How much did you weigh when you started here?"

I informed him.

"Ah," he stumbled, "…in that case it would appear that you have lost…"

He cleared his throat.

"Nothing!"

"What, nothing as in nothing at all?"

"Seems like it Chris."

"But why?" I implored. That damn question again. Of course it should have been 'why not?' to be totally correct in terms of grammar.

(That reminds me of a joke, actually. A teacher is handing back marked work of a punctuation exercise completed by Johnny in 8X. 'This work's appalling Johnny: where on earth is your grammar?' to which Johnny piped up: 'she's in bed with grandpa!')

Quick thinking on the part of the Instructor though led to a glimmer of hope for me!

'What you *have* done though Chris, is to replace the *wrong* type of weight with a *good* type of weight!'

This explanation confused me somewhat, and got me thinking of the wrong type of snow or the wrong type of leaf! However, what it *did* confirm was that I, and any other establishment calling itself a gym, or fitness centre, was never to be acquainted again! I am sure that these places have their benefits, but not for me. I know my limits!

A good equivalent to the gym is to join something like a walking club. Most towns have these, and they are devised for fitness purposes, not for completing a marathon or walking the sub four minute mile! In my experience, they progress at whatever rate you want them to go at; there is always a walk leader and a walk 'end-marker', so there is no chance that you will get left behind, or, heaven forbid, lost; or heavenly heaven please dear God forbid, that you will collapse into an undignified heap with nobody noticing!

So, tip number three is simple:

- Take care of yourself like you never have done before, and be serious about it. If a professional has advised you to do something which may not have been a feature of your life pre-hospitalisation, they are doing so for a reason. Do not dismiss the advice you are offered out of hand. In other words, don't be so 'bloody pig-headed' about your health! If you've been told to cut down on your food in-take, then do it. Start with a hardly noticeable reduction in the quantity of roast potatoes, say nine instead of ten! (it is amazing the psychological difference reducing one's potato intake from double to single figures can have!) and then work towards the magical number of three (in your, and my, dreams!) gradually! The same principle applies to other vastly enjoyable foodstuffs as well like Pizza, Fish and Chips, Take-aways, Curries of all varieties, and Gypsy Tart (one for the kids old and young there; do you remember this delicious pudding at school: it was basically burnt sugar in a pastry and was very, very 'tasty' shall we say!) Everything in moderation is the mantra here: well, *almost* everything in moderation: one or the exceptions do come to my mind which I will not elaborate here: it is neither the time nor place, as the actress said to the Bishop!

So, I have finally arrived at the end of my story.

Some time has now elapsed since I lost my hospital virginity, and quite a lot of water has gone under the bridge.

- I am still here! I don't say that flippantly. I say it because, if you had asked me before my stroke, what I thought about the condition, I would have replied 'It's a killer!' Wrong, Christopher! It can result in serious changes to the lifestyle one has become accustomed to. Sometimes you will feel 'down' because of the restraints it will put on your everyday activities, but remember: other days, you will feel very much 'up': thankful for what you have and grateful to those who have helped you.
- At times, I have felt frustrated, and have asked that question of myself that has no satisfactory answer: why *me*? Am I being punished? The answer to the first question is answered by another: why *not* me? The reply to the second question is: don't be so bloody silly! People have accidents; people get ill: that is the long and short of it: the notion that injury or illness is some sort of divine retribution is a lot of tosh! Don't feel ashamed by feelings of this nature.

And, so to my final comment:

- Enjoy life! Celebrate life! Revel in its pleasures! *Do* 'pass go'; *do* 'collect two hundred pounds!' Buy *Mayfair* if you can! Build hotels on it! Just because you are no longer a hospital virgin, do not look back with anger. Look forward with your new found personal respect and enjoy the ride!

I hope this book has been useful to you, and an enjoyable read. If so, tell your friends and neighbours so that they too will rush out and buy multiple copies, which will necessitate a new print run and increased royalties for yours truly!

If your opinion is not quite so favourable, do me a favour and keep quiet!

Post Script

This is just an afterthought really. However, as circumstances would have it, the situation I have described below re-calls an event which happened after my discharge, and the subsequent exchange of letters between two people who know of each other but very rarely meet, largely because of the geographical difference between where we live. It is a prime example of something I hold very dear to my heart, and that is, the power of conversation, in this case via the written word in the form of a simple letter.

What's the thought that goes through your mind when the letterbox rattles and in drop a handful of postal communications: if you are anything like me, I suspect your line of comment goes something like this:

'Bill, bill, rubbish, bill, more rubbish...why do they keep on sending me this stuff? I told them over the phone that I neither want nor need a stair lift because, due to the fact that I live in a bungalow, I do not possess stairs that I need lifting up!'

These communications very quickly become re-cycled.

But, every now and again, perhaps once or twice a year, a hand-written envelope might land on the floor. This is intriguing, isn't it? You look for clues: do I recognise that hand-writing? Where has it been sent from? Don't think you can become Morse overnight by concluding that because something is post-marked 'Peterborough' for example, the person who has sent it actually lives there! Post-codes cover a wide area!

When I first became aware that girls weren't 'silly' and 'annoying', but actually rather nice and sort of attractive; that would be when I was about thirteen years of age, or so, I might send a 'Valentine day's' card to my intended recipient via somebody else's mother or father who worked in a different postal area! Yes: I'd had a cunning plan! I wasn't really 'on the ball' though because I only signed the card with a huge 'X' which stood for two things: a big smacker and a way of securing my anonymity!

What a prize idiot! As Del-boy probably said in *Only fools and horses'*: what a plonker!

The result of this secretive card sending exercise would invariably have the net effect of persuading the girl of my dreams to think that some other spotty oik had sent the card: not me! *And* I had paid for it out of my pocket money, *and* I had paid for the stamp as well!

I'll take 'time out' here to whisk you back to schoolboy humour. In the playground, a jolly wheeze would be to approach some unsuspecting younger and smaller person than yourself and then, in all sincerity, say to said pupil/victim:

"Do you want a thrupenny stamp for free?"

"Yes please!" the victim would generally reply, working on the basis that anything 'free' had to be a good thing.

Thereupon, the originator of the gag, which at this point, it transparently *was,* would proceed to take great delight on bringing one's whole wait down upon one of the feet of the victim via a strategically placed stamp!

'Ouch!', or words to that effect, the victim would say, followed up by: 'I'm telling teacher of you!' which, of course never materialised, or the teacher would never accept that such a sweet, innocent child like my good self, would do such a thing!

How funny! I thought as I walked away in triumph.

I do believe that this individual character went on to become a tax inspector, putting his stamp on people's monetary affairs! I like to think that I had some bit part to play in his ultimate career route!

I have digressed!

Again!

Please accept my most humble apologies!

That also applies to *any* person's foot I delivered a hefty blow to in the manner just described, in the pursuit of a cheap, petty laugh!

Sorry! (I mean that most sincerely, folks!) Good old Hughie Green and *Opportunity Knocks.*

Anyway: back to this hand-written letter. This item of post is treated with utmost respect. It is carefully opened: perhaps with a paper knife even (in my opinion, one of the most stupidest inventions ever made!) The paper is withdrawn from the envelope with the curiosity mounting. It is unfolded. You quickly scan the letter. What fascinating hand-writing! For the unaware, the art of hand-writing is fading away: a dying skill, and is being replaced by text messages, with its maximum usage of one hundred and forty characters, and computers. This is a particular process whereby you acquire a sheet or two of actual 'writing paper' ('My name's Bond: *Basildon Bond;* man of letters!) and a 'fountain pen' filled with *'Quinck'*. One then finds time to sit down, reflect, and write a personal communication to another human being. It takes time: it cannot be sent as an 'attachment' but what results is a unique and personal document, a transcript no less, sent to the intended recipient, hopefully with love.

A letter of this nature can be 'life-affirming'. It can inspire happiness humour and confidence in a person who perhaps feels just a wee bit down. It also generates a feeling of warmth and integrity in the person who has written it.

So, what follows below, is an exchange of letters that occurred between a lovely lady called Pat, who, with my Mum, have developed an enduring friendship, and myself. To put this into perspective: I had just been released from hospital. Mum then told me about Pat, who basically at the same time as me, was going through some health issues. I have always liked Pat: as I have said, a very close friend of my Mum's, with whom I would generally exchange Christmas wishes with over the phone on that special morning. On this occasion, however, I wanted to write to her, personally, and this is a transcript of what I said.

Dear Pat,

Surprise surprise! It's Chris here, Sadie's son!

I usually start my letters by saying: 'how are you?' It's usually just a way of starting a letter, isn't it? But, in your case, I know the answer: you have been a little bit poorly, haven't you Pat? I became aware of this tonight. Mum had left me a message on my answer phone, asking me to get back to her about an entirely different issue, which, as a loyal son, I duly did! But then, she told me about you: how you had been admitted to hospital with heart and lung problems, and I was very sorry to hear that. I know that you and Mum are dear friends; a friendship which goes back many a year to the days of 'PPP' I think. She always talks about you in the fondest of terms, so, any friend of Mum's is a friend of mine! I also understand that you are a bit worried about what will happen after you 'make good your escape!' Pat, I am writing to you just to try to re-assure you that you will be perfectly alright. I know this because of my little escapade in hospital recently.

I know that Mum told you about my recent hospitalisation. Yes: I had a stroke. A very minor one, thank God. I just kept falling over Pat; four times in one day! I thought that was beyond co-incidence;

one fall clumsy, two falls stupid and as for four in the space of a couple of hours, I guessed something was not 100%. So, I phoned 111. I didn't phone 999 because it was not an emergency as far as I was concerned: I just kept falling over! The paramedics came round; the rest, as they say, is history.

Whilst I was in hospital, the care I received was top notch. Good old NHS eh?

I had specialists of all variety coming to my bedside, every day.

More importantly though, when I was discharged, I was told that arrangements had been put in place to support me when I got home.

Believe me Pat, you will be looked after when you are at home. There are so many different agencies that get involved. They will look after your every need. You will not be allowed home, however, until they are totally sure that you are able to look after yourself, and this is a good thing!

Being single, as you are, Mum is, and I am (not through choice incidentally) flags up certain concerns to the medics: will you be OK by yourself? Can you cope with seemingly menial tasks? Are you in the right state of mind to be on your own?

Pat: everything is considered by the experts! You will be fine: I promise!

I have been inundated with visits from various people since I got home, and I am very grateful for all that they have done, and will continue to do. The same will be the case for you, Pat, so try not to worry, even though, like me, you probably will for a while: that is to be expected!

I, am now, fully recovered! I just get short of breath at times, which is annoying, because most of the time, I am sat on my bottom, either doing my radio shows or at home. I now realise that I have been a lazy so and so: nature has given me an 'eye opener', and a call to make alterations to my lifestyle, which I will. That means exercise and diet control for me. You will be given advice as well. Take it and embrace it with open arms Pat!

Blimey: I am beginning to sound like my Mum now! She is 84 (ish) and has her own problems to cope with. I am a mere 'chick' at the ripe young age of 60. You guys have just a few years over me, and are real battlers!

There is a song, Pat, which goes like this: 'I get knocked down, but I get up again, ain't nothing gonna keep me down!' Elton John also recorded a song called: 'I'm still standing'. These are my mantras! You are, Mum is, and I am, which is nice to know, isn't it?

Pat, I wish you a speedy recovery; as speedy as mine has been!

When I was in hospital, to stop myself being bored, I got someone to bring me a pad of A4 paper and a biro, so that I could write down my thoughts about being in hospital. I like writing, as it gives me something to think about!

Anyway, when I got home, I began to type my jottings down. Now, I have just about finished doing it. It has taken quite a long time: I type with two fingers only. I can only dream and be amazed at the way Mum used to type using all fingers at an incredible speed: no doubt like you! But what I have produced is a book! It is about 60,000 words long! It is funny in places, sarcastic and realistic elsewhere! All I need to do is to get a publisher for it! I promise to let you have a copy of it in some form, published or not, so that you can have a grin! It will take a little while, but I won't forget!

Pat: I know that you enquire after me when you chat with Mum over the phone. I really appreciate that! So, here I am, asking about you! I know you will be fine. Just give it time and accept the help you will be given! With love, Chris.

Have written it, I posted it (obviously: no point *not* posting it, having written it!) I then thought no more about it. About two weeks passed.

Then, one morning, I heard the letter box being opened: it creaks under the pressure, you know! That particular instance, it seemed like the postman was delivering an avalanche of post: he took two attempts to deliver the communications addressed to me. I felt really excited when I approached the door.

There it was in all its glory:

- Un-solicited mail
- Un-requested leaflets
- Bills (well, mine, actually!)
- More stair lift catalogues
- Funeral plan details (really subtle this one!)

But, as I was sifting through this venerable mountain of postal items, and re-cycling them accordingly, I noticed that a small, yellow, hand-addressed envelope slipped out from between them. I went through the process for uniquely written correspondence as described before. The person's hand-writing was very distinctive indeed: a sweeping, gregarious style; a written encapsulation of the author. I soon discovered who take taken so much time and effort in composing this work of art: it was beautiful. This is what Pat wrote:

My very dear Chris,

Wow! A letter from a lovely fella. What a joyful overwhelming surprise. That you would take some of your precious time to write to me: well, how's that for being a really caring person? Thank you so much.

I was in desperate need of re-assurance about 'what happens after' and you have done just that. I guess it's the unknown, Chris that makes you feel so 'iffy'.

Bev and Richard [my sister and brother-in-law] *have been so kind and understanding and as for your Mum, well, she is something else, so special to me. We talk on the phone nearly every weekend which is like a tonic for me.*

Some weeks I don't talk to anyone for three to four days and then on Sunday there is your Mum's happy voice asking how I am. Always this lovely lift in her voice, no matter how she is feeling: amazing.

Now: there's a funny thing. I [am] *writing to you as though we do this all the time – how lovely for me to feel so comfortable corresponding with you. Please take this as a great compliment*

There is one thing we do have in common. I love to write and used to write the prayers for Church and articles for the magazine.

Just know that your book will be great; can't wait to read it. Told your sister [that] *your letter had a lovely splattering of humour in it. We all love a good 'giggle' as your dear Mum calls it.*

Take great care of yourself – make the most of each and every day. I will be thinking of you .

I send you my love
Patxxxx

There you have it. A simple exchange of letters.

Each person reaching out in so many ways.

Of benefit to the reader and the writer.

As someone else commented: 'the pen is mightier than the sword' (probably Bill S, I should think!)

And here's another reference which I have made earlier in this book, but right now, it seems absolutely the right thing to do is to repeat *The Beatles'* mantra:

'And in the end, the love you take, is equal to the love you make.' (Or, is it the other way round? One to google, perhaps, but therein lies a point worth making.

The simple act of writing a letter does not require an academic degree. It doesn't matter if you make the odd mistake; no-one is judging you. In fact, due to your efforts in writing, however difficult you might find it, your efforts will be appreciated. There are no qualifications needed in order to pick up a piece of paper and write a few heart-felt words on it. The recipient will probably read, re-read, and re-read again, your words and sentiments, and will react accordingly. It makes not the slightest bit of difference whether you know the correct way of using a semi-colon or apostrophe. Neither is it of any importance whatsoever whether you are not top of the class in spelling or cannot exactly define what a split infinitive is (for your information, incidentally, a split infinitive is when one uses a phrase like 'to boldly go', like Jim said in the *Star-trek'* opening credits! Apparently, I used to employ the use of split infinitives at a particular school when I was a young teacher, much to the annoyance of the head teacher, who was a stickler for traditional English grammar!). My advice is this: make someone happy: write a letter!